Living Resurrected Lives

Living Resurrected Lives

What It Means and Why It Matters

Veronica Mary Rolf
and Eva Natanya

CASCADE *Books* · Eugene, Oregon

LIVING RESURRECTED LIVES
What It Means and Why It Matters

Copyright © 2020 Veronica Mary Rolf and Eva Natanya. All rights reserved.
Except for brief quotations in critical publications or reviews, no part of this book
may be reproduced in any manner without prior written permission from the
publisher. Write: Permissions, Wipf and Stock Publishers, 199 W. 8th Ave., Suite 3,
Eugene, OR 97401.

Cascade Books
An Imprint of Wipf and Stock Publishers
199 W. 8th Ave., Suite 3
Eugene, OR 97401

www.wipfandstock.com

PAPERBACK ISBN: 978-1-7252-5324-7
HARDCOVER ISBN: 978-1-7252-5325-4
EBOOK ISBN: 978-1-7252-5326-1

Cataloguing-in-Publication data:

Names: Rolf, Veronica Mary, author. | Natanya, Eva, author.

Title: Living resurrected lives : what it means and why it matters / Veronica Mary
Rolf and Eva Natanya.

Description: Eugene, OR: Cascade Books, 2020 | Includes bibliographical refer-
ences and index.

Identifiers: ISBN 978-1-7252-5324-7 (paperback) | ISBN 978-1-7252-5325-4 (hard-
cover) | ISBN 978-1-7252-5326-1 (ebook)

Subjects: LCSH: Jesus Christ—Resurrection. | Paschal mystery.

Classification: BT872 .L4 2020 (print) | BT872 (ebook)

Manufactured in the U.S.A.   OCTOBER 8, 2020

For all those who yearn
To live their lives—even now—
As sons and daughters of the resurrection.

Table of Contents

Preface

WHEN I FINISHED WRITING the last chapter of my previous book, *Suddenly There is God: The Story of Our Lives in Sacred Scripture* (Cascade Books, 2019), I knew I had only begun to develop the theme of resurrection and its immediate relevance to our lives. The topic of resurrection is often fraught with confusion and controversy, grave misunderstanding and sharply divergent views, even among faith-filled Christians. My extensive research for *Suddenly There is God* had raised more questions about resurrection than I could address in that book. I had to write a companion volume.

During lengthy conversations with my daughter and coauthor, Eva Natanya, I realized that there were many aspects of resurrection that needed to be re-confronted, re-clarified, and re-defined so that laity and students, as well as preachers and spiritual guides, might have a clear and contemporary explanation of what resurrection means and why it matters. Eva and I bounced ideas off each other for months; then I wrote and we revised, editing together with great energy and enthusiasm. Over several years of creative collaboration, Eva's challenging questions and insightful answers contributed immeasurably to the ideas and arguments in this book. Her academic training as a systematic theologian and a scholar of comparative religion suggested fresh and exciting ways of reinterpreting ancient Christian teachings on the nature of identity and the resurrected body, while remaining true to apostolic tradition.

In addition, Eva's many years of contemplative practice and solitary retreat inspired her to record the guided meditations on resurrection in Part Two, which I then transcribed. These highly imaginative meditations, combined with Eva's instructions on how to create a daily contemplative practice, offer readers a deeply personal way to experience Christ's resurrection. They also serve to affirm faith in our own resurrection as a vibrant reality here and now, rather than merely a distant promise. I am forever grateful that Eva was willing to collaborate with me on this project. Her contribution has been invaluable.

I also want to acknowledge the theologians, historians, and Scripture scholars whose masterful works on resurrection have challenged and inspired my own thinking and writing: Gerald O'Collins, N. T. Wright, Michael Licona, Xavier Léon-Dufour, Caroline Walker Bynum, Stephen T. Davis, Sandra Schneiders, Rowan Williams, Pheme Perkins, Luke Timothy Johnson, Brant Pitre, Richard B. Hays, and Joachim Jeremias, to name a few.

Once again, I am indebted to Rodney Clapp, my editor for *Suddenly There is God*, for guiding this new manuscript through the editorial process with his usual expertise and kind appreciation. Great thanks are also due to the entire production and marketing team at Wipf and Stock Publishers, especially Matthew Wimer and Joe Delahanty, for their thorough professionalism, courtesy, and good humor.

Finally, I want to express my boundless gratitude to my husband, Frederick, and our son, David. Their loving and unconditional support of the work Eva and I have undertaken has been a source of immense courage and creativity. Thank you!

Introduction

THROUGHOUT THE FORTY DAYS of Lent, Christians fast and pray, do penance and give alms in anticipation of Easter. On Holy Thursday we celebrate the Last Supper and first Eucharist, keep watch with Christ in the garden of Gethsemane, and lament over the reality of suffering in every age. On Good Friday we stand at the foot of the cross with the women and the Beloved Disciple, and when Jesus gives up his spirit, we feel utterly bereft. Then, at the Holy Saturday Vigil and on Easter Sunday morning, we switch abruptly into singing "Alleluia!" and wishing each other "Happy Easter!" We know that our joy is not only about the return of warmer weather, the beauty and abundance of spring flowers, family reunions, and children hunting for colored Easter eggs. We proclaim that because Christ is risen, he has conquered death once and for all. He will never die again. Even more pertinent to our immediate situation, we are told that if we have been like Christ in our sufferings and eventually our own deaths, we shall also rise with him.

But do we believe it? And do we live as if we believe it?

Perhaps we are much too realistic, too caught up in the demands of daily life in our materialist culture, to begin to fathom what resurrection might mean. We are only too aware that even if Christ *has* risen, right now our personal suffering, our family problems, and our own fear of dying are definitely not solved. The death and burial of every loved one has been utterly convincing. Death certainly looks and feels awfully final to us. Indeed, from our perspective, death appears much more real than the hope of resurrection.

But is it?

What is death, after all? What actually dies? What lives on? What transforms? Do we have any idea? Just because we cannot see the persons we love becoming "a new creation" after their final breath, does that mean it is not happening? When we breathe our last, will our awareness suddenly stop? Will the spirit that has informed our body simply disappear into thin air? Will we continue to exist? Can any disease, accident, or natural disaster kill that which is not physical, namely the mind, or spirit? But if spirit does continue, does that mean it is immortal? Are we not just a little bit curious about *how* one might die and still continue to be aware? When the body returns to the dust, where does the spirit dwell? Even more, how can a decomposed or cremated body ever be reunited with the spirit at the resurrection of the dead? What kind of body would it be? A resuscitated body, a transfigured physical body, or a spiritual body? In short, *what has Christianity revealed about the process of death and resurrection?*

To become authentic and relevant to our daily lives, Easter faith must go far, far deeper than mere wishful thinking that at some moment in a timeless eternity, God will reassemble our scattered ashes from the four winds, reunite them with our disembodied souls, put new flesh on our dry bones, and give us bodies that can no longer sin, suffer, or die; bodies that will be reunited with our loved ones in heaven forever. While this may in some sense be true, we must try, no matter how challenging it may be, to anticipate what it might actually *mean* to enter a glorified body that is capable of dwelling in the timeless vision of God. And even more immediately, *How might we live our whole lives for this glorious purpose?*

Furthermore, can we believe in resurrection enough to be ready to give our lives to it? That's the biggest hurdle by far. As we see throughout the world right now, thousands of people are being brutally martyred for their faith in the risen Christ. Like Christian witnesses throughout history, they die in the hope that they will rise again and be united with God for eternity. What about the rest of us who live mostly normal lives? What would it take for us to believe so passionately in resurrected life that our lives would change radically *right now?*

To attempt answers to these questions, we must first dig into the history of Judeo-Christian thought in order to understand the roots of the ideas we might almost take for granted from church teaching today. Only then may we examine what elements of those ideas form the rock-bottom foundation of our faith, and what parts developed later, evolving across the complex history of theological reflection. Only when we can understand something of the cultural context in which philosophical interpretations of Christian revelation developed in the past, may we legitimately imagine how those ideas might continue to be reinterpreted and re-understood in the context of our contemporary global cultures and worldviews.

Thus our exploration in Part One will seek to build the basis for belief in resurrection, both the resurrection of Jesus Christ and our own. If resurrection is to become for us what the Gospels tell us it is—the foundation, inspiration, and goal of our sojourn on earth as Christians—then we must be informed about how the idea of resurrection first developed from the Old to the New Testaments. Chapter 1 lays the groundwork with a brief historical overview of what has been meant by resurrection since ancient times. It explores a range of notions about what might happen after death, from the philosophical theories of the Greeks and Romans to the references (or implied references) to resurrection in the Hebrew Bible.

Chapter 2 examines in detail the Gospel narratives depicting the discovery of the empty tomb, discusses the inconsistencies, and questions whether the accounts might still agree in principle. We evaluate the fear and silence of the women in Mark's account and the possibility that they were delusional or even visited the wrong tomb and found it empty. We touch on persistent debates concerning what might have happened to Christ's body and whether or not the idea of an empty tomb was a pious legend added later by the evangelists. We also consider whether the empty tomb stories can ever actually serve as "proof" of Christ's resurrection—or whether they simply establish that the preponderance of historical evidence does not contradict but rather supports our faith. In chapter 3, we address some revisionist theories of "what happened" at the resurrection, then delve into the dramatic accounts of Christ's appearances to the two Marys, to Mary Magdalene, to the disciples on their way to Emmaus, in the upper room, and on the beach by Lake Tiberias. Along the way, we examine convincing reasons for accepting their authenticity.

Chapter 4 investigates what many modern Christians tend to believe about the resurrection and how some contemporary scholars seek to explain the resurrection appearances in more "rational" terms. Were they a mass hallucination? Self-delusion? Group fantasy? Or real experience? In contrast, we establish the bedrock of Christian faith about resurrection: what we *can* believe. In chapter 5, we look at Paul's letters to the skeptical Corinthians in response to their own questions about bodily resurrection: "How are the dead raised? With what kind of body do they come?" (1 Cor 15:35). We enter into the apostle's heated debate with the doubters of his time and consider his understanding of what the resurrection body will be like. We discuss Paul's crucial distinction between the natural body and the spiritual body as well as his sublime teaching about the glorified body. We also examine the process of divinization and consider what it promises for believers.

Then in chapter 6, we grapple with the philosophical problem that traditionally lies at the root of all discussions of resurrection: how can continuity of the same bodily matter be assured, given the complete *dis*continuity that occurs through the decaying process of the corpse? In addition, how can the unique identity of the individual person be restored from scattered dust and bones? This leads to the all-important existential question: Wherein does identity lie? Based on logic used by several theologians of the past, we propose a new way of understanding resurrection as a radical transformation of both body *and* mind, which must begin even now in our active practice of the spiritual path in this life.

In chapter 7 we seek to discover how we might begin to inhabit a divine dimension on a daily basis. We consider the essential virtues that, once developed, might empower us to think, feel, and act as liberated sons and daughters of the resurrection. We explore the eucharistic liturgy as the supremely transformative process by which we become incorporated into the mind and mystical body of the risen Christ. And we reflect on the necessity of weaving a daily practice of contemplative prayer into our busy lives.

Part Two goes on to outline an actual method of contemplative practice and offers guided meditations on the resurrection experience that can help us to prepare our minds and hearts for the daily journey towards resurrected life. We contemplate scenes, characters, and key moments of coming to faith in resurrection as these are dramatized in the Gospel narratives. Practicing such meditations in a progressive sequence and on a consistent basis can bring us to a deeper confidence in the reality of Christ's resurrection and, by extension, our own. Such meditations may also inspire greater experiential clarity about what we, as Christians, profess to believe.

One thing appears certain: if we confess that Christ really died on the cross on Good Friday and really rose from the dead on Easter Sunday, then this affirms that he has in fact defeated death once and for all. Church teaching has always assured us that this means Christ has vanquished our own death as well—in a dimension beyond our current perspective.

But what does this mean for us now? Easter faith proclaims that since the Lord is risen, we, too, shall rise. If this is true, then our efforts to do Christ's work of love on earth take on an entirely new significance. Once we dare to believe what we profess to believe—namely that God raised Christ from the dead as the "first fruits" of all the rest of us—we cannot go about our lives anymore as if nothing had changed. *Everything* about our human situation has changed in light of our faith, whether we are fully aware of it yet or not.

If we seize the opportunity to make our resurrected destiny the driving force behind every aspect of our earthly lives, then our entire being will expand in capability, deepen in certainty, and soar in divinely grounded expectation. We will love more intensely, savor our joys more thankfully, and find meaning in our struggles and sufferings. We will be able to trust in the dark what has been revealed in the light. Most of all, we will develop a more intimate relationship with the risen Lord that no one can ever destroy. That is why faith in the resurrection of Jesus—combined with the longing for it to become actualized in each one of us—matters so much! Without it, we have no ultimate hope; with it, nothing is impossible.

The challenge before us is to discover how an informed, vibrant, well-considered belief in resurrection might enable us to see everything in our world through a more enlightened mind and more compassionate heart. Such a faith will allow us to begin living our lives in a new dimension: a divine dimension. Nothing less.

PART ONE

The Basis for Belief in Resurrection

By Veronica Mary Rolf

1

What Does Resurrection Mean?

"I BELIEVE IN THE resurrection of the body and life everlasting." This statement of belief is what Christians profess when reciting the ancient Apostles' Creed. But do we understand what it implies? Even if we do, let's be honest with ourselves: Do we really believe it? The Nicene Creed (325 CE) goes even further: "I look forward to the resurrection of the dead and the life of the world to come." Do we really *look forward* to resurrection, in spite of having to die to experience it, and "the life of the world to come," even if we cannot possibly imagine what it will be like? The first Creed of Epiphanius (c. 374 CE) states: "He was crucified for us under Pontius Pilate, and suffered, and was buried; and the third day He rose again according to the Scriptures; and ascended into heaven." The second Creed of Epiphanius specifies that Christ "suffered in the flesh; and rose again, and went up into heaven in the same body."[1]

What do these phrases, "resurrection of the dead," "life of the world to come," and rising "in the same body" actually mean? Even more, what might resurrection mean *for us*? Not only after we and our loved ones die, but right here and now, while we are alive on this earth? Moreover, if we can understand what resurrection implies and accept its personal relevance, how are we to live every day of our lives actually looking forward to being resurrected from the dead? Before we attempt to answer these crucial questions, we need to consider how the age-old idea of resurrection was understood, disbelieved . . . and believed.

1. Epiphanius, "The Creeds of Epiphanius."

Ancient Ideas about the Afterlife

The noun "resurrection" (Greek, *anastasis*) means a "raising or standing up," either from a seated position or from the dead. As a verb, "to resurrect" implies causing someone to stand up, to awaken, or to rise again, either from sleep or from death. For Greeks, Romans, Jews, and Christians living in the first century of the Common Era, the term *resurrection* referred specifically to a human being "rising up" from the dead in bodily form with the same personal identity as before. However, resurrection did not imply a state of new life immediately following death, but rather, "new life *after* a period of being dead."[2] It is important to note that the Jewish people never expected *anyone* to rise from the dead until the end of the world.

Greeks and Romans emphatically denied the possibility of any such phenomenon as resurrection. For them, as for postmodern skeptics, once people died, they stayed dead. It was understood as far back as the Greek poet Homer (c. eighth century BCE) that resurrection simply could not and did not happen. Achilles warns Priam (after having killed Priam's son, Hector): "Bear up and do not grieve ever ceaselessly in your heart; for nothing will you accomplish by grieving for your son, and you will not bring him back to life; before that you will suffer some other ill."[3] Similarly, the playwright Aeschylus put these definitive words into the mouth of Apollo: "But when once a man has died and the dust has sucked up his blood, there is no rising again."[4] Indeed, for the ancient Greeks the very idea of a resurrection of a rotted corpse was abhorrent: "Resurrection of the flesh appeared a startling, distasteful idea, at odds with everything that passed for wisdom among the educated."[5] The dead might live on through tales of their brave deeds in war, or through their philosophical writings, or in mythic stories, but the commonsense thinking was: "Dead men don't rise."

Moreover, they cease to exist. Greek Epicureans considered that the soul, like the body, was composed of the smallest particles of physical matter. When the matter of body and soul disintegrated at death, so did the person.[6] The dead became no more than a shadow of their former

---

2. Wright, *The Resurrection of the Son of God*, 31, emphasis added.

3. Homer, *The Iliad*, Vol. II, 24:549–51, 603.

4. Aeschylus, *The Eumenides*, 437.

5. MacMullen, *Christianizing the Roman Empire*, 12.

6. Wright, *Resurrection*, 34.

selves or "shades" (Greek, *skiai*); wandering ghosts (*psychai*); or phantoms of the imagination (*eidola*). Though they might "appear" in human form in various myths and tales, they were never considered to be real, nor could they be grasped and held onto, for the appearance was only an illusion, utterly deceptive.[7] These non-bodily phantoms were thought to dwell forever in Hades, where they existed in a miserable inhuman state, sometimes tormented for earthly crimes, with no hope of escape or salvation. "Death did not mean complete oblivion for the individual, but the conventional notions of the afterlife offered little comfort for the dying or the bereaved."[8] Hades, then, was certainly not a place one longed to reach after death. It was deemed a place of hopelessness and despair—a ghostly hell.

Egyptian mythology, on the other hand, told stories about the reemergence of the dead back into this life (after an indeterminate period of being dead). "The Egyptians were essentially religious optimists, believing fervently in the 'resurrection' of the dead as an individualised, embodied self, with the whole purpose and point of the funeral rite being to rejoin the *ba* (soul) with the body. Cremation was abhorrent, reserved for evil-doers who would thereby be rendered totally non-existent."[9] The Egyptian practice of mummification implied that the dead person was still "alive" in a bodily sense (in spite of appearances to the contrary) and would, at some future date, reemerge as an embodied self. "The point of the funeral was to accomplish the 'going out into the day', the new life with Osiris and as Osiris, in the delights of eternity."[10] Thus, for Egyptians, the boundaries between life and death were indistinct, even amorphous. Death was thought to be merely a continuation of earthly life. Since the mummy was not considered technically dead, its reemergence could not be called a resurrection *from* the dead. Rather, it would signify a sort of mummified resuscitation among the gods.

Immortality of the Soul

The influence of the philosopher Plato (late fifth to early fourth century BCE) cast a startling new light on Greek views of the afterlife. Plato

7. Wright, *Resurrection*, 43.

8. Price, *Religions of the Ancient Greeks*, 101.

9. Davies, *Death, Burial and Rebirth*, 34.

10. Davies, *Death, Burial and Rebirth*, 34–35.

inquired whether death was nothing but the *separation* of the soul from the body: "The body's having come to be apart, separated from the soul, alone by itself, and the soul's being apart, alone by itself, separated from the body? Death can't be anything else but that, can it?"[11] He also suggested: "Isn't the body liable to be quickly dissolved, whereas soul must be completely indissoluble or something close to it?"[12] Thus in Plato's worldview, it was not the body but the *soul* that was destined for immortality. Whereas in Homer, the locus of the individual "self" was the physical body rotting in the ground while the phantom ghost descended into the kingdom of the shades in Hades, for Plato it was exactly the opposite: the locus of the self was in the soul.

In Platonic thinking, the soul is the form that temporarily "informs" matter, awakens its potential to form a body, and enables the human being to exist at all. The "true self" resides in the non-corporeal soul and the corpse in the grave is merely the physical remnant, the cast-off clothing as it were, of the real person. Plato taught that the soul is superior precisely because it is immaterial and immortal. Furthermore, "given that the immortal is also indestructible, wouldn't soul, if it proves to be immortal, be imperishable as well?"[13] Plato considered that the soul existed before the body and will continue to exist eternally after the body decays. Throughout its earthly existence, however, the soul (Greek, *soma*) remains imprisoned in the body as in a living tomb (Greek, *sema*), forgetting its true origin, and longing to be set free by death. "For some say that the body is the grave of the soul which may be thought to be buried in our present life . . ."[14]

Thus for Plato, it was *earthly* life that was full of delusion, fraught with suffering and constant danger.

> For there is no radiance in our earthly copies of justice or temperance or those other things that are precious to souls: they are seen through a glass dimly; and there are few who, going to the images, behold in them the realities, and these only with difficulty.[15]

---

11. Plato, *Phaedo*, 64c, 8–9.

12. Plato, *Phaedo*, 80c, 29.

13. Plato, *Phaedo*, 106e, 61.

14. Plato, *The Dialogues: Cratylus*, Vol. 2, 400c, 148.

15. Plato, *The Dialogues: Phaedrus*, Vol. 2, 250b, 267.

Because of human ignorance, injustice, and intemperance, Plato judged it essential to educate and discipline the human soul. He was convinced this could only be done through the study of philosophy and the practice of virtue. He argued that the quality of happiness or misery the soul would experience in the next life depended on its accomplishments or failures in this one. "But the company of gods may not rightly be joined by one who has not practiced philosophy and departed in absolute purity, by any but the lover of knowledge."[16] Plato held that if the soul is in that "pure state" at death: "then, does it not depart to the invisible, which is similar to it, the divine and immortal and wise; and on arrival there, isn't its lot to be happy, released from its wandering and folly, its fears and wild lusts, and other ills of the human condition, and . . . does it not pass the rest of time in very truth with gods?"[17]

According to the Platonic scenario, death should be anticipated as the liberation of the immortal soul from the sufferings of earthly life, much to be desired. For those who had become wise, fulfilled their civic duties, and shown courage in battle, dying was deemed the *triumph* of a good life, not a tragedy. Furthermore, for those who had lived good lives on earth, Hades was considered a place of extreme pleasure and a center for philosophical discourse. For those who had been wicked, however, Hades meted out severe punishments. Still, these sufferings were considered to be necessary for the triumph of justice and therefore, distinctly positive.[18] In the afterlife, righteous souls would finally be set free from their bodies and might ascend to the place of the immortal gods and become divine. Such divinized souls were believed to be so content they did not even want to return to the world of space, time, and matter.

In Plato's dualistic philosophy, immaterial and immortal forms (ideas) took precedence over material and thus mortal matter. Hence, there was no need nor was there any desire for bodily resurrection after the soul had finally escaped the prison of the body. Why would there be? It would have been absurd to hope for the soul to be weighed down yet again by another physical body. According to Plato, even the great pleasures of the human body could not be compared to the pure bliss of the soul's contemplation of eternal forms in the Isles of the Blessed. Why

---

16. Plato, *Phaedo*, 82b, 32.

17. Plato, *Phaedo*, 81a, 30.

18. Wright, *Resurrection*, 52.

should an immortal soul ever long for a resurrected body? Indeed, the world of abstract and pure ideas was, for Plato, the only *real* world.

Plato's most famous student, Aristotle, attempted to undercut the Platonic dualism of soul and body by teaching that the soul (form) was not independent of or superior to the physical matter of the body. He defined soul as the *substantial form* of the body, the organizing principle of the matter—that which, in fact, enlivened the body. Therefore, the individual person was essentially made up of *both* body and soul. Nevertheless, Aristotle still acknowledged the innate superiority of mind over matter: "the highest aspect of reason might be immortal and divine."[19] Even with Aristotle's respect for the nature of matter and his understanding of the complete human person as consisting of both soul and body, he did not suggest the possibility of resurrection and the reunification of soul and body in a life after death. It was too bizarre to bear discussion.

Transmigration of Souls

Another ancient theory that needs mentioning is that of transmigration or reincarnation (Greek, *metempsychosis*) of souls into new bodies. This passage of a disembodied soul into a *different* body might occur immediately or it might take place at any time from a few years to a millennium after death. Based on the ideas of Pythagoras (sixth century BCE), the notion of the transmigration of souls gained popularity within the secret Greek Orphic religious cults as well as among some philosophers. It was also a tenet of the Druids in Gaul. However, it never seems to have caught on with the general populace.[20]

Ancient Greek theories of matter and form, body and soul, may appear tiresomely dualistic to us postmodern people who try to focus on the wholeness and integrity of the individual. Nevertheless, we can appreciate that Greek philosophers sought to define the nonmaterial dimension of the human person, the spiritual aspect that thirsts for continuance in some form after death. They articulated the yearning of the human heart for immortality (preferably one that would involve eternal happiness, not everlasting punishment) and the longing of the human mind to contemplate reality with true wisdom. The idea of becoming "one with the stars," which is found in ancient Babylonian,

19. As quoted in Wright, *Resurrection*, 53.
20. Wright, *Resurrection*, 78.

Egyptian, and Greek sources, became a potent expression of the universal hope of transcending death in a new and exalted life.

However, while the majority of ancient people may have wished for some kind of life in another sphere (after a period of being dead), no one ever expected the dead to return to *this* earth, their spiritual identities preserved but their once-mortal bodies radically transformed into glorified bodies. Such a concept would have been unthinkable, as unthinkable as resurrection of the body would seem to a contemporary materialist. Although the souls of emperors, statesmen, philosophers, and the virtuous might be said to dwell among the stars with the immortal gods, their bodies were either buried or burned. No one expected the fresh graves of national heroes to be found empty and the bodies of rulers did not customarily rise from their funeral pyres.

From our brief overview, we may deduce that among ancient philosophers there was no consistent thinking about what happens after death. The one thing everyone seemed to agree upon was that there was no such thing as the bodily resurrection of a human being who had previously died and been buried. That would have been thought impossible.

Biblical Ideas of Resurrection

Now we turn to theistic views of resurrection. What did the ancient Israelites believe about resurrection? How did they develop a unique understanding of what might happen after death? Are there prophecies of bodily resurrection in the Hebrew Bible?

For those expecting to find a host of statements about the afterlife, it is somewhat disappointing to realize that the concept of resurrection never became a central issue in the Hebrew Scriptures. There is scant mention of the word for resurrection (Hebrew, *techiyah*). Nevertheless, it is possible to trace, albeit circuitously, a gradual development in beliefs about the afterlife and bodily resurrection. Biblical scholars suggest that, in the earliest phase of Hebrew thought, the dead were thought to descend into Sheol, the realm of eternal darkness, gloom, and endless sleep (a place similar to Homer's idea of Hades), from which they would never emerge. In the next phase, devout Israelites began to hope that the mutual love between Yahweh and the Israelites was so strong and enduring that nothing could break that bond, not even death. Yahweh, the God of loving-kindness and abounding in mercy, simply would not let such love perish. Psalmists suggested there might be a disembodied but nevertheless blissful afterlife with Yahweh following death. Finally, in the third phase, prophets envisioned that, after an interim period of waiting, the dead would rise to a new and *bodily* life.[21] Admittedly, none of these phases of thought was clear cut or moved directly from one interpretation of the afterlife to the next in a sequential development. However, if we examine these different positions we might recognize the range of ideas that Israelites of the first century CE entertained about resurrection from the dead.

Psalmic Intuitions

Some of the psalmic literature may date back to the reign of King David in the tenth century BCE. Surprisingly, many of these ancient psalms hold no promise for resurrection, but suggest only an endless state of despair and forgetfulness following death, where one is irrevocably cut off from the presence of Yahweh forever: "For in death there is no remembrance of you; in Sheol who can give you praise?" (Ps 6:5). And again: "The dead do not praise the LORD, nor do any that go down into silence" (Ps 115:17). These gloomy predictions do not seem to be that different from Homer's desolate view of the afterlife. The dead were "asleep" in their graves, unaware of having ever been alive, and cut off from the memory of Yahweh. King David was said to have "slept with his ancestors" which implies that he had gone to a nether world to rest with Abraham, Isaac, and Jacob. While the dead might be given food and other provisions at the time of burial, thereafter any effort to communicate with or "awaken" the sleeping dead to gain knowledge of the future was considered extremely dangerous and strictly forbidden. An injunction against veneration of the dead was deemed necessary to protect Israel from Canaanite necromancers and the cult of ancestor worship. Israel's God was believed to be the sole source and arbiter of life and death, the only one who could know the future. It was considered an insult to Yahweh to consult the dead for signs and prognostications.

Other psalms, however, convey a buoyant hope that eventually the dead would be rescued from the eternal death of Sheol through the all-powerful Creator of life:

21. See Wright, *Resurrection*, 86.

Therefore my heart is glad, and my soul rejoices;
   my body also rests secure.
For you do not give me up to Sheol,
   or let your faithful one see the Pit,

You show me the path of life.
   In your presence there is fullness of joy;
   in your right hand are pleasures forevermore. (Ps 16:9–11)

For the foolhardy and false, death will mean everlasting despair in Sheol;
but for the righteous, Yahweh will bring salvation:

But God will ransom my soul from the power of Sheol,
   for he will receive me. (Ps 49:15)

In another passage, the psalmist sings even more confidently of his total
trust in the Lord who will welcome him into glory after a period of resting
in death:

Nevertheless I am continually with you;
   you hold my right hand.
You guide me with your counsel,
   and afterward you will receive me with glory.
(Ps 73:23–24, emphasis added)

Here we find a firm conviction that "afterward" (that is, after death), there
will be a final judgment followed by the faithful being received into the
glory of God. More directly than any others, these three psalms (Pss 16,
49, and 73) point toward an emerging faith and hope in the restoration
of bodily life after death. This hope is not based on having an immortal
soul that will necessarily live forever (as the Platonists believed); it is
grounded purely in the love and faithfulness of Yahweh, who will restore
his people to the fullness of life in newness of flesh. It should be noted
that Psalm 16:10 would be cited in the New Testament as an ancient
prediction of Christ's own resurrection: "Foreseeing this, David spoke of
the resurrection of the Messiah, saying, 'He was not abandoned to Hades,
nor did his flesh experience corruption'" (Acts 2:31).

Even such a small sampling of psalms suggests that Israelite belief
in resurrection became inextricably linked to the exaltation of divine
justice. Resurrection was considered essential to reveal Yahweh's supreme
power over life and death, heaven and earth. If there were no other realm
but Sheol, how would Yahweh reveal his victory over death? If there were
no final judgment, how would the lowly be raised up from their misery,

and the godless (who so often seem to prosper in this life) be brought low? If there were no hope of divine vindication, how would Yahweh offer just fruits to the faithful? In short, if there were no life after death, how would good triumph over evil?[22]

Again and again, in the midst of crisis, illness, invasion, and the fear of death, the psalmist expresses confidence that God is "my refuge, my portion in the land of the living" (Ps 142:5). Because of his unshakeable trust in the love of God, the psalmist hopes that Yahweh will carry him over the threshold of death into the next life. This is because "Yahweh holds his pious one fast, and remains his God in every situation in life, and even death cannot remove the communion vouchsafed to him."[23] Thus the idea of resurrection became inextricably linked to belief in *divine redemption*.

Prophetic Voices

The earliest explicit Old Testament reference to bodily resurrection appears in a prophecy from Hosea, dating perhaps to the eighth century BCE:

> Come, let us return to the LORD;
>   for it is he who has torn, and he will heal us;
>   he has struck down, and he will bind us up.
> After two days he will revive us;
>   *on the third day he will raise us up,*
>   that we may live before him. (Hos 6:1–2, emphasis added)

While at the time this passage probably alluded to a physical renewal of an entire people, for later Jewish-Christians it would be read as a direct prophecy of Christ's own resurrection "on the third day."

Likewise, First Isaiah (eighth to early seventh century BCE) expresses the hope of a final victory by Yahweh over Israel's oppressors and suggests the salvation of *all* the nations:

> In days to come
>   the mountain of the LORD's house
> shall be established as the highest of the mountains,
>   and shall be raised above the hills;
>   all the nations shall stream to it. (Isa 2:2)

22. See von Rad, *Old Testament Theology*, Vol. I, 406.

23. von Rad, *Old Testament Theology*, Vol. I, 406.

After describing a too-familiar scene of disaster, death, and destruction, Isaiah holds out hope that Yahweh will finally destroy the "shroud" of death, the winding sheet that covers every nation, excluding none. All suffering peoples—not just the Israelites—will be rescued; their tears and their disgrace will be "wiped away." They will be invited to celebrate at a holy banquet that the Lord will provide on the mountain of Zion (Isa 25:8). Furthermore, the prophet declares that after a period of great trials and chastisement the day will come when all those who seek Yahweh will receive the reward of a *bodily* resurrection:

> Your dead shall live, their corpses shall rise.
>   O dwellers in the dust, awake and sing for joy!
> For your dew is a radiant dew,
>   and the earth will give birth to those long dead. (Isa 26:19)

Apocalyptic Visions

In the biblical literature that deals with the destruction of the world and the final judgment, we find more explicit references to the expectation of bodily resurrection. The prophet Ezekiel (seventh century BCE) experiences a vision in which he understands that after an interim period, the "dry bones" of the dead would be infused with divine breath, given new sinews, flesh, and skin, and rise again to life and knowledge of God. While written as an allegory, the message is clear: Yahweh, the Creator God, is able to resurrect dead bones, re-clothe them with flesh, and restore them to new life.

> The hand of the LORD came upon me, and he brought me out by the spirit of the LORD and set me down in the middle of a valley; it was full of bones. He led me all around them; there were very many lying in the valley, and they were very dry. He said to me, "Mortal, can these bones live?" I answered, "O Lord God, you know." Then he said to me, "Prophesy to these bones, and say to them: O dry bones, hear the word of the Lord. Thus says the LORD God to these bones: I will cause breath to enter you, and you shall live. I will lay sinews on you, and will cause flesh to come upon you, and cover you with skin, and put breath in you, and you shall live; and you shall know that I am the LORD." (Eze 37:1–6)

The prophet does as Yahweh tells him and prophesies that these bones shall, indeed, *live*. Then "suddenly there was a noise, a rattling, and the bones came together, bone to its bone" (Ezek 37:7). Ezekiel looks and sees that there is sinew and flesh and skin on the bones, but as yet no breath of life in the bodies.

> Then he said to me, "Prophesy to the breath, prophesy, mortal, and say to the breath: Thus says the LORD God: Come from the four winds, O breath, and breathe upon these slain, that they may live." I prophesied as he commanded me, and the breath came into them, and they lived, and stood on their feet, a vast multitude. (Ezek 37:9–10)

Yahweh reveals to Ezekiel that these "dry bones" belong to the whole house of Israel, all who have lost hope and are cut off from life in the land of Israel. Yahweh directs the prophet:

> Therefore prophesy, and say to them, Thus says the Lord God: *I am going to open your graves, and bring you up from your graves, O my people*; and I will bring you back to the land of Israel. And you shall know that I am the LORD, when I open your graves, and bring you up from your graves, O my people. *I will put my spirit within you, and you shall live*, and I will place you on your own soil; then you shall know that I, the LORD, have spoken and will act, says the LORD." (Ezek 37:12–14, emphasis added)

Through this elaborate metaphor, Ezekiel prophesies that Yahweh would resurrect an entire nation that had been presumed "dead," bring its scattered tribes back from foreign lands to the soil of Israel, cleanse their impurities, and infuse them with the living spirit of God. This revelation evokes the story of Genesis when "the LORD God formed man from the dust of the ground, and breathed into his nostrils the breath of life; and the man became a living being" (Gen 2:7). Once restored to life, the people will surely know that Yahweh is the God who saves. Ezekiel's vision became a persistent allegory for resurrected life.

Like the book of Ezekiel, the much later apocalyptic book of Daniel (second century BCE), dramatizes the ongoing agony of the Jewish people. It recreates the destruction and exile of the Babylonian captivity as a "cover story" for the brutal persecution and martyrdom of Jews during the reign of the Greek king of the Seleucid Empire, Antiochus Epiphanes IV (175–164 BCE). Daniel predicts that the Messiah will come to judge the nations and rule over a new and everlasting kingdom.

> I saw one like a human being
>> coming with the clouds of heaven.
> And he came to the Ancient One
>> and was presented before him.
> To him was given dominion
>> and glory and kingship,
> that all peoples, nations, and languages
>> should serve him.
> His dominion is an everlasting dominion
>> that shall not pass away,
> and his kingship is one
>> that shall never be destroyed. (Dan 7:13–14)

What the righteous might expect after a time of great anguish, suffering, and death was nothing less than *divine* deliverance. Daniel also envisions the angelic prince Michael coming to the aid of the desperate Israelites and vanquishing their enemies. The prophet clearly predicts a *bodily* resurrection; that some would be raised to everlasting life and some to endless shame.

"Many of those who sleep in the dust of the earth shall awake, some to everlasting life, and some to shame and everlasting contempt. Those who are wise shall shine like the brightness of the sky, and those who lead many to righteousness, like the stars forever and ever" (Dan 12:2–3). Just as being asleep "in the dust of the earth" was a metaphor for death, so "shall awake" was an implied reference to bodily resurrection. Those who were "wise" and had lived according to the law of righteousness, as well as those who had taught and led others on the path of virtue, were destined to "shine like the brightness of the sky" and "like the stars forever." However, these two similes did not mean (as they would have meant for Plato) that the souls of the righteous would depart immediately after death and become one with the stars, enjoying a disembodied "astral immortality." On the contrary, these images implied that, after an undefined period of being dead ("asleep in the dust of the earth"), the wise would be re-awakened by Yahweh and live forever in a new and glorious *bodily* form.[24] No doubt, this was written to convince the Jewish people that its martyrs had not died in vain and that they would never be forgotten by Yahweh.

We must emphasize that resurrection from an interim state of "being dead" did not signify mere *resuscitation* from the dust of the earth and a

---

24. See Wright, *Resurrection*, 110–11.

return to the same bodies the dead had known before, bodies that would have to suffer and die all over again. Nor did it suggest *transportation* of the human body to a heavenly dimension, without passing through death, such as had happened to Enoch (Gen 5:24; Heb 11:5) and Elijah (2 Kgs 2:11). Resurrection in the book of Daniel meant that the righteous ones of Judea would be raised to a radically *transformed* bodily state and would enjoy a completely different relationship with the world. The allusion to shining like "the brightness of the sky" suggests that resurrected martyrs and righteous ones would become heavenly beacons of wisdom and light for those on earth still suffering in ignorance and darkness.

Martyrdom and Resurrection

The second book of Maccabees (late second century BCE) depicts a dramatic story of faith in resurrection as the driving force through the sufferings and martyrdoms endured under Antiochus Epiphanes. According to the historian Josephus (first century CE), the context of the story is that Antiochus had pillaged Jerusalem, killing eighty thousand men, women, and children, while selling another eighty thousand into slavery. Thereafter, the king had himself desecrated the holy Temple, set up Greek idols on the altar, and stolen eighteen hundred talents from the temple treasury. He ordered Jerusalem's Temple renamed the temple of Olympian Zeus, and forbade Jews to keep the Sabbath and celebrate religious festivals, practice circumcision, or even declare themselves Jews. Antiochus demanded sacrifices of swine's flesh to be made to Greek gods upon the temple altar, which was, of course, a grave violation of the Law of Moses. He also commanded that Jews be forced to eat the sacrifices.[25]

In a poignant tale of faith and courage, a Jewish mother and her seven sons were arrested and threatened with death by Antiochus for refusing to eat the pork that had been sacrificed to idols. Even though whipped and tortured, one after another the sons (and eventually the mother) professed that they would rather die than transgress the Mosaic Law. Furthermore, they declared that they had no fear of death because they were confident that they would be given back their bodies at the resurrection. The second son confronted Antiochus:

25. Josephus, *Jewish Antiquities*, 6:2, 139–41.

> "You accursed wretch, you dismiss us from this present life,
> but the King of the universe will raise us up to an everlasting
> renewal of life, because we have died for his laws." (2 Macc 7:9)

The third brother spoke as he held out his tongue and hands to be cut off:

> "I got these from Heaven, and because of his laws I disdain them,
> and from him I hope to get them back again." (2 Macc 7:11)

Likewise, the fourth brother insisted:

> "One cannot but choose to die at the hands of mortals and to
> cherish the hope God gives of being raised again by him. But for
> you there will be no resurrection to life!" (2 Macc 7:14)

And so it went, down to the seventh son, to whom the king promised great wealth, political influence, and even personal friendship if only he would transgress the ways of his ancestors. The mother implored her youngest child not to submit:

> "Accept death, so that in God's mercy I may get you back again
> along with your brothers." (2 Macc 7:29)

Last of all, the mother, too, was killed, and the narrator concludes tersely: "Let this be enough, then, about the eating of sacrifices and the extreme tortures" (2 Macc 7:42).

Here there is no doubt that for righteous Jews of the second century BCE, *bodily resurrection was the expected reward of martyrdom.* Resurrection implied not only liberation of the soul but a return of dismembered body parts to complete wholeness sometime after death. It was no longer solely a metaphor for the restoration of the land of Israel, the renewal of the covenant, and the dream of political self-rule. The idea of resurrection had become very literal and very physical.[26] Now it was about getting back one's individual body reunited with one's soul, in a new and glorious form, with one's personal identity intact. Indeed, it was this burning faith in the power of the Creator of life who grants bodily resurrection to the righteous that would inspire extraordinary acts of courage in generations of Jewish zealots in their revolutionary uprisings against tyrannical rulers, whether Greek or Roman.

---

26. Wright, *Resurrection,* 202.

Why Resurrection?

In considering these few but significant biblical prophecies of resurrection, we may be inclined to ask: "Why did the Israelites come to believe in bodily resurrection?" In a broad sense, the foundation for Israelite belief in bodily resurrection may be traced all the way back to the revelation of the Creator God who brought forth all that is, who created humankind in the divine image and likeness, and who "saw that it was good" (Gen 1:31); to a wise God who knew what would provide the most perfect happiness for human beings; to a saving God who rescued a remnant from the great flood; to a mighty God who led Abraham into a new land, promised to make him the father of many nations, and blessed him and his wife Sarah with a son in their old age; to a liberating God who commissioned Moses to lead the Israelites out of slavery in Egypt; to a merciful God who raised up prophets to urge repentance when the people sank again and again into sin; to a faithful God who brought the Israelites back from exile in Babylon; and to a loving God who promised a Messiah who would free his people from the scourge of sin and teach them the path to wisdom.

Eternal life would not be granted because of any human merits or achievements, or even as a result of martyrdom for the faith, but solely because of the goodness and mercy of Yahweh. The God of Israel created humankind out of the earth in the beginning; likewise, the same Divine Power could and would *recreate* human life at the end of the world—from the scattered bones and dust of the earth.

> He raises the poor from the dust,
>   and lifts the needy from the ash heap,
> to make them sit with princes,
>   with the princes of his people. (Ps 113:7–8)

While only a few psalms may refer specifically to bodily resurrection, almost all the psalms sing of boundless trust in Yahweh's power over death. The Israelites knew only too well that earthly life involved famine, persecution, exile, and sometimes, martyrdom. They attributed their suffering to their own willful breaking of the covenant with Yahweh, their lack of obedience to the Law of Moses, and their apostasy from the faith. In fact, in the book of Daniel, the account of the Babylonian Exile became an extended metaphor for the even more deadly breaking of the covenantal union with God. Only Yahweh could end the physical and spiritual exile. Only Yahweh could forgive the people and bring them back home. It was precisely because Yahweh is full of mercy and loving-kindness that the Israelites believed that Yahweh would come to the people's rescue, liberate them from the bonds of their oppressors, and return them to their native land. Likewise, the love of Yahweh would triumph over death, reunite body and soul, and reward the righteous with everlasting life.

Unlike the Greek hope of disembodied immortality, the biblical hope of life after death was not connected to the idea of the human being already possessing an immortal soul that could survive forever without a body. Judaism did not favor such a body-soul dualism. For Israelites, *the complete human person consisted of a body and spirit conjoined,* as in the creation of Adam. The body expressed the spirit and the spirit enlivened the body. When the spirit was taken from the body, the body disintegrated into bones and ashes. When the body died, the spirit "slept" in the divine embrace, waiting for bodily resurrection. The book of the Wisdom of Solomon (written between the second century BCE and mid-first century CE) evokes this transitional passing into a divine dimension:

> But the souls of the righteous are in the hand of God,
> and no torment will ever touch them.
> In the eyes of the foolish they seemed to have died,
> and their departure was thought to be a disaster
> and their going from us to be their destruction;
> but they are at peace.
> For though in the sight of others they were punished,
> their hope is full of immortality. (Wis 3:1–4)

For the Israelites, to be rescued from the disaster of death and to hope for immortality meant that *both* body and soul, the whole person, would be saved and become immortal. While the book of Wisdom considers that "the hope of the ungodly is like thistledown carried by the wind, and like a light frost driven away by a storm" (Wis 5:14), the writer expresses confidence that those who remained faithful to the divine covenant will see their hope in eternal life realized.

> But the righteous live forever,
> and their reward is with the Lord;
> the Most High takes care of them.
> therefore they will receive a glorious crown
> and a beautiful diadem from the hand of the Lord,
> because with his right hand he will cover them,
> and with his arm he will shield them. (Wis 5:15–16)

We see this steadfast faith in the Creator redeeming, restoring, and recreating life throughout the entire Hebrew Bible. The story of salvation is not merely a biblical metaphor. For the Israelites, it was the *true history* of Yahweh's steadfast love. Thus as a natural extension of that faith in divine love, Israelites came to believe that Yahweh would rescue them— even from the exile of death.

In a very real sense, all the stories, psalms, and prophecies of salvation are only one story: the gift of life freely given; the sacred covenant established with God, then broken by disobedience; the necessary chastisement of exile and suffering; and the return of the people to the covenant, the land, and the nation of Israel. The basic refrain is that, because God is always faithful, "I believe that I shall see the goodness of the LORD in the land of the living" (Ps 27:13). For Israelites (as later for Christians), faith in a just and loving God naturally engendered the hope of vindication, restoration, and bodily resurrection. Hope in the eventual triumph of divine life over human death was grounded in the certainty that the Creator is all-powerful. What God creates, God can and will redeem and recreate. Sin and death have no hold over Yahweh.

The Prayer of Jerusalem

In considering the various attitudes toward resurrection in Judaism, we must also mention the prayers that were being recited during the Second Temple period, from c. 530 BCE until the Temple's destruction in 70 CE. The Sabbath and weekday prayers included the most fundamental testimony of Jewish faith, *Shema Ysrael*: "Hear, O Israel, the LORD our God, the Lord is one" (Deut 6:4) and the *Tefilat HaAmidah* ("The Standing Prayer") or simply *hatefila* ("Prayer"), which was recited three times a day. It is called the standing prayer because it was recited standing and facing the ark that encloses the sacred books of the Torah. The *Amidah* blesses, praises, and petitions Yahweh in a series of Eighteen Benedictions. The second Benediction is called "powers" (Hebrew, *Geburot*) and directly extols the mighty deeds of the One who revives the dead:

> "Thou art mighty forever, O Lord: Thou resurrectest the dead; art great to save. Sustaining the living in loving-kindness, resurrecting the dead in abundant mercies, Thou supportest the falling, and healest the sick, and settest free the captives, and fulfillest Thy faith to them that sleep in the dust. Who is like Thee, master of mighty deeds and who may be compared

unto Thee? King sending death and reviving again and causing salvation to sprout forth. Thou art surely believed to resurrect the dead. Blessed be Thou, O Lord, who revivest the dead."[27]

Such exalted faith in bodily resurrection and the ultimate vindication of the righteous sustained the Israelites through wars, persecutions, exiles, the destruction of the Second Temple, and the fall of Jerusalem. However, no Jew in the turbulent first century of the Common Era ever expected resurrection to occur *before the final judgment.*

> Ancient Judaism did not know of an anticipated resurrection as an event of history. Nowhere does one find in the literature anything comparable to the resurrection of Jesus. Certainly resurrections of the dead were known, but these always concerned resuscitations, the return to the earthly life. In no place in the late Judaic literature does it concern a resurrection to glory as an event of history.[28]

Furthermore, apart from what would take place for all the dead at the end of the world, no Jew anticipated that resurrection would ever happen to a *single* person first—not even the Messiah. Until it did.

> *And he will destroy on this mountain*
> *the shroud that is cast over all peoples,*
> *the sheet that is spread over all nations;*
> *he will swallow up death forever.*
> *Then the LORD God will wipe away the tears from all faces,*
> *and the disgrace of his people he will take away from all the*
> *earth,*
> *for the LORD has spoken.* (Isa 25:7–8)

27. Adler and Hirsch, "Shemoneh 'Esreh" in the Jewish Encyclopedia, available online at www.jewishencyclopedia.com/articles/13561-shemoneh-esreh.

28. Jeremias, "Osterüberlieferung," 194.

2

Looking Into the Empty Tomb

THE GOSPEL ACCOUNTS CONCERNING the discovery of the empty tomb do not intend to supply a precise historical account of facts; that is, an exact description of what was seen or a word-for-word transmission of what was said. Written decades after the event, how could they? Rather, the Gospels testify to deeply personal experiences of *faith*. They provide short, evocative dramatizations of the earliest, most basic, and most sacred oral traditions: that women discovered the tomb was empty; that the risen Christ appeared to Peter, and to the other disciples; and that later (according to Paul), Jesus appeared to James as well as to five hundred people gathered at one time.

What runs through all four Gospel accounts is that Mary Magdalene and a few other women were the original witnesses to the empty tomb, the very first to bear the good news that Jesus was risen. This, in itself, is astounding. In the ancient world, the word of a woman was never to be trusted. A woman could not give testimony in a court of law because she could not be counted on either to know or to tell the truth. The first-century historian Josephus had added to the ancient law of witnesses (Deut 19:15): "From women let no evidence be accepted, because of the levity and temerity of their sex."[1] That all four evangelists identify Mary Magdalene and other women (by different names, but nonetheless, a small group of devoted female followers of Jesus) as the first witnesses to the resurrection has the ring of authenticity. No disciple or later evangelist would have willingly chosen to recount the revelation of Christ's resurrection based on the testimony of mere women if it had not

1. Josephus, *Jewish Antiquities*, 4:10, 219.

been well known that they were, in fact, the first to discover the empty tomb. Such a story would not have been fabricated because it was such a colossal embarrassment for the young church. Indeed, this is called by scholars the "criterion of embarrassment" and heavily weights the truth of the testimony in its favor. Furthermore, after Jesus was seen by all the disciples gathered together, it became perfectly obvious that Mary Magdalene's announcement of the risen Lord—at first denied by the men as idle talk—had been true after all. The indisputable agreement among the four evangelists on this point lends credence to the validity of their story.

Divergent Accounts

Nonetheless, it has long been observed that there are disparities in the resurrection accounts. The four canonical Gospels diverge not only in details, but in personal viewpoints. For some readers, these variations have given rise to doubt and even disbelief. What is the historical bedrock of each resurrection story? What is dramatization for effect? What is symbolic embellishment to evoke a more spiritual understanding? What is the elaboration of tradition by the early church?

Before we examine these discrepancies, we must be very clear that no one actually *witnessed* the moment of resurrection:

> Yet, *as far as we know*, no one saw what happened to the body; what the first witnesses experienced was not the resurrection-event itself, but an encounter with Jesus, an encounter which they then interpreted as meaning that Jesus was risen, had previously been raised so as to be in a position to encounter them.[2]

Furthermore, we may assume that the astonishing stories of Easter morning were told over and over again and, in the retelling by different people, independent traditions arose among the disciples. Then the Gospel writers assembled the basic oral traditions—and perhaps a collection of the "sayings of Jesus" from the hypothetical Q source[3]—and shaped them to express their own theological and pedagogical priorities.

2. Wedderburn, *Beyond Resurrection*, 12.

3. From the German *Quelle*, meaning "source." Scholars believe that the common material found in the Gospels of Matthew and Luke derived from this hypothetical Q document, essentially an early collection of the sayings (*logia*) of Jesus.

Do different versions necessarily mean basic disagreement? Was the empty tomb a nonhistorical legend concocted later in the first century by the evangelists? Was it merely designed as an imaginative prelude to the resurrection appearances? Do minor inconsistencies indicate such fabrication on the part of the early church? Or could they simply point to the development of theological understanding over the years?

While these are all valid questions, the main point we need to consider is: *Does each of the Gospel stories bear witness to Jesus Christ risen from the dead?* If so, then the diverse ways of dramatizing the details of the resurrection story—who saw and heard what and when— matter less than the essential meaning and message of the story itself. Inconsistencies do not rule out truthfulness. Some might even say they add to a story's authenticity. No two individuals recount the same life-transforming experience in exactly the same way. We know that reports about major historical events continue to undergo reevaluation. Furthermore, it is certainly not unusual for writers, be they first-century evangelists or postmodern scholars, to reinterpret a historical event in the light of current circumstances in order to discover a deeper relevance. It was also inevitable that the earliest witnesses told their stories simply, roughly, perhaps even confusing certain initial impressions. The shock and exhilaration of finding an empty tomb and then of encountering Jesus alive and in the flesh must have been overwhelming to the human psyches of those who saw him. Each person remembered and recounted the experience differently. Each attributed greater or lesser importance to certain aspects of the revelation. But all who saw the risen Jesus contributed in some way to the earliest oral tradition. All were convinced that the Jesus they had known before had now returned from the dead, utterly transformed but entirely recognizable. They knew this to be true because they had seen him with their own eyes.

Then, as the early Christian communities grew and developed, a theology of the salvific ramifications of Christ's resurrection evolved as a result of shared experience, discussion, communal prayer, eucharistic liturgy, and the ongoing inspiration of the Holy Spirit. Thus new layers of meaning entered into the resurrection stories. Indeed, some inconsistencies may indicate that each evangelist was determined to retell the resurrection story in his own particular way, with his own unique emphasis, articulating his own theological viewpoint.[4] Generally,

4. O'Collins, *The Easter Jesus,* 19–20.

the Gospels of Matthew and Luke were written in more apologetic and pedagogical language than the earlier and leaner Gospel of Mark. And the Gospel of John—while containing the simplest and therefore most probably the *earliest* account of what Mary Magdalene saw and heard— reveals a more highly developed Christology, as well as symbolic signs and mystical insights. But these teaching agendas did not change the essential story of what had happened. On the contrary, the *kerygma*—the apostolic "proclamation" of teaching about the risen Christ—was the core tradition from which all the Gospels were written.

Nevertheless, scholars disagree on the literary nature of the Gospel stories: Are they imaginative reconstructions of eyewitness accounts? Written versions of pre-Gospel templates? Reports of divine or angelic apparitions employing traditional Jewish elements? Commissioning narratives designed to inspire early Christians?[5] Indeed, the resurrection stories may be any or all of these. While we need not delve into controversial questions concerning literary genre, it may be beneficial to examine some of the obvious discrepancies in the resurrection stories to discover if they are really as problematic as they might first appear.

Time and Motivation

First of all, the Gospels do not agree on the exact time of day when the empty tomb was discovered. Mark describes it as after the Sabbath, "very early on the first day of the week, when the sun had risen" (Mark 16:2); Matthew specifies that it was after the Sabbath "as the first day of the week was dawning" (Matt 28:1); Luke indicates it was "on the first day of the week, at early dawn" (Luke 24:1); and John (probably for symbolic reasons) sets the scene "early on the first day of the week, while it was still dark" (John 20:1). Yet all four evangelists concur that Mary Magdalene and the other women's arrival at the tomb took place "very early *on the first day of the week,*" that is, on Sunday.

Second, the Gospels differ on the women's motivation for visiting the tomb. In the Gospels of Mark (16:1) and Luke (23:56; 24:1), the reason given that the women came to the tomb was to anoint the body of Jesus with spices they had prepared after the Sabbath. In Mark, Jesus had already been anointed by Mary Magdalene, in anticipation of his death (Mark 14:3–9). Still, Mark's mention that the women "bought" spices after

5. See Perkins, *Resurrection,* 114.

the Sabbath may have been the traditional reason given for their going to the tomb. In Matthew's Gospel, however, no intended anointing by the women is mentioned, nor would it have been possible, since the tomb had already been sealed with a large stone and a guard set to prevent the theft of the body. Presumably, in Matthew, the women returned that morning for no other reason than "to see the tomb" (Matt 28:1) and perhaps recite psalms of the dead while keeping watch over the corpse.[6] Likewise, in the Gospel of John, no reference is made to Mary Magdalene bringing spices for anointing since the body of Jesus had already been anointed at his burial with "a mixture of myrrh and aloes, weighing about a hundred pounds" (probably a symbolic, not a realistic, number) by Joseph of Arimathea and Nicodemus (John 19:39). Thereafter the corpse was wrapped in winding cloths and laid in the tomb, "according to the burial custom of the Jews" (John 19:40). Mary Magdalene simply came to the tomb alone to mourn her beloved Lord and discovered that the great stone had been rolled back. Immediately assuming that the body had been stolen, she ran to alert Peter and the other disciples.

What all the narrators describe is that early on the first day of the week, Mary Magdalene (and possibly some other women) came to the tomb on their own before any male disciples.

Women and Angels

How many women were there? In the Gospel of Mark, *three* women went to the tomb: "Mary Magdalene, Mary the mother of James, and Salome" (Mark 16:1). The names of these women do not exactly match those Mark placed at the very end of the crucifixion narrative, namely "Mary Magdalene and Mary the mother of Joses [who] saw where the body was laid" (Mark 15:47). However, the three names are congruent with those the evangelist mentioned as having seen the crucifixion: "There were also women looking on from a distance; among them were Mary Magdalene, and Mary the mother of James the younger and of Joses, and Salome" (Mark 15:40). This slight discrepancy may be explained by Mark working from different traditions with conflicting lists of women who accompanied Mary Magdalene from Galilee. Notably, Magdalene is the

6. Some scholars have suggested that the annual Easter celebration by Jerusalem Christians included a visitation to the empty tomb of Jesus; however, there is no evidence to support such a speculation. See Léon-Dufour, *Resurrection and the Message of Easter*, 113.

only name that appears consistently in all four Gospel accounts. Mark may have been attempting to harmonize the various names of the women who stood at the foot of the cross with those who saw where the body was laid on Good Friday and who then returned to the tomb on Easter Sunday.[7]

"They had been saying to one another, 'Who will roll away the stone for us from the entrance to the tomb?'" (Mark 16:3). Mark had previously indicated that "a stone" had been rolled against the door of the tomb (Mark 15:46), perhaps in order to set the stage for its miraculous removal and to show that nothing is impossible with God. According to Jewish thought, the sepulcher signified Sheol, that place of darkness and sleep into which the dead were believed to descend.[8] The stone rolled in front of a tomb both sealed the body for its journey into Sheol and acted as a deterrent to grave robbers. Now the women spoke of who would remove the great stone. As in numerous biblical stories, just when the desperate needed it most, a heavenly presence appears: "When they looked up, they saw that the stone, which was very large, had *already* been rolled back" (Mark 16:4, emphasis added). When the three women stooped and entered the dark tomb, they saw one "young man in a white robe" (Mark 16:5) sitting on the right side of the slab where Jesus had been placed. Who was this "young man"? Most likely Mark was suggesting an angelic presence, commonly depicted in Jewish writings as wearing white, and appearing and disappearing at will.[9] Quite naturally, the women "were alarmed" (Mark 16:5), a typical reaction to divine intervention throughout Mark's Gospel. However, the women were not only terrified because of the unexpected appearance of the young man in white, but because they *saw no corpse*. "But [the young man] said to them, 'Do not be alarmed. You are looking for Jesus of Nazareth, who was crucified'" (Mark 16:6). As so often in Scripture, the angelic apparition provided reassurance with the words, "Do not fear."

Even though the women had just been told by a divine apparition not to be afraid, they *still* needed an explanation for the missing body. The angel continued: "He has been raised; he is not here. Look, there is the place they laid him." (Mark 16:6). Then, probably using words from the oral kerygma, the angelic young man commissioned the three

7. Perkins, *Resurrection*, 116.

8. Léon-Dufour, *Resurrection*, 110.

9. Perkins, *Resurrection*, 118.

women: "But go, tell his disciples and Peter that he is going ahead of you to Galilee; there you will see him, just as he told you" (Mark 16:7). Just as Jesus had walked ahead of his disciples on the way to his crucifixion in Jerusalem (Mark 10:32), so now Mark indicates that Jesus will be going ahead of them into Galilee, the place where his ministry began and to which they must now return. In fact, wherever the disciples might go from then on, the risen Christ would always go ahead of them, especially if their witnessing might lead to suffering and death. This is Mark's message to the fearful Christian community.

In Matthew's version, only *two* women are mentioned: "Mary Magdalene and the other Mary" (Matt 28:1). These are just two of the many female disciples who "had followed Jesus from Galilee and had provided for him," and then stood by and watched the crucifixion: "Among them were Mary Magdalene, and Mary the mother of James and Joseph, and the mother of the sons of Zebedee" (Matt 27:55–56). These two, Mary Magdalene and the other Mary, had also observed Joseph of Arimathea bury Jesus, while sitting opposite the tomb (Matt 27:61). Now, at dawn, they had returned in order to keep watch and pray opposite the sealed sepulcher. They had no expectation of the stone being rolled back or of entering the tomb. Perhaps they were fulfilling a religious obligation to visit the tomb on the third day, in order to confirm that the deceased was indeed dead and buried.[10] "Suddenly there was a great earthquake; for an angel of the Lord, descending from heaven, came and rolled back the stone and sat on it. His appearance was like lightning, and his clothing white as snow" (Matt 28:2–3). Thus the stone becomes "the object of an intervention of the divine power over death: the angel of the Lord rolls it away and is sitting on it triumphantly."[11] Notably, Matthew is the only evangelist who depicts the women witnessing the stone being rolled back by an angelic presence. He is also the only evangelist who mentions that there were guards who shook and became "like dead men" at the terrifying event (Matt 28:4).

We may recall that Matthew had previously described a violent earthquake as the land itself felt the shock waves of the Savior's death: "At that moment the curtain of the temple was torn in two from top to bottom. The earth shook, the rocks split" (Matt 27:51). The curtain of the

---

10. This would have been done according to a first-century tradition of burials and confirmed by later rabbinic teaching. See Longstaff, "The Women at the Tomb," 278–81.

11. Léon-Dufour, *Resurrection*, 110.

Temple separated the Holy of Holies, where God's earthly presence was believed to dwell, from the rest of the Temple where worshipers came to offer sacrifices for sin. The sudden rupture may have indicated that Christ's sacrificial death would put an end to the old cultic practice of sacrificing animals as penitential offerings. With the violent earthquake, the evangelist depicted the overwhelming power of God in Jesus the Messiah—breaking open the very substructure of the earth to rise triumphant over the power of death. "Yet once more I will shake not only the earth but also the heaven" (Heb 12:26).[12] A new creation was dawning, the time of salvation!

The crucifixion earthquake also recalls the words of the prophet Ezekiel: "So I prophesized as I had been commanded; and as I prophesied, suddenly there was a noise, a rattling, and the bones came together, bone to its bone" (Ezek 37:7). And again: "Therefore prophesy, and say to them, 'Thus says the Lord God: I am going to open your graves, and bring you up from your graves, O my people; and I will bring you back to the land of Israel'" (Ezek 37:12). As we have seen, originally this prophecy promised the return of the exiled and "once-dead" Israelites to Palestine. But in his Gospel, Matthew made use of it to proclaim a much greater realization of that prophecy: "The tombs also were opened, and many bodies of the saints who had fallen asleep were raised. After his resurrection they came out of the tombs and entered the holy city and appeared to many" (Matt 27:52–53). Thus Matthew linked the opening of the tombs of the saints at the moment of Jesus' death with the beginning of the new "messianic age," to be completed by Christ's resurrection and exaltation into glory. By referencing familiar biblical allusions, the evangelist also affirmed that all righteous sufferers who ever lived would eventually rise with the Messiah, the Son of God. Then the ancient promises of salvation to Israel would finally be fulfilled.[13] One scholar commented: "The experience of the days of Easter by the disciples as an earnest of the coming day of God and the beginning of the great resurrection was presumably their original reaction and not a later interpretation."[14]

12. See also Mark 13:8; Rev 6:12; 11:13, 19; 16:18.

13. Perkins, *Resurrection*, 125. For other biblical descriptions of the earth responding to manifestations of divine power, see: Judg 5:4; Ps 77:18; Isa 25:5, 24:18; Ezek 37:12–13, 38:19; Jer 4:23–24; Joel 2:10; 1 Kgs 19:11–12; Zech 14:4; Nah 1:5–6; Dan 12:2.

14. Schlatter, *Der Evangelist Matthäus*, 785, as quoted in Jeremias, *New Testament Theology*, 309.

For Matthew, all these miraculous signs attested to the divine nature of the one who had died on Calvary: Jesus Christ, Lord and ruler of heaven and earth. No giant stone or guard could impede his resurrection. Even the descent into Sheol could not hold back the Savior. Just as in the infancy narrative, where Matthew had depicted an angel of the Lord appearing to Joseph in a dream saying, "Joseph, son of David, do not be afraid to take Mary as your wife, for the child conceived in her is from the Holy Spirit" (Matt 1:20), so now the evangelist describes an angel of the Lord telling the women not to be afraid: "Do not be afraid; I know that you are looking for Jesus who was crucified" (Matt 28:5). Then the angel announced the good news of what had happened to Jesus: "He is not here; for he has been raised, as he said. Come, see the place where he lay" (Matt 28:6). Presumably, the two women entered and inspected the sepulcher and found it to be empty. The angel urged them not to delay: "Then go quickly and tell his disciples, 'He has been raised from the dead, and indeed he is going ahead of you to Galilee; there you will see him.' This is my message for you" (Matt 28:7).

In Matthew's story, the women obeyed, leaving the tomb "quickly with fear and great joy, and ran to tell his disciples" (Matt 28:8). Unlike the instruction given by Mark's "young man" that Jesus was going ahead of them and would only be seen in Galilee, in Matthew's account, Jesus himself appeared to the women on the road, greeted them, and imparted the same directive again. "And they came to him, took hold of his feet, and worshiped him. Then Jesus said to them, 'Do not be afraid; go and tell my brothers to go to Galilee; there they will see me'" (Matt 28:9–10). For Matthew, it became crucial that the disciples, male and female, return to Galilee and its Jewish people who lived in "the land of the pagans," where Jesus' own earthly mission had begun.

Remembering and Recognizing

In Luke's Gospel, *several* women—Mary Magdalene, Joanna, Mary the mother of James, as well as others who were unnamed—arrived at the tomb with the spices they had prepared to anoint Jesus. As in the Gospels of Mark and John, they found that the stone had already been rolled away from the entrance. Unique to Luke's Gospel, the women entered the tomb by themselves, and discovered that it was empty even before they perceived the angelic presences.[15] Suddenly, they saw not one angel but *two men* in dazzling clothes (again, a typical biblical indication of angelic visitors) standing beside them. The women became terrified, falling on the ground and hiding their faces. The two men said to them, in a tone of rebuke: "Why do you look for the living among the dead? He is not here, but has risen" (Luke 24:5). Possibly using a familiar preaching formula, Luke employed the angelic visitors to recall Christ's prophecy of his death and the necessity of his resurrection: "Remember how he told you, while he was still in Galilee, that the Son of Man must be handed over to sinners, and be crucified, and on the third day rise again" (Luke 24:6–7). In Luke, *remembering* becomes a key factor in bearing witness to the fact that Jesus who was once dead is now alive. In his account of the Last Supper, Luke alone among the evangelists had Jesus add, after the consecration of bread and wine: "Do this in remembrance of me" (Luke 22:19). Now Luke's angels speak in one voice to urge the women to *remember* all that Jesus had foretold so that they might link what they had seen at the crucifixion and burial with what they were now witnessing at the empty tomb. The necessity of the Lord's crucifixion can only be understood in the light of his resurrection. To become Christ's witnesses, the women must treasure all these words and ponder them in their hearts, as had Jesus' mother (see Luke 2:19). They must never forget what they had seen and heard.

Notice that Luke's angels made no mention of Jesus going before the disciples into Galilee. On the contrary, Luke will have Jesus himself tell the disciples to remain in Jerusalem: "And see, I am sending upon you what my Father promised; so stay here in the city until you have been clothed with power from on high" (Luke 24:49). Unlike Matthew, Luke did not have Jesus appear to the women while on their way to tell the disciples. Prompted by the angelic voices, the women remembered the words of Jesus about his resurrection, "and returning from the tomb, they told all this to the eleven and to all the rest" (Luke 24:9). The disciples scoffed at the women's reports: "But these words seemed to them an idle tale, and they did not believe them" (Luke 24:11). Nevertheless, Peter was compelled to get up and run to the sepulcher. He looked into the empty tomb, saw the linen cloths lying there by themselves, and went home, "amazed at what had happened" (Luke 24:12). He did not understand. He did not yet believe. He had not yet seen. Notably, in Luke's tradition,

15. Perkins, *Resurrection*, 153.

at some point Jesus appeared to Simon Peter before he showed himself to the other disciples, thus suggesting Peter's primacy among his brethren.

In John's Gospel, as in Mark and Luke, the tombstone had already been rolled back by the time only *one* woman—Mary Magdalene—came to the tomb "early on the first day of the week, while it was still dark" (John 20:1). (As mentioned, because this is the *simplest* account of the empty tomb, free of illustrative clarification, it is most probably based on the *earliest* tradition.[16]) Entering the tomb and seeing that there was no body and assuming it had been stolen, Mary Magdalene "ran and went to Simon Peter and the other disciple, the one whom Jesus loved, and said to them: 'They have taken the Lord out of the tomb, and *we* do not know where they have laid him'" (John 20:2, emphasis added). Notice that the evangelist switches from referring to a single woman to implying that at least one other woman was with Mary Magdalene. (The sudden use of the first person plural might have drawn on the synoptic form of the tradition which speaks of several women. Alternately, the plural might have been a mistranslation of a Galilean Aramaic idiom that regularly substitutes "we" for "I."[17]) Peter and the Beloved Disciple came running, entered the tomb, and realized that it was empty. The Beloved Disciple "saw and believed" (John 20:8) that something extraordinary had occurred. Then both men left, but "as yet they did not understand the scripture, that he must rise from the dead" (John 20:9). This comment sounds credible because no evangelist would have dared to mention it if it had not been true. According to the criterion of embarrassment, such a lack of faith in Christ's resurrection placed the male disciples in a poor light.

As we shall consider in chapter 3, Mary remained at the tomb, finally gained courage to look inside, and discovered "two angels in white sitting where the body of Jesus had been lying, one at the head and the other at the feet" (John 20:12). The angels did not actually tell Mary that Jesus had risen from the dead, but rather questioned her reason for weeping. It was the appearance of Jesus himself that testified to his resurrection. And it was Jesus, not the angels, who personally gave Mary the commission to go tell the disciples.

Thus we see that while the number of angelic visitors and their exact words varied in the four Gospels, the message, whether spoken or unspoken, was basically the same: He is not here. He has been raised. Tell

16. Jeremias, *New Testament Theology*, 304–5.
17. Jeremias, *New Testament Theology*, 304–5, n9.

the disciples. He will go before you. However, the *reaction* of the women in each gospel story was starkly different. This requires more detailed discussion.

Silence of the Women

☩The resurrection story in the Gospel of Mark 16:1–8 is considered by most New Testament scholars to be the earliest version upon which Matthew and Luke based their own narratives, although, as mentioned earlier, several other Scripture scholars suggest that it belongs to a later stage in the Easter tradition.[18] Either way, in examining Mark's version of the event, we must deal with a dilemma. Mark's original ending left the women dumbstruck and so overcome by fear-filled alarm and awe that they were unwilling to tell anyone what they had seen and heard at the empty tomb. Following the commission by the "young man" to go and tell Peter and the disciples that Jesus would "go ahead of them" to Galilee and that there they would see him, we read: "So they [the women] went out and fled from the tomb, for *terror and amazement* had seized them; and they said nothing to anyone, for they were afraid" (Mark 16:8, emphasis added). What was the cause of this "terror and amazement" the evangelist described? We can certainly appreciate that the appearance of an angelic presence attesting that Jesus was not dead but alive must have struck the women like a lightning bolt, producing a mixture of shock and trembling. Yet, at the same time, the news was exceedingly joyful. The tomb was empty precisely because Jesus their beloved Lord was no longer dead, but alive. Would that not have produced exultation?

In these two descriptive words, "terror and amazement," it seems that Mark sought to evoke in the reader or listener the same combination of fear and trembling that the women would have experienced at such a manifestation of divine power: Christ had triumphed over his own death. This is how *we* should feel when hearing the story, full of awe and wonderment in the face of such a discovery. Indeed, the evangelist described a very human reaction that we all have experienced in some measure. Do we not say "It's unbelievable!" when we are stunned by a sudden, inexplicable turn of events—while at the same time, feeling overjoyed that something beyond our wildest hopes has just occurred? However, since the news so far exceeded their comprehension, why did

18. Jeremias, *New Testament Theology*, 304–5.

Mark write that the women ran away and said "nothing to anyone, *for they were afraid*"?

The Women's Fear

Why were the women so afraid? Perhaps Mark depicted them as afraid that they would not be believed by the disciples if they recounted what they had seen and heard. On this point they certainly proved to be correct. But is that Mark's last word on the resurrection, that the women told no one because *they were afraid* (Greek, *ephobounto gar*)? Since Mark's Gospel has three explicit predictions of Christ's impending suffering and death as well as his promise to rise again "after three days," it is hard to believe that the evangelist was not working up to the Lord's triumph and total vindication in resurrection.[19] At his trial before the High Priest and all the Sanhedrin, Mark records that when Jesus was asked if he was, indeed, the Messiah, he answered: "I am; and 'you will see the Son of Man seated at the right hand of the Power,' and 'coming with the clouds of heaven.'" (Mark 14:62). According to this passage, Jesus foresaw his eventual triumph over death. "It is therefore credible that he predicted not only his death but also his resurrection."[20] Yet the fact remains that there are no resurrection *appearances* recorded in the oldest and shortest Gospel of Mark.

There is another point concerning the women's fear. Throughout his Gospel, Mark recorded Jesus telling people *not* to be afraid: for example, the woman with the hemorrhage, and the crowd mourning the dead twelve-year-old girl. When Jesus calmed the violent storm at sea, his disciples were astounded. He said to them, "Why are you afraid? Have you still no faith?" (Mark 4:40). Here, fear is not a positive reaction, but implies deep misunderstanding or persistent disbelief. In another scene, when Jesus walked on the water toward the terrified disciples in the boat, he told them: "Take heart, it is I; do not be afraid" (Mark 6:50). Mark would not have wanted *fear* to be his final statement about Jesus' life, death, and resurrection. For this evangelist, fear was a sign of mistrust and lack of faith in divine ability to accomplish anything and everything. It must be replaced by a burning faith and hope. Further, when Mark's angel announced to the women that Jesus was going ahead of them into

19. See Mark 8:31; 9:31; 10:34.
20. Dodd, *The Parables of the Kingdom*, 73.

Galilee and "there you will see him, as he told you" (Mark 16:7), does this message not raise expectations of just such an encounter? Surely Mark was not setting them up for a devastating disappointment.

It is possible that the evangelist may not have intended to end his narrative at this point. Perhaps his appearance stories were never completed, or deliberately excised for whatever reason. Mark may have been arrested or died before finishing his account. It is also conceivable that the last page of Mark's original manuscript was lost. Unless there is an extraordinary archaeological discovery, we will never know for sure. We simply have to accept that what happened to the culmination of Mark's Gospel is an unsolved mystery.

Mark's Silence

There is yet another possibility. New Testament scholar Joachim Jeremias suggests that Mark's silence about the resurrection appearances may have been deliberate. He may have exercised restraint because any further information about the risen Lord would have revealed *esoteric knowledge*, not to be given to the uninitiated or the disbelieving.[21] "Esoteric teachings were not isolated theological writings, but great theological systems, great doctrinal constructions, whose content was attributed to divine inspiration."[22] In Mark's time, some Hebrew Scriptures, legal requirements, and apocalyptic writings were deemed so sacred that Jewish scribes, fully aware of their role as guardians of secret knowledge, taught them only in private to one or two privileged students. These sublime teachings might not be read aloud, even in Hebrew; or they might only be read in Hebrew but not in Aramaic translations that the public could understand. They might only be discussed in a whisper with covered heads.[23]

Throughout the Gospels, the evangelists took great care to distinguish Jesus' public discourses to the crowds from his "private" or "secret" teachings to his closest disciples. According to the synoptic Gospels, Jesus did not discuss his messiahship in public. After Peter's profession of faith that Jesus was indeed "the Messiah," Jesus commanded his disciples "not to tell anyone about him" (Mark 8:29-30). Again, after his transfiguration on Mount Tabor, as Peter, James, and John were

---

21. Jeremias, *Jerusalem in the Time of Jesus*, 240-41.

22. Jeremias, *Jerusalem*, 239.

23. Jeremias, *Jerusalem*, 237-38, 239-40.

coming down the mountain, Jesus "ordered them to tell no one about what they had seen, until after the Son of Man had risen from the dead" (Mark 9:9). Only when questioned on trial before the Sanhedrin: "Are you the Messiah, the Son of the Blessed One?" did Jesus proclaim publicly: "I am" (Mark 14:61–62). Likewise, Jesus' predictions of his passion and death were strictly limited to private teachings for his disciples (Mark 8:31–33; 9:30–32; 10:32–34). And his eschatological prophecies about how to recognize the signs of the coming of the end times and final judgment were only given to his four closest disciples, Peter, James, John, and Andrew (Mark 13:3–37). In Mark's depiction, Jesus seems to insist repeatedly that secrecy was necessary to protect those teachings and prophecies that were not meant for a hostile public. According to Jeremias, "This is probably the solution of the abrupt ending of Mark at 16:8. Although the appearances of the risen Lord formed a fixed part of the teaching of the faith, Mark felt that they were among the things which should not be disclosed to pagan readers."[24]

In the farewell discourses in the Gospel of John (John 13:31–17:26), Jesus revealed the hidden meaning of his earthly mission and his approaching departure only to those present at the Last Supper.[25] Furthermore, it is also evident that none of the four evangelists dared to discuss the divine nature of Jesus Christ or describe how the resurrection took place.[26] Such topics were considered too sacred for a public text. John does not even reveal the words of institution of Eucharist, allowing only an earlier teaching by Jesus on the eucharistic words—a sermon which would have been completely obfuscating to those who had not been initiated into the sacred mysteries.[27]

We see this same concern to protect esoteric teachings in the letters of Paul. In First Corinthians, the apostle declares that only "among the mature" (that is, those who possess the Spirit) does he speak of "God's wisdom, secret and hidden, which God decreed before the ages for our glory" (1 Cor 2:6–7). He asserts that these things are being revealed "in words not taught by human wisdom but taught by the Spirit, interpreting spiritual things to those who are spiritual" (1 Cor 2:13). He acknowledges that until now, he had only given the Corinthians "milk" (basic teachings)

24. Jeremias, *The Eucharistic Words of Jesus*, 132.

25. See Jeremias, *Eucharistic Words*, 129–30.

26. Jeremias, *Eucharistic Words*, 132.

27. Jeremias, *Eucharistic Words*, 136.

because they were not yet ready for the solid food of "wisdom" for the "mature" (1 Cor 3:2). And finally he reveals a secret revelation: "Listen, I will tell you a mystery! We will not all die, but we will all be changed" (1 Cor 15:51). If Paul had kept such esoteric wisdom from the Corinthians, even though they had been Christians for years, we may assume that he would never have preached about such secrets before non-Christians.[28] In 2 Corinthians, Paul dares to mention his own mystical experience of being "caught up to the third heaven," where he "heard things that are not to be told, that no mortal is permitted to repeat" (2 Cor 12:2–4). And in his letter to the Romans, Paul hints that he was the recipient of secret knowledge concerning the divine plan of redemption for all of Israel (Rom 11:25–27). Similarly, the letter to the Colossians longs for "their hearts to be encouraged and united in love so that they may have the knowledge of God's mystery, that is, Christ himself, in whom are hidden all the treasures of wisdom and knowledge" (Col 2:2–3). And the whole book of Revelation was considered to be an eschatological secret.[29]

Thus it may well be that Mark decided not to reveal any details ✗ of the private and mysterious resurrection appearances, lest they be misreported and misinterpreted by those who did not believe.

The Angel's Message

Nevertheless, even if we do not have resurrection appearances in Mark, from what we have of his empty tomb story (followed very closely by Matthew and Luke), we see that the essential factor was *not* the women's fear of the angel, but their total astonishment at the angel's message that Jesus had risen—plus the angel's commission to go and tell the disciples "He has been raised; he is not here" (Mark 16:6). It was imperative for Mark to depict the women as truth-bearers to Peter and the other disciples. They must *speak*, not remain silent. Then they and the disciples would see Jesus. Yes, they may have fled in shock and confusion, as we might run away if we visited the grave of a dearly loved one and found it standing open, with the body gone, and a blazing angelic presence telling us that the person we mourned is alive and already on his way home before us. We might be so confused that we could not trust what we had seen and heard, lest our senses had deceived us. We might not know how

28. Jeremias, *Eucharistic Words*, 130–31.
29. Jeremias, *Jerusalem*, 240–41.

to tell anyone, at least not at first. But eventually, we would not be able to contain the good news.

Thus we may assume that very soon the women told their story to Peter and the disciples. How else did such an earth-shattering narrative become the bedrock of the earliest oral tradition? We must also not forget that these eyewitnesses were real flesh and blood individuals with their own unique ways of seeing, hearing, and describing what they had experienced. These were honest, devoted women who had followed Jesus from Galilee and had ministered to him for years. Consequently, they would not and could not have been capable of telling lies about what they saw and heard that first Easter morning. Their "oral tradition" was not a highly developed treatise on the theological implications of the resurrection, but a collection of *vivid memories*. Some accounts may have been as simple as: "We went to the tomb, the stone was rolled back, the body was gone, and we felt the presence of angelic beings telling us that Jesus had risen from the dead. We were told to tell the disciples that Jesus would see them in Galilee. We were overcome with fear and ran away."

Likewise, Peter and the other disciples who were in the upper room must have told the story of what they had experienced that Easter evening for the rest of their lives. Every time they preached, they must have relived the fear, awe, and ecstatic joy of seeing the risen Jesus in a transformed body. This is how the oral tradition brought the reality "alive" for those who heard the disciples. The sheer honesty, exuberance, and passionate conviction they had in the telling convinced many that these men and women were not perpetrating a hoax; they were bearing witness to the truth. Jesus of Nazareth had risen from the dead. He must be the Messiah of Israel, the very Son of God.

Additional Endings

To address Mark's missing or incomplete or deliberately silent ending, a short finale was added years later to the last verse: "And all that had been commanded them [the women] told briefly to those around Peter. And afterward Jesus himself sent out through them, from east to west, the sacred and imperishable proclamation of eternal salvation" (Mark 16:8). Note that the text implies that Jesus sent the proclamation out through *the women* as well as the men, from east to west. While women were not able to travel freely in the ancient world without a male escort, this inclusive reference indicates that they, like the male disciples, testified that Jesus was truly risen and exalted, having triumphed over death.

To further expand Mark's ending and introduce a reference to the resurrection appearances of Jesus that would parallel those of the later evangelists, yet a second editor added an even longer ending, perhaps in the early second century. In spite of the late date, this ending was written strictly in accordance with the already well-established tradition.

> Now after he rose early on the first day of the week, he appeared first to Mary Magdalene, from whom he had cast out seven demons. She went out and told those who had been with him, while they were mourning and weeping. But when they heard that he was alive and had been seen by her, *they would not believe it.* After this he appeared in another form to two of them, as they were walking into the country. And they went back and told the rest, but *they did not believe them.* (Mark 16:9–13, emphasis added)

Twice more, we read the startling report that the disciples did not believe—either Mary's testimony or that of the two disciples on the road to Emmaus. "Later he appeared to the eleven themselves as they were sitting at the table; and he upbraided them for their lack of faith and stubbornness, because they had not believed those who saw him after he had risen" (Mark 16:14). It is significant that in spite of the embarrassing depiction of the apostles' disbelief, these appearances to Mary Magdalene and the disciples on the Road to Emmaus (which we shall discuss in chapter 3) became so deeply embedded in the tradition of the early church that they could not be omitted from this last addition to Mark's Gospel. Far from trying to *suppress* the scandal of the apostles' stubborn lack of faith, the redactor wanted the truth known: the women believed, the men did not.

Belief in the Empty Tomb

We may ask: *What exactly did they believe?* Scholars tend to consider that any discussion of "what actually happened" on Easter morning lies outside the purview of historical verification. Because acknowledgment of Jesus' resurrection seems to presuppose faith in an all-powerful God who intervened in the natural order of things to bring a human corpse back to life, such inquiry is deemed to be beyond the jurisdiction of historians who deal in certifiable events, data, and facts. Nonetheless, we are well aware that the documentation of events, data, and facts is heavily colored by the religious or political horizon or viewpoint of any particular historian. No scholar (indeed, no individual) is without a lens through which he or she organizes and interprets the so-called facts, and then judges which are reliable and which are not. By profession, historians research and analyze world events such as the rise and fall of monarchies and kingdoms, revolutions, wars and their probable causes, sociopolitical and economic factors, and long-term results. Given this dedication to what can be known (however ancient and reliable the original sources may be), still, for the historian, "the hypothesis 'God raised Jesus from the dead' is 'imponderable.'"[30]

Nevertheless, historians may be able to generate from reliable data a profile of a historical core event that must have occurred in order to produce the verifiable long-term results that we do in fact witness. With this in mind, we may consider: *What must have happened* for previously disbelieving and terrified disciples to become empowered to preach the gospel of Jesus' resurrection, thus courting their own persecution and even martyrdom? *What must have happened* for faith in an obscure rabbi from Galilee who was crucified and buried to be suddenly proclaimed throughout the known world as the Lord and ruler of heaven and earth? *What must have happened* for a small band of Jews to become convinced that this man was divine, the long-awaited Messiah, the Anointed One, the Son of God? *What must have happened* for men and women to form clandestine house churches from Palestine to Rome and be willing to undergo harassment from both Jewish and Roman authorities as well as excommunication from their own synagogues? *What must have happened* for Greek Gentiles (who, as we have discussed, could not fathom the physical resurrection of a corpse) to come to believe in the testimony of itinerant preachers that one man did, in fact, rise from the dead, and that he appeared in the flesh to his followers? *What must have happened* for belief in the risen Christ to have spread so quickly over the then-known world, and still be spreading to millions in our current age? In essence, *what was the foundational event that propelled Christianity from its inception?* The answer, as New Testament scholar N. T. Wright affirms, lies in the fact that "the early Christians believed that something

---

30. Licona, *The Resurrection of Jesus*, 184.

happened to Jesus after his death, something to which the stories in the four canonical Gospels are as close as we are likely to get."[31]

Objections to the Empty Tomb

It was essential to the evangelists to explain that the tomb of Jesus had been visited first by the women and found to be *empty*. This is because there were other stories circulating at the time. One was that the body had been stolen to make it look as if Jesus had risen. In John's Gospel, Mary Magdalene voiced this fear aloud: "they have taken the body out of the tomb, and we do not know where they have laid him" (John 20:2). Some nineteenth-century critics suggested that the body was stolen by the gardener. Bizarre as this may seem, Matthew also called attention to the story of the "theft" of Christ's body:

> While [the women] were going, some of the guard went into the city and told the chief priests everything that had happened. After the priests had assembled with the elders, they devised a plan to give a large sum of money to the soldiers, telling them, "You must say, 'His disciples came by night and stole him away while we were asleep.' If this comes to the governor's ears, we will satisfy him and keep you out of trouble." So they took the money and did as they were directed. And this story is still told among the Jews to this day. (Matt 28:11–15)

Ironically enough, because Matthew chose to include this information in his Gospel, he undercut the very stories of collusion presented by modern skeptics. If there had been any truth to the notion that the disciples stole the body and then concocted a resurrection tale, Matthew would never have dared suggest such a thing. But because Matthew saw fit to feature the scenario near the end of his Gospel, it lends credence that the theft story in circulation was a total fabrication. In addition, everything we know about the early Christians bears witness that they were not a clique of thieves and liars bent on a colossal deception. That would have nullified everything Jesus had ever taught them. Even more, would they have been willing to suffer persecution and go to their deaths as martyrs for what they knew to be a hoax?

Another objection: the late second-century to the late fourth-century Gnostic Gospels held that the Word did not become flesh at

---

31. Wright, *Resurrection*, 614–15.

the incarnation, but only *assumed* the appearance of a physical body.[32] Therefore, Christ was not really a human being, but merely a heavenly illusion. His body had no physical substance, either in life or in death. Thus at the crucifixion, he did not really die. Rather, another died in his place while he returned to heaven and was never even buried.[33] These Gnostic viewpoints denied not only the human nature of Jesus Christ and his crucifixion, death, and burial; they refuted the possibility of his bodily resurrection at all. If Christ was not a human being, he could not die; if he did not die, he was not really buried; if he was not dead and buried, he could not have risen from the dead. If there was no resurrection for Christ, there certainly would be no hope of resurrection for us.

An alternate theory from the nineteenth century tried to explain away the empty tomb by fabricating a fantastic scenario about how Jesus did not actually *die* on the cross but only went into a "swoon" or perhaps a coma. Scholars who hold this theory maintain that Jesus was taken down from the cross *before* he died (despite Roman soldiers standing watch at the crucifixion) and buried, but then somehow came out of the swoon and, still bleeding from his extreme wounds, had the strength to roll back the stone from the inside and escape from his tomb. Such stories are too far-fetched to be considered seriously.

In fact, the great majority of modern exegetes agree that the account of Jesus' death by crucifixion is reliable and historically reasonable. In John's Gospel, according to an eyewitness testimony: "one of the soldiers pierced his side with a spear, and at once blood and water came out" (John 19:34). All the evidence that Jesus died as a result of crucifixion is convincing—and this from both ancient Christian and non-Christian sources. There is no historical report to contradict it. "Even those scholars and critics who have been moved to depart from almost everything else within the historical content of Christ's presence on earth have found it impossible to think away the factuality of the death of Christ."[34]

---

32. These ancient texts are a collection of some fifty-four fragments, written one to three centuries after the four canonical Gospels. They were found in the archaeological discovery at Nag Hammadi in 1945. They include excerpts from the Gospel of Thomas, the Gospel of Truth, the Gospel of Philip, and the Gospel of Judas. Another Gnostic work is the Gospel of Mary, of which only one remnant was recovered in 1896 and published in 1955.

33. Gnostic ideas seem to have been derived from Docetism.

34. McIntyre, "The Uses of History in Theology," 7.1.8.

Another consideration is that after crucifixion, Roman soldiers usually threw the bodies of criminals into a mass grave or lime pit near Golgotha. However, it is a known fact that Roman authorities would, on occasion, allow family and friends to take away the body of an executed criminal, once it could be ascertained that he was really dead. The tradition about the body of Jesus and Joseph of Arimathea remains very strong:

> When evening had come, and since it was the day of Preparation, that is, the day before the sabbath, Joseph of Arimathea, a respected member of the council, who was also himself waiting expectantly for the kingdom of God, went boldly to Pilate and asked for the body of Jesus. Then Pilate wondered if he were already dead; and summoning the centurion, he asked him whether he had been dead for some time. When he learned from the centurion that he was dead, he granted the body to Joseph. (Mark 15:42–45; see also, Matt 27:57–60; Luke 23:50–53, John 19:38–42)

However, some scholars have suggested that later, Joseph of Arimathea *stole* the body from where it had lain in his newly carved tomb. It seems preposterous to imagine that a devout Jew of the stature of Joseph of Arimathea, a respected member of the Sanhedrin (and a secret disciple of Jesus who had voted *against* condemning him to death), would suddenly change his mind about Jesus, return to his family tomb after celebrating the Passover, roll back the heavy stone, and remove the decaying corpse in order to bury it somewhere else. To what purpose? First of all, such an act would have been a crime of desecration to the body of a well-known rabbi, however hated Jesus may have been by the Sanhedrin and disgraced by a Roman crucifixion. Secondly, Joseph had already risked his position in the Sanhedrin by going to Pilate and asking for the dead body of Jesus, then burying it in his family tomb. He would not have wanted to cross the authorities any further. Thirdly, if Joseph *had* hidden the body elsewhere for whatever reason, once he heard the disciples speaking publicly about Christ's resurrection, he would have been duty-bound to come forward and expose the story as an outright hoax.[35]

Alternately, if Jesus had *not* risen on Easter morning and a story had been spread abroad that the tomb was empty, Joseph would certainly have invited members of the Sanhedrin to inspect his family tomb to verify

35. O'Collins, *Jesus Risen*, 124.

that the corpse of Jesus was still in place. All things considered, the details given of Jewish anointing practices and burial in a family tomb by Joseph of Arimathea, based on the deep respect of one Jew for the ritual burial of another before the feast of Passover, seem perfectly plausible. Joseph and Nicodemus were simply following Hebraic law: "When someone is convicted of a crime punishable by death and is executed, and you hang him on a tree, his corpse must not remain all night upon the tree; you shall bury him that same day, for anyone hung on a tree is under God's curse" (Deut 21:22–23).

A further objection to the empty tomb is that the women were delusional or completely confused. Overcome by the emotion of grief, they saw what wasn't there: an *empty* tomb. Yet Matthew's Gospel clearly makes the point that at the burial, "Mary Magdalene and the other Mary were there, sitting opposite the tomb" (Matt 27:61) and Luke specifies that "the women who had come with him from Galilee followed, and they saw the tomb and how his body was laid" (Luke 23:55). Even so, it has been suggested that on Easter morning, the women *forgot* which tomb it was. So they went to the wrong tomb, which just happened to have the stone that was in front of it rolled back, with no body inside. Then they ran to the disciples, told the tale of the body being gone, and the story gained traction. It is just not plausible. Jewish family tombs were tightly sealed and not left wide open with the stone rolled back for fear of vandals stealing and desecrating the bodies or scattering the ossuaries containing the bones of already-decayed corpses.

To counteract whatever erroneous stories were circulating at the time, all four first-century evangelists specified that the actual tomb of Jesus had been carefully observed by men and women at its sealing. It was revisited by the women on Sunday morning, then later viewed by Peter and the Beloved Disciple and found to be empty. Very few scholars would agree that Mark or anyone else fabricated the empty tomb story to lend credence to a bodily resurrection. There is simply no historical evidence that the Jewish authorities ever disputed that the body was, indeed, *gone*.[36]

Even ancient anti-Christian writers never suggested that the corpse was still in the tomb. It seems to have been a recognized fact that the tomb was, in fact, empty. The burning question was (and is) not, "Was the body still in the tomb?" but "Who took it away?" As we have seen, in order to

---

36. See Craig, *Assessing the New Testament Evidence*, 197–201, 360–61.

explain the disappearance, the embarrassed authorities spread the story that Jesus' disciples had stolen it. Could it be that the disciples actually broke into the tomb and stole the body away in the night to make it seem as if Christ's prophecy that he would rise again had actually been fulfilled? No, and for one very good reason: the disciples never even *expected* Jesus to rise from the dead! Even though the disciples had heard Christ predict his own passion, death, and resurrection on numerous occasions, all the evangelists concur that the disciples did not believe him. Furthermore, to suggest that a band of terrified and disheartened disciples would have been capable of overpowering armed soldiers, stealing the body, and keeping it successfully hidden, seems not only improbable but well-nigh impossible.

New Testament scholar and theologian Rudolf Pesch painstakingly assessed all the available evidence and came to an insightful conclusion about Mark 16:1–8:

> The burial story *looks forward with expectancy* to the empty tomb: Joseph's laying the body in the tomb *anticipates* the angel's proclamation, "He is not here; see the place where they laid him"; the mention of the roll-stone *anticipates* the women's question in v.3 and the open tomb in v.4, and the women's witnessing the location *prepares for* the visit on Sunday morning. . . . it is unthinkable that the passion story could end in defeat and death with no mention of the empty tomb or resurrection. . . . Thus, there seem to be very strong reasons for taking the empty tomb account as part of the pre-Markan passion story. . . . All these factors point to a very old tradition concerning the discovery of the empty tomb.[37]

A Later Account?

A few modern scholars have suggested that the empty tomb story was merely a "pious legend" created by the evangelists long after the fact, as a late first-century reinforcement of the resurrection appearances. Rudolf Bultmann argues that in particular, Mark's ending is not only "a quite secondary tradition," but even an "apologetic legend," which seeks to "prove the reality of the resurrection of Jesus by the empty tomb."[38]

37. Pesch, *Das Markusevangelium*, 2:519–20, as quoted in Craig, *Assessing*, 198–201, emphasis added.

38. Bultmann, *History of the Synoptic Tradition*, 284, 287.

However, if the empty tomb had been a concoction by the evangelists, would not the Jewish leaders of that later period have been quick to produce strong evidence that the bones of Jesus were still in place in the tomb's ossuary? Indeed, modern exegesis has shown that such a hypothesis fails on many counts.[39] For example, even from our brief exploration, we can see that the story of the empty tomb did *not* provide a well-defined, carefully articulated message. On the contrary, it caused great confusion at the time, not greater clarity or certainty. It produced a mixture of fear and trembling in the women. It only met with a tentative faith on the part of the Beloved Disciple and stubborn disbelief from the other disciples. This obvious disarray and inconsistency in the telling is not typical of legends that have been carefully constructed to present a well-honed message.

Nor are the story lines the result of fine-tuned rewriting. If the evangelists (especially Matthew, Luke, and John) had fabricated their empty tomb accounts in the fourth quarter of the first century, they would certainly have been careful to eliminate all inconsistencies in order to be in perfect accord with one another. They would have made sure that the stories were consonant in every aspect. They would not have left us with so many missing explanations, wide-open gaps, and unanswered questions. They would have reworked the basic material to provide smoother and more cohesive narratives. Most importantly, they would have cited two or more *men* as the first witnesses at the tomb, rather than women. They would have created a dramatically viable scene in which an angel appeared to trusted leaders of the community like Peter and James who believed the words of the angel immediately. At the very least, the evangelists would have carefully *deleted* the uncomfortable aspects of the oral traditions before setting them down on papyrus. Obviously, they did not. They did not dare nullify the basic facts of the oral tradition because the faith of Christianity rested firmly on the bedrock of these well-known early accounts concerning the empty tomb. Thus the Gospels' very simplicity, incongruities, and lack of artifice actually attest to their authenticity.

> The stories exhibit, as has been said repeatedly over the last hundred years or more, exactly that surface tension which we associate, not with tales artfully told by people eager to sustain a

---

39. See a comprehensive discussion of the arguments in Davis, *Risen Indeed*, 63–84. See also O'Collins, *Jesus Risen*, 125–27 and Perkins, *Resurrection*, 93–94.

fiction and therefore anxious to make everything look right, but with the hurried, puzzled accounts of those who have seen with their own eyes something which took them horribly by surprise and with which they have not yet fully come to terms.[40]

Furthermore, the story of the empty tomb never seems to have been used *apologetically* in the New Testament as conclusive proof of the resurrection. Neither was it ever presented as the fulfillment of any scriptural prophecy. Notably, these empty tomb accounts (even though written by the evangelists after Paul's letters in the mid-fifties of the Common Era) do not contain any carefully developed theological understanding of Christ's resurrection such as we read in Paul's letters. The most plausible explanation for this lack of Pauline influence is that the empty tomb and resurrection stories as told in the Gospels were founded on much *earlier* sources than Paul's own writings. Besides, once again, if the empty tomb had been invented as a later legend to help prove the resurrection, why would all four evangelists have made the same glaring error of naming women as the first witnesses?

Oral Tradition

It appears much more reasonable that the accounts of the empty tomb arose from oral transmissions about what actually happened that first Easter morning. These testimonies were stark, simple, and undeveloped—and thus very early. They were well-known and probably based on recollected accounts of eyewitnesses. By the time the evangelists were writing their Gospels in the mid-to-late first century, these empty tomb stories had been told and retold in house churches for decades.

> The information from 1 Cor 15:3–5 and the sermons in Acts suggest that the empty tomb was implicit in the kerygma, even if it was not explicitly proclaimed. What was proclaimed was Christ and what he *did*, namely, rose and appeared, not the empty grave left behind. . . . The evidence suggests that both Paul and the formula he transmitted reflect knowledge of the historical fact of Jesus' empty tomb.[41]

Indeed, the evangelists had too much respect for these stories to alter their core message. As we have discussed, even though narrative details

40. Wright, *Resurrection*, 612.

41. Craig, *Assessing*, 360, emphasis in original.

in the four empty tomb stories reveal inconsistencies, they recount *the same general sequence of events*. This makes the discrepancies all the more plausible as very early testimonies. Moreover, in spite of their surface inconsistencies, the stories all agree on the essential fact: The tomb was empty for only one reason—Jesus had risen from the dead. The empty tomb was not merely a symbol of a spiritual arising; nor was it a fabrication or a feel-good story. In fact, one cannot begin to "explain" belief in Christ's resurrection among the disciples and within the early church *unless* the tomb was actually empty: empty of the seeming finality of death, empty of supposed failure over the powers of evil. "On the available evidence the substantial factuality of the empty-tomb tradition has much to be said for it and no convincing argument against it."[42]

At the same time, it is certainly possible that the evangelists themselves (who were most probably *not* eyewitnesses) took some dramatic liberties and used familiar biblical devices such as an earthquake, blinding lights, and angelic appearances to express the inexpressible: the mighty power of God overturning the natural order to raise the Son from the dead. Indeed, the embellishing of details by an individual author was an accepted convention in the ancient world for the writing of *bioi*, historical biographies of extraordinary people.[43] Nevertheless, the basic tradition of the tomb being empty and the women receiving divine directives remains the unwavering foundation of all four versions. There is also the distinct possibility that the extraordinary phenomena described in the Gospels actually did occur and were part of the oral tradition. The empty tomb and the angelic revelation that Jesus had been raised from the dead by the power of God shattered all natural and rational rules for what had previously been considered possible. They still do.

Examining the Evidence

Within a mere two months after Easter, on the Jewish feast of *Shavuot*, preaching about the resurrection of Jesus by the apostles generated great excitement among "devout Jews from every nation under heaven living in Jerusalem" (Acts 2:5). Such preaching also resulted in the apostles being questioned, threatened, and incarcerated by the Jewish authorities (Acts 4:1–31). Certainly this new threat to the temple authorities provided

42. O'Collins, *The Easter Jesus*, 38–39.

43. Licona, *Resurrection*, 338.

a powerful incentive to prove that Jesus' corpse was still in the tomb. Having handed Jesus over to the Romans to be killed, the Sanhedrin wanted to silence all his disciples who were stirring up the crowds. Since we have no record of either Jewish or Roman authorities ever displaying Jesus' decaying corpse to disprove the disciples' teaching, "we can infer, then, that the apostles' proclamation of the resurrection was successful precisely because (among other things) nobody was able to produce the corpse. The tomb was empty and the body nowhere to be found."[44]

In summary, we may review the four basic elements that appear in all the stories. First, the women discovered the empty tomb and were the first witnesses to the resurrection. This fact was both deeply embarrassing and highly convincing precisely because it was such a major displacement of the superior male position in the ancient world. The physical proof of the authenticity of the women's experience was that the tomb was really empty and the body really gone. If this had not been true, it would never have been fabricated and then told and retold by those wishing to authenticate the leadership of Peter and James in the early church. For either a Jewish or a Gentile audience, basing the story of the empty tomb on the witness of some "hysterical women" would have been sheer madness.

Second, all four Gospels agree that the women experienced a supernatural presence and heard an inspired locution that told them Jesus had been raised from the dead and that they would see him. Women, not men, were recorded as the first to be entrusted with the good news of the resurrection by angelic visitors and given the mission to tell the other disciples.

Third, the women related the good news to the male disciples . . . and fourth, the disciples did not believe them, did not understand, or doubted. Because of the double criteria of embarrassment concerning the women as the first witnesses and the stubborn disbelief of the disciples, we are well-justified in accepting that the empty tomb story was not a later fabrication by the evangelists.

Finally, we may consider that the empty tomb stories are convincing as they were written precisely because they do *not* try to be everything we want them to be. They do not attempt to answer all our prying questions. They convey the incomprehensibility of mystery, not step-by-step explanations or rational arguments. They recount oral traditions of what

44. Davis, *Risen Indeed*, 80.

firsthand witnesses saw, heard, and felt. They are so idiosyncratic that they would never have been concocted in that way if they were designed to convince skeptics. They are so preposterous, they seem positively believable.

The Testimony of Experience

Having examined all this, we might ask: Is the story of the empty tomb essential to our understanding of the resurrection of Jesus Christ? Does it really matter? Absolutely. If the physical body of Jesus had remained in the tomb and he had only appeared as a ghostly apparition following his death, it would mean he had not truly risen from the dead and we in turn could only hope for a spiritual life after death, not a bodily resurrection. However, because the physical corpse of Jesus was transformed into a glorious physical body that was able to be seen, heard, and touched by his disciples, then we, too, may believe in the possibility of a bodily resurrection.

In addition to what we can ascertain from historical evidence and the evangelists about the empty tomb, there is yet another way of approaching the resurrection story: through the accounts of personal experiences of the risen Lord. It was not until Christ's actual *appearances* to the women and to the other disciples that they understood that he was truly alive in a transformed but recognizable body. In short, for all its dramatic content and essential facticity, the discovery of the empty tomb did not "prove" the resurrection. On the contrary, only the resurrection *appearances* provided plausible explanation for the empty tomb.

*When once you have taken the Impossible into your calculations
its possibilities become practically limitless.*[45]

---

45. Saki (H. H. Munro), *The Chronicles of Clovis*, 104.

3

"We have seen the Lord!"

HOW DID JESUS RISE from the dead? Did his new body break into or out of his old body? Did his corpse become saturated with divine light? Did he discard the winding cloths soaked with his blood and clothe himself in heavenly garments? Did his divine power roll back the heavy stone guarding the tomb or did an angel do it? There are no clear answers to these questions. The most profound realities are those hidden from our current understanding. They are mystery and we must respect them as such. They cannot be explained by rational theories, but affirmation of such mysteries can sometimes be shown to be the most "rational" interpretation of events, as we shall see.

From the testimony of the first Christians, we may surmise that at some point over that historic weekend, the glorious divinity of the Son of God transformed the battered, crucified, and deceased humanity of Jesus of Nazareth. His physical body was not just restored, re-invigorated, or resuscitated, but thoroughly *re-created*. This glorified body could no longer experience pain. It could no longer be limited by time and place, past or future, or any physical impediment. It could never again suffer and die. Yet it remained individual, and was not utterly diffuse.

During his lifetime on earth, the divine powers of Jesus Christ had been largely hidden by his humanity (except for those transcendent moments when his divinity shone through, such as when he walked on water, raised the dead, or was transfigured on Mount Tabor). At the resurrection, in some inconceivable way, Christ's concealed divinity overcame the lifelessness of his physical remains, suffused the stiffened corpse, and transformed it into a living and radiant body. The wounds of the nails in his hands and feet were still there, but now they were turned into glorious marks of triumph over suffering. The imprint of the lance still marked his side, but now it became the symbolic entry point into the very heart of God. The deep gashes on his head remained from the crown of thorns, but now they emanated beauty and light. Every aspect of Christ's human existence was transfigured as he appeared to the women, his other disciples, and the crowd of five hundred men, women, and probably children. Yet he could still be seen, heard, touched, and embraced by mere mortals. Though he was changed in mysterious ways, he was eventually recognizable to those who knew him as the very Jesus they had followed during his lifetime.

Naturally, we all seek to understand: *What did the witnesses see that convinced them that Jesus had risen?* Scholars and exegetes, apologists and ecclesiastics, preachers and lay folk have been trying to figure this out for centuries. Let us examine the appearances one by one and try to discover what we can (and admittedly, cannot) know. Let us consider if the stories are convincing and if they may be judged worthy of our belief.

The Two Marys

In Matthew's account of the empty tomb, closely following Mark's, there is a dramatic difference in the women's reaction from the original Markan ending we discussed in chapter 2. After hearing the angel's message to tell the disciples that Jesus had been raised from the dead and would be going ahead of them to Galilee, and "there you will see him" (Matt 28:7), in Matthew's Gospel, Mary Magdalene and the other Mary ran off quickly "with fear and great joy." As we have seen, on the way they encountered Jesus:

> Suddenly Jesus met them and said, "Greetings!" And they came to him, took hold of his feet, and worshiped him. Then Jesus said to them, "Do not be afraid; go and tell my brothers to go to Galilee; there they will see me." (Matt 28:9–10)

In this version, the angel's directive to go to Galilee was repeated by Jesus himself, and even though it was not stated that the women followed the commission, we may assume they did. The two Marys are not depicted as being paralyzed by fear as they are in Mark; their joy overcomes their initial shock and they rush off eagerly to tell the disciples what they have seen and heard. As a result, they all must have journeyed to the mountain in Galilee "to which Jesus had directed them" (Matt 28:16). When Jesus finally appeared to them, the "eleven" disciples (minus Judas) worshiped him. Matthew adds, somewhat cryptically, "but some doubted" (Matt 28:17). Again, we find the intrusion of disbelief into the resurrection story. Did some disciples see him and still doubt that it was really Jesus? Was he so transformed they could not recognize him? Was their skepticism so ingrained that they could not believe their own eyes? Was this "doubt" similar to the women's "fear" in Mark? Or does it refer to those in Matthew's own Judeo-Christian community who still did not fully believe? Whatever the intended meaning of this phrase, Matthew finishes his Gospel with a hope-filled message that is a far more optimistic ending than that of Mark's original last words.

> And Jesus came and said to them, "All authority in heaven and on earth has been given to me. Go therefore and make disciples of all nations, baptizing them in the name of the Father and of the Son and of the Holy Spirit, and teaching them to obey everything that I have commanded you. And remember, I am with you always, to the end of the age." (Matt 28:18–20)

Here, the disciples are given three distinct commands. First, they are to make disciples "of all nations," extending the commission to preach the good news beyond Jewish communities to include all the Gentile nations. Second, they are to baptize them not only "in the name of Jesus," but "in the name of the Father, and of the Son, and of the Holy Spirit." This rite of initiation replaces that of circumcision. Third, for the first time in the Gospels, the triadic formula equates Jesus, the Son of God, with the Father and the Holy Spirit. While such specific directives were most probably *not* spoken by Jesus at his parting exactly as they were later expressed in written form, this sweeping commission suggests what was already happening by the second half of the first century, following the influential teaching of Paul and other disciples. By the time Matthew finished writing his Gospel in the last quarter of the first century, it had become clear to the burgeoning church that the Holy Spirit *was* the abiding presence of Jesus in the world. This Spirit was inspiring disciples to go out into the whole known world and spread the good news of salvation, baptizing without regard to race or former creed. Having been excommunicated from their synagogues, Jewish Christians as well as Gentiles were coming together to form faith communities that assembled for worship in house churches throughout Palestine and Antioch, all the way to Greece and Rome. Men and women who called themselves "Christians" believed that the Lord's own power would enable them to persevere through persecution and suffering, because Jesus would be with them always, until the end of time.

Magdalene's Mistake

We are not alone in desiring God to work in one way and not recognizing divine revelation when it appears to us in quite a different way. According to the Gospel of John, even Mary Magdalene, who was probably closer to Jesus than many of his male disciples, did not recognize him at first. As we saw in chapter 2, when she went to the tomb in the dark on the first morning of the week and found that the stone had been removed, she was terrified that the Lord's body had been stolen away. Then she ran to tell Peter and the Beloved Disciple, and they came and saw that the tomb was empty. They left, not understanding what had happened. But Magdalene stayed and wept. Bitterly. Not only had she witnessed the Lord she loved suffer and die on a cross, now she thought his enemies had dared to desecrate his final resting place and steal his corpse!

She bent down to look into the dark, cold, empty space inside. "She saw two angels in white, sitting where the body of Jesus had been lying, one at the head and the other at the feet" (John 20:12). The angels, speaking as one, questioned her: "'Woman, why are you weeping?' She said to them, 'They have taken away my Lord, and I do not know where they have laid him'" (John 20:13). Greatly distraught, Mary seemed totally unaware that she was addressing heavenly visitors. As we have mentioned, in John's version the angels did not tell Mary that the Lord had risen, as they did in the synoptic Gospels. They merely questioned her, so that she could dig deep down into her soul and express her innermost longing.[1]

Then Mary *turned around* in the dark. This might be a symbolic action to indicate a turn of mind; a *metanoia* or change of heart that makes spiritual insight possible. She saw the silhouette of a man she assumed must be the gardener, for the tomb was in a garden. This stranger asked Mary the same question as had the angels: "Woman, why are you weeping? Who are you looking for?" (John 20:15). Could it have been the Lord's voice all along? At this point, Mary was so overcome by grief and desperation that she did not recognize the voice. She begged the stranger: "Sir, if you have carried him away, tell me where you have laid him, and

1. Léon-Dufour, *Resurrection*, 176–77.

I will take him away" (John 20:15). (One wonders how Mary thought she could single-handedly carry away the corpse of a man.) She still had no idea she was speaking to Jesus. She must have *turned away* from him again to stoop down again and peer into the tomb. It was only when the stranger called her softly by name—"Mary!"—that she realized who it was who stood behind her, barely visible in the pre-dawn darkness. Now she recognized the voice, even before she saw his face. Again Mary "*turned* and said to him in Hebrew, 'Rabbouni!' (which means Teacher)" (John 20:16, emphasis added). With this cry of jubilation and overflowing love, Mary ran to Jesus and embraced him.

How we long for such a moment! How we wish Jesus would call our own name so that we could run and embrace him. How often we pray and implore and plead for weeks, months, years, and perhaps think our prayer has not been heard, or that it has been refused by God. But could God ever refuse our love? Sometimes, in the depth of silence or in the tender voicing of our name by someone who knows us really well, we receive—suddenly!—the answer to our prayer and the reassurance we had sought for so long. We run and cling, just like Magdalene.

But "Jesus said to her, 'Do not hold on to me, because I have not yet ascended to the Father'" (John 20:17). How that must have cost her! Jesus was physically alive, able to be heard, felt, seen, and touched. How could she ever let him go? Heartbreaking though it may seem, Jesus was telling Mary that he must return to the Father. He would not be visibly walking the earth day after day as he had done during his human lifetime. From now on Mary, and indeed all the disciples, must not cling to the physical presence of Jesus, no matter how beloved. None of them would be able to be transformed into what Christ *is* until he himself had returned to the Father and in turn sent the Paraclete, his Holy Spirit, to be with them. They would not come into their own until their Teacher was no longer in their midst, at least in the flesh. But once Jesus returned to the Father, then the disciples would be empowered to do what he had done. Then they would become his mystical body on earth.

In her moment of letting go, of obedient surrender, Mary was given a personal commission: "But go to my brothers and say to them, 'I am ascending to my Father and your Father, to my God and your God'" (John 20:17). Here Jesus seems to imply that henceforth all his followers in every generation might become as intimate with God the Father as Christ is himself. Now he must return to the Father to be glorified and to transform all things into himself. At the Last Supper, Jesus had prayed to the Father in anticipation of being lifted up and exalted on the cross: "I glorified you on earth by finishing the work that you gave me to do. So now, Father, glorify me in your own presence with the glory that I had in your presence before the world existed" (John 17:4–5). For John the Evangelist, the life, crucifixion, resurrection, and return to the Father formed one incomparable mystery: the exaltation and glorification of Jesus as the Christ, the Messiah. Since the Prologue, John's consistent theme had been that Jesus, the Word, was sent from God and must return to God. Jesus had told his disciples that unless he went away, the Holy Spirit could not come. Therefore, it was essential that he return to the Father.

Yet we must not think of the "return" as taking place in a linear time sequence, in the sense that Christ would soon "ascend" to the Father. If that were the case, Christ would have had to leave the Father to return to earth and appear to the disciples on Easter evening. Theologian Xavier Léon-Dufour calls the Lord's words to Mary a "literary projection"[2] to suggest that Jesus can no longer be "held on to" as he once was; he is not in an earthly body, but in a glorified body. And that changes everything. In this moment of divine revelation, Mary understood what she had to convey to Peter and the other disciples, and that she must not delay in doing it. She was being commissioned to tell them that not only was Jesus risen from the dead, but that he was being glorified by God the Father! She must announce the good news quickly: "I have seen the Lord" (John 20:18). In doing so, she became the apostle to the apostles.

The fact that Magdalene did not immediately recognize the very person she so longed to see tells us that, like the other disciples, she had *no expectation* that Jesus would rise from the dead. The narrative detail that Mary only knew it was Jesus by the way he called her name sounds so authentic, it may well have had its foundation in her own account of the experience. Indeed, in John's post-resurrection appearance stories, "Mary is the only one who is brought to recognize the risen one, not by sight or touch nor even by the sound his voice (for he speaks in v. 15a) but by his *naming her personally* (v. 16a)."[3] In so doing, John bears witness that the loving human relationships that existed before the crucifixion between Jesus and his disciples, both male and female, have survived the grave. Finally, Magdalene's calling out in Aramaic, "Rabbouni!" makes

2. Léon-Dufour, *Resurrection*, 178.

3. Catchpole, *Resurrection People*, 159.

her "very consciously a representative of the Jewish Christians within the community . . . it is a confessional statement whereby she acknowledges and commits herself to the whole corpus of revelation that the Son has brought from the Father. In this she, just *one*, just one *woman*, speaks for *all*, the whole community of faith."[4] Some scholars consider this scene of a *single* woman visiting the tomb to be the oldest of all the empty tomb and resurrection appearance stories. There is no embellishment; just a simple and sublime encounter between a weeping woman and her risen Lord.

One can imagine how often Mary Magdalene would have told this story: to Jesus' mother, to the other women, to the disciples, and to anyone else who would listen to her. She must have relived the experience of meeting the risen Jesus countless times, remembering more details, just as we often do about a transformative experience that was overwhelming at first. Then, as the story was told and retold among the early Christians, it became an oral tradition, perhaps as part of the community of the Beloved Disciple. It remains one of the most affecting scenes in the whole of John's Gospel.

The Disappointed Disciples

Luke's artistic ability to paint a dramatic portrait reaches its height in the story of the two disciples, possibly husband and wife, walking on the dusty road toward the town of Emmaus, about seven miles from Jerusalem. They were desolate, disappointed, and disillusioned by the fact of Jesus' brutal death and burial. They were discussing the heartbreaking events of the previous Friday, just before the feast of Passover, for which they had traveled to Jerusalem. The condemnation of Jesus by the Sanhedrin and his deliverance to the Romans to be crucified had been a terrible shock to all who had loved him. The two disciples could not come to terms with the tragedy.

Suddenly, out of nowhere, a man joined them on the road. "And he said to them, 'What are you discussing with each other while you walk along?'" (Luke 24:17). Of course, it was Jesus, looking like any other ordinary Jewish man returning home from Jerusalem after the Passover; but the two disciples did not recognize him. They stood still and looked very mournful. Then one of them named Cleopas said, with

4. Catchpole, *Resurrection People*, 162.

a hint of rebuke: "Are you the only stranger in Jerusalem who does not know the things that have taken place there in these days?" (Luke 24:18). Jesus wanted to open their hearts so that they would describe what had happened in their own words, so he asked, "What things?" The answer came pouring out of them, as perhaps they interrupted one another, amazed that this man on the road from Jerusalem did not know what every other Jew must have known—that Jesus of Nazareth had been crucified. They, like so many others, had thought he was a prophet "mighty in deed and word before God and all the people" (Luke 24:19). But their chief priests had condemned him as a blasphemer and handed him over to the Roman authorities to be executed. The disciples expressed their disillusionment: "But we had hoped that he was the one to redeem Israel" (Luke 24:21). Such a sense of profound loss in those three words: *we had hoped*. Clearly, that hope was gone.

However, just before they had left Jerusalem, the two disciples had heard a report too bizarre to be believed. Some women in their group had reported that they went to the tomb that morning and had discovered that the corpse was gone. They even described a vision of angels who insisted that Jesus was alive. Of course, the women's story was "nonsense," except that some of the men (Peter and the Beloved Disciple) had gone to the tomb to examine it for themselves and found it to be just as the women had testified: empty. The two disciples on the road must have discounted the story themselves. Otherwise, they would have stayed in Jerusalem in the hope of seeing the risen Jesus.

> Then he said to them, "Oh, how foolish you are, and how slow of heart to believe all that the prophets have declared! Was it not necessary that the Christ should suffer these things and then enter into his glory?" Then beginning with Moses and all the prophets, he interpreted to them the things about himself in all the scriptures. (Luke 24:25–27)

Here is a total stranger, walking side by side with the two disciples on the road, explaining the meaning of the Scriptures in a profoundly personal way, such as they had never heard anyone do before. Imagine what this scriptural exegesis must have been like: the risen Jesus telling his own life story in terms of the hidden import of biblical prophecies and ancient expectations of the Messiah. Jesus explained why it was necessary that the Christ, the anointed one of Israel, the Messiah, had to suffer and die at the hands of his enemies, instead of conquering and reigning over them like any other earthly king. Here Luke was unique among the evangelists in writing explicitly of the Messiah (Greek, *Christos*) as *suffering*. Some scholars believe this passage, as well as others in Luke, was based on early church preaching concerning the Suffering Servant of Deutero-Isaiah 53, and the necessity of the Messiah having to suffer in order to enter into his glory.[5] This very teaching of the church may well have had its foundation in what Jesus revealed to the two disciples along the road, which they later taught openly. Like so many other *logia* (that is, divinely inspired teachings), this one depicting the Messiah as the Suffering Servant may have come from the lips of the Lord himself.

At the time, however, the two disciples had been deaf and blind to the idea of the Messiah having to suffer and die. As devout Jews, they thought that the Messiah would come and save his people by a military defeat or a miraculous intervention. Certainly not by suffering! Indeed, the disciples "had no conception of a dying, much less a rising, Messiah, for the Scriptures said that the Messiah would reign forever (Isa 9:7; compare John 20:34)."[6] The shameful condemnation and crucifixion had destroyed their belief that Jesus was the Christ. And like Magdalene, the two disciples had *no expectation* that Jesus would or could rise from the dead.

> As they came near the village to which they were going, he walked ahead as if he were going on. But they urged him strongly, saying, "Stay with us, because it is almost evening and the day is now nearly over." (Luke 24:28–29)

The travelers could not bear to think of this charismatic stranger leaving them. His words had penetrated deep into their hearts. They wanted to hear more of his scriptural interpretation of Jesus' death. They longed for his infusion of hope. Besides, it was getting dark. The roads were unsafe, especially at night. They offered him hospitality; if they were, indeed, a married couple, they probably welcomed him into their own home. "So he went in to stay with them" (Luke 24:29). They set a meal before him: bread, and wine, and perhaps some dried fish. "When he was at the table with them, he took bread, blessed and broke it, and gave it to them" (Luke 24:30). Perhaps there was something about the way Jesus said the *berakhah*, the customary Hebrew blessing over the bread; something about the way he prayed as if speaking to Yahweh personally, as his *Abba*

5. Perkins, *Resurrection*, 160–61.

6. Craig, *The Son Rises*, 127.

(Daddy); something about the characteristic way he broke the bread and handed it to each of them. This common ritual of an opening blessing, breaking of bread, and distribution by the host signified the unity of fellowship at table. However, Jeremias suggests "it would be unusual of Jesus, as a guest, to take the place of the master of the house, and the disciples might have recognized him by this."[7] Could it also be that in the breaking of the bread—and only then—they first noticed the marks of the nails in his hands? Was it then that they identified the sound of his voice? Was it at that moment that they looked at him, *really* looked at him, as if for the first time? While they never said his name aloud, at last they knew who he was. "Then their eyes were opened, and they recognized him; and he vanished from their sight" (Luke 24:31).

In the instant of graced recognition, he was gone. He was no longer sitting in front of them. The bread and wine were still there where he had blessed them. How did it happen? The two disciples must have looked at each other in total shock. Had they seen a ghost? No, they had walked and talked with this stranger for miles. They had heard him interpret the stories of the Hebrew Bible in words that set them aflame with renewed faith. "They said to each other, 'Were not our hearts burning within us while he was talking to us on the road, while he was opening the scriptures to us?'" (Luke 24:32). He had accepted their invitation to stay with them. He had sat down to eat. He had prayed aloud, giving thanks to God for the meal. The two disciples had fully expected he would eat, sleep a while, and still be there in the morning. But he had vanished from their sight!

There was only one explanation: It must be true that Jesus had risen from the dead, for they had seen and finally recognized him with their own eyes. There was only one thing to do. No matter the unfinished meal, the late hour, their former fatigue, the darkness and dangers on the road back to Jerusalem. Now they were newly exhilarated with a divine mission:

> That same hour they got up and returned to Jerusalem; and they found the eleven and their companions gathered together. They were saying, "The Lord has risen indeed, and he has appeared to Simon!" Then they told what had happened on the road, and how he had been made known to them in the breaking of the bread. (Luke 24:33–35)

7. Jeremias, *Eucharistic Words*, 120–21, n3.

A Eucharistic Meal?

Some scholars have associated "the breaking of the bread" with the eucharistic liturgy as it was practiced in the early church. While the phrase may simply have referred to the customary Jewish ritual before meals, "in view of the Lukan usage of 'the breaking of bread' (Acts 2:42) and 'to break bread' (Acts 2:46; 20:7, 11), it is more probable that the phrase refers to the Eucharist. The risen Lord grants the Emmaus disciples fellowship at his table and 'during the holy meal' . . . 'their eyes were opened, so that they recognized him' (Luke 24:31)."[8] Luke might have been implying that the two disciples understood Jesus as saying "This is my body." The evangelist may have been indicating that the way to see and recognize Jesus with the eyes of faith is precisely in the eucharistic banquet, the primary celebration of Christian unity and fellowship (Greek, koinonia). In fact, three evangelists testified that Jesus "showed himself present at meals (Luke 24:30; 41–43; John 21:9–13; Mark 16:14) so that his disciples recognized him in the breaking of the bread (Luke 24:35)" and this "may be related to the belief in his coming at the celebration of the eucharist."[9]

However, it may be countered that since these two Emmaus disciples were probably *not* among the twelve at the Last Supper, how could they have known about the institution of Eucharist?[10] Moreover, just when we might "expect to find the clearest reference to the meal fellowship of Jesus with some of his disciples . . . after the Resurrection, the chief character disappears and the two travelers return to Jerusalem to tell the good news."[11] Perhaps Luke wanted to imply that Christ "vanished" into the bread he gave them and once they ate of it, they were empowered to bear witness to his resurrection. Luke might have meant that from now on all Christ's disciples are able to recognize Jesus in the breaking of the bread, even though he is no longer visible to physical eyes.[12]

Indeed, throughout Luke's Gospel, meals are depicted either as miraculous events (when Jesus feeds the multitudes), as opportunities for Christ to teach his disciples, or as intimate experiences of table fellowship. "These meals tie together Jesus' earthly ministry, the period of the resurrected One's appearances to the disciples, and the eucharistic

8. Jeremias, *Eucharistic Words*, 121, n3.

9. Brown, *An Introduction to the New Testament*, 288–89.

10. Waterman, *The Empty Tomb Tradition of Mark*, 25, n58.

11. Alsup, *The Post-Resurrection Appearance Stories*, 197.

12. Licona, *Resurrection*, 356.

experiences of Lukan Christians."[13] Yet it can also be argued that since there were no recorded words of consecration of the bread, "the assured lines of contact with the words of institution and the practice of the church in its eucharistic fellowship with the resurrected One are simply missing."[14]

There seems to be no satisfactory explanation for the Lord's sudden disappearance right after the disciples had recognized him, except that it was part of "Luke's theme of incognito/appearance, recognition, disappearance."[15] Since this is the only account of the Emmaus disciples, we cannot compare it to any other version, except for Pseudo-Mark, which might have been a direct reference to the Emmaus disciples: "After this he appeared in another form to two of them, as they were walking into the country. And they went back and told the rest, but they did not believe them" (Mark 16:12–13). There may indeed have been other versions of this appearance among the earliest pre-Gospel sources. Luke may have been working from a tradition other than Mark's, but close to John's depiction of a post-resurrection meal on the beach (John 21:9, 12, 13). This story of Jesus breaking bread with his disciples may have been widely circulated in the early church, especially while the Emmaus disciples were still alive.

It is also possible that Luke may have created this story as an allegorical narrative to describe how Christians may meet Jesus in disguise on the road of life. However, it seems much more plausible that the appearance had its foundation in real experience and oral tradition. Luke, like the other evangelists, would have been too respectful of well-known traditions to create totally fictional scenarios about the risen Jesus meeting his disciples on the road and sharing a meal with them. Besides, all the actual apparitions were far more marvelous than any fictionalized accounts could ever have been. "While many have argued that Jesus' post-resurrection appearance to the Emmaus disciples may have been invented to describe the early church practice of the Eucharist, we may say that this is possible but that there is nothing to commend this interpretation over an actual appearance."[16]

---

13. Perkins, *Resurrection*, 162.

14. Alsup, *Post-Resurrection*, 197.

15. Alsup, *Post-Resurrection*, 197.

16. Licona, *Resurrection*, 358.

Recognizing Christ

How are we to interpret this resurrection narrative? Often, we think of the first disciples, male and female, as being especially privileged to be near the physical Jesus during his lifetime—and of course, they were. But from all accounts, they often failed to recognize who the Lord was in their midst, either before or after his resurrection. The real point of the two disciples on the road to Emmaus may be that we, like them, must grow more and more consciously aware that Jesus walks along the road with us and within us, with every step we take. We may not recognize him at first, but if we are willing to listen with a burning heart, Jesus will reveal the hidden meaning of his life in the Scriptures to us. His Spirit will also explicate the deeper story of *our own lives*: why it was necessary that this or that happened in the process of our maturing and purification in order that God might be made manifest in us. If we allow Jesus to travel with us—and invite him to *stay* with us—he will show us how God is being glorified in everything we think, feel, and do. Then, through a deepening of faith, and a warm welcoming of "the stranger" in hospitality, as well as by coming together in eucharistic fellowship, we will more readily recognize Jesus in the breaking of the bread.

The Upper Room

The appearance to the "twelve" (the traditional term for the original apostles, in spite of the loss of Judas) in the upper room is considered to be very early. It is the best attested of all the appearances and is strongly supported by many different sources.[17] In John, it is implied that this appearance occurred in Jerusalem, while Matthew places it on a mountain in Galilee and limits it to the "eleven" (Matt 28:16). The specific details and even the location of the appearance, whether in Jerusalem (Luke and John) or Galilee (Mark and Matthew), may be moot; however an almost unanimous consensus of scholars agrees that "subsequent to Jesus' execution, a number of his followers had experiences, in individual and group settings, that convinced them Jesus had risen from the dead and had appeared to them in some manner."[18] Historian and religious scholar Paula Fredriksen asserts: "The disciples' conviction that they had seen the

17. 1 Cor 15:5; Mark 16:7; Matt 28:16–17; Luke 24:33–51; John 20:19–29. See Licona, *Resurrection*, 372, n330.

18. Licona, *Resurrection*, 372.

Risen Christ, their permanent relocation to Jerusalem, their principled inclusion of Gentiles *as* Gentiles—all these are historical bedrock, facts known past doubting about the earliest community after Jesus' death."[19]

Immediately following the Emmaus story, Luke transports us to the house where the "eleven and their companions" were gathered. As cited, the moment the two Emmaus disciples arrived, they were told by the others, "The Lord has risen indeed, and he has appeared to Simon!" (Luke 24:34). Notably, no narrative exists of this appearance to Simon Peter. Even more puzzling, some ancient texts do not include this verse concerning Simon Peter at all. The other evangelists never mention a private apparition to Peter, although Paul does do so in his description of the tradition he had received from Peter and James (1 Cor 15:5). Thus it may have been authenticated by Peter himself. We do not know if, in Luke's tradition, it happened after Peter ran to the tomb, looked in, and saw the linen cloths lying by themselves without a corpse, and returned home "amazed at what had happened" (Luke 24:12). Unfortunately, the first appearance to Peter remains undocumented.

On hearing of this apparition, the Emmaus disciples revealed that the Lord had also appeared to *them* on the road and illuminated the Scriptures about himself, after which he made himself known in the breaking of the bread. The combination of euphoria and awestruck fear at such a manifestation of divine power must have been overwhelming. And there is more:

> While they were talking about this, Jesus himself stood among them and said to them, "Peace be with you." They were startled and terrified, and thought that they were seeing a ghost. He said to them, "Why are you frightened, and why do doubts arise in your hearts? Look at my hands and my feet; see that it is I myself. Touch me and see; for a ghost does not have flesh and bones as you see that I have." (Luke 24:36–39)

The first reaction of the disciples was always fear and doubt. This is a common theme throughout the Gospels to any out-of-the-ordinary experience. Yet the stunned disciples could see that it was, indeed, Jesus. "It is I myself" echoes the familiar scriptural self-identification of the earthly Jesus—"I am he"—and links this same identity directly with the risen Lord. "The identity of the risen Christ with the earthly Jesus, hence the unbroken path of the Saviour, inaugurated at Luke 9:51, is

---

19. Fredriksen, *Jesus of Nazareth*, 264.

being proclaimed in each phase of our pericope: narrative, instruction, finale."[20] This presence before them was no ghost, no product of their imaginations. The disciples could see and hear him as undeniably as they could one another. But his body was clearly not subject to the same laws of physicality as were their own bodies. So they could hardly believe what they saw.

> And when he had said this, he showed them his hands and his feet. While in their joy they were disbelieving and still wondering, he said to them, "Have you anything here to eat?" They gave him a piece of broiled fish, and he took it and ate in their presence. (Luke 24:40–43)

In this dynamic scene, Luke is concerned to make four things clear. First, the disciples recognized Jesus as the same person who had taught, healed, and forgiven sins throughout his earthly mission; then had been crucified, died, and was buried. The disciples could still see the marks of the nails in his hands and feet. Second, the Jesus who stood before them was not a ghost, a hallucination, or a phantasm of the real Jesus, but a physical body that could be seen and touched. Third, Jesus wanted to eat something in the disciples' presence, not because he was hungry, but because he wished to prove to them that he had indeed risen with the same identity, in a body that could still engage in the physical functions of the human world—though in a transformed way. And fourth, since a shared meal was a sign of close fellowship and resulted in renewed strength, by wanting to eat with them Jesus revealed his great joy in being alive again and reunited with his disciples, as well as his eagerness to impart his new life.[21] In succession, the Lord invited his disciples "to look on him, then feel him, then give him to eat."[22]

Following the meal, Jesus gave his personal exegesis of the Scriptures, just as he had done for the two disciples on the road.

> Then he said to them, "These are my words that I spoke to you while I was still with you—that everything written about me in the law of Moses, the prophets, and the psalms must be fulfilled." Then he opened their minds to understand the scriptures, and he said to them, "Thus it is written, that the Christ is to suffer and to rise from the dead on the third day, and that repentance

20. Dillon, *From Eye-Witnesses to Ministers of the Word*, 193.

21. Léon-Dufour, *Resurrection*, 165–67.

22. Dillon, *From Eye-Witnesses*, 194.

and forgiveness of sins is to be proclaimed in his name to all
nations, beginning from Jerusalem. You are witnesses of these
things." (Luke 24:44–48)

Here again, Luke reiterated the importance of remembering the Scriptures
concerning the necessity of a suffering and rising Messiah. He also
summed up the preaching message that would already have been familiar
to Christian communities by the third quarter of the first century. How
the disciples must have listened in awe as Jesus explained all that had
been closed to them before! How many generations have been inspired
by these same teachings! Jesus was well aware that he would soon have to
leave his disciples on their own to do all that he expected them to do; to
baptize and to proclaim the forgiveness of sins to all the nations. But he
would not leave them without divine help. He would send the Holy Spirit.
He gave them a final commission: "And see, I am sending upon you what
my Father promised; so stay here in the city until you have been clothed
with power from on high" (Luke 24:49).

The reference to the sending of what the Father promised is Luke's
anticipation of the coming of the Holy Spirit at Pentecost, fifty days after
Easter. At the very beginning of Acts, Luke again mentions the promise
of the Father to the disciples: "you will be baptized with the Holy Spirit
not many days from now" (Acts 1:5). Once they received the power of the
Spirit on Pentecost, the disciples were emboldened to become witnesses
"in Jerusalem, in all Judea and Samaria, and to the ends of the earth"
(Acts 1:8). We must realize that this group of disciples in the upper
room was not only the "eleven," but also "their companions." Thus Luke
must have included the women who had followed Jesus from Galilee,
although they were not specifically mentioned. These women, too, were
commissioned by Jesus. "Their inclusion reflects the important role of
women as missionaries in the earliest period, as attested to in both the
Pauline letters and in Acts."[23]

If all these witnesses who had seen the risen Lord had not been
willing to convey what they had personally experienced, how could
those who had *not* seen the resurrected Jesus ever have known about
the resurrection? Two thousand years of Christian evangelization rest
on the testimony of these men and women, the first disciples, the first
Christians. If they had not dared to speak, to write, to suffer, and to give
their lives for what they knew to be true, we would never have known

23. Perkins, *Resurrection*, 167. See also Fiorenza, *In Memory of Her*, 160–204.

what happened that first Easter. The fact that these frightened disciples became such courageous witnesses—preaching the gospel "to the ends of the earth"—is perhaps the most convincing proof we have of Christ's resurrection.

Behind Locked Doors

John the Evangelist has a very different version of Jesus' second resurrection appearance. We have seen that in John's account, Magdalene was the first to see the Lord and spread the good news to Peter and the others. While John sets the appearance to the disciples on the evening of "the first day of the week," just as Luke did, John describes a much more disturbing scene. He depicts the disciples hiding behind locked doors, terrified of being arrested, questioned, and condemned to death by the Jewish authorities as followers of Jesus. The disciples had not believed Magdalene's story, even though she was probably part of their gathering, along with Mary, Jesus' mother, and the other women who had come with Jesus from Galilee for the Passover. Maybe Magdalene was still trying to convince the disciples of what she had seen that morning: the empty tomb, the angelic presences, the linen cloths lying neatly folded where the body had been, and Jesus appearing to her in person, risen from the dead. Perhaps Peter and the Beloved Disciple were still struggling to make sense of the empty tomb they had visited at dawn. No doubt, emotions ran high. There may have been some intense arguments.

Suddenly, without warning, Jesus appeared in the room. He did not come *through* the locked doors; he simply "stood among them." One moment he was not there; the next moment he was. As in Luke, Jesus' first words to his disciples were "Peace to you," the familiar Hebrew greeting, *Shalom*. This is what the disciples needed most, the assurance of the Lord's peaceful presence among them. Then Jesus showed them his hands (his feet are not mentioned), and the wound in his side from the soldier's lance.

> Jesus said to them again, "Peace be with you. As the Father has sent me, so I send you." When he had said this, he breathed on them and said to them, "Receive the Holy Spirit. If you forgive the sins of any, they are forgiven them; if you retain the sins of any, they are retained." (John 20:21–23)

John focuses on Jesus giving the disciples a mission. As Christ was sent by the Father, so Christ is now sending them. They must unlock the doors of fear in their hearts and go forth in courage. In John's version, Christ's transformative action of *breathing* on the disciples signifies the imparting of the Holy Spirit (as Luke describes again at Pentecost). Every time Jesus appeared, he poured out his Holy Spirit on those who believed in him. Just as God breathed life into Adam at the creation, so now the Son of God breathed his resurrected life into the disciples. Likewise, this life-giving breath occurred on "the first day of the week," after the Lord had rested in the tomb from his labors on the cross. John wants us to recognize that Easter is the *first day* of a whole new creation.[24] From now on, Christ's disciples in every age, male and female, would be called upon to live the resurrected life of Christ—his very Spirit—and to continue his mission in the world.

Matthew's Gospel had commissioned the disciples to go forth to all nations and baptize them in the name of the Father, Son, and Holy Spirit, teaching them to obey everything that Christ had taught them (Matt 28:19–20). In Luke's version of Christ's words, "repentance and forgiveness of sins is to be proclaimed in his name to all nations, beginning from Jerusalem" (Luke 24:47). In John's narrative, when Christ breathed upon the disciples, they were most urgently commissioned to forgive sins. To any Jew, the idea that a human being, even acting in the name of God, could forgive sins would have been anathema. Christ had been sharply criticized for doing just that: "Who is this who is speaking blasphemies? Who can forgive sins but God alone?" (Luke 5:21). In John's resurrection account, Jesus assured the disciples that in his name they could, in fact, forgive sins because henceforth the Holy Spirit would pour forth mercy from Christ's own perfect sacrifice on the cross through them to the whole world. It should be noted that John does not list the disciples to whom Jesus gave this power, either by name, gender, or number; nor does he limit this divine action of mercy to just one generation of disciples, namely those gathered on that Easter evening in the upper room. He was addressing all disciples of Jesus yet to come.[25]

What is meant by "if you retain the sins of any, they are retained"? Unfortunately, this is a mistranslation dating back to the third century, which was then codified by the decrees of the Council of Trent. As New

24. See Wright, *Resurrection*, 667.
25. Moloney, *The Gospel of John*, 534, n19.

Testament scholar Sandra Schneiders points out: "The text of John 20:23 does not say anything about 'retaining sins.' Translated literally it says: 'Of whomever you forgive the sins, they are forgiven to them; whomever you hold are held fast.'" [26] She explains that the verb "to hold" (Greek, *kratein*) does not mean "retain," but rather, "hold fast," "grasp," even "embrace." In keeping with this sacred mission, Schneiders observes: "The community that forgives sins must hold fast those whom it has brought into the community of eternal life. This may be a reference to baptism, but hardly to penance."[27] Thus the essence of the church's mission, as the living presence of Jesus Christ in the world, must be one of forgiving, embracing, holding fast, guiding, and sustaining believers in the faith by the power of the Holy Spirit. The church community must be a place of refuge, of witness, of justice—especially for the poor, the outcast, and the marginalized. It must carry on Christ's own mission of boundless mercy and compassion for a sinful, suffering humanity.

The Doubting Disciple

One of the disciples was not there in the upper room. He is the only one actually named by John the Evangelist in this scene; not Peter, not the Beloved Disciple, not James, not Magdalene or any of the other women, nor any of the original eleven. "But Thomas (who was called the Twin), one of the twelve, was not with them when Jesus came" (John 20:24). For some unexplained reason, Thomas had separated himself from the group, perhaps even from his twin brother or sister. Thus he had not heard Magdalene's report, nor Peter and the Beloved Disciple's confirmation of the tomb being empty. Presumably, Thomas had been so devastated by the news of Christ's shameful death that he could not bring himself to face the others. He could not even bear to mourn with them. He remained alone, cut off, and in hiding.

At some point during Easter week, the "other disciples" sought out Thomas and told him, "We have seen the Lord" (John 20:25). Thomas's depression and sense of loss were too great to be so easily consoled. He could not accept their oral testimony, lest he be duped into a false euphoria like theirs. He would not consider such an outrageous claim, even on the basis of trustworthy eyewitnesses. He wanted to confirm the

26. Schneiders, "The Resurrection (of the Body)," 186.

27. Schneiders, "The Resurrection," 186–87.

story for himself. "Unless I see the mark of the nails in his hands, and put my finger in the mark of the nails and my hand in his side, I will not believe" (John 20:25). Unless his stipulations were met, he refused to believe. That was his non-negotiable position.

It is interesting to note that in Mark's Gospel the women at the tomb doubted out of fear; in Matthew, even to the very last, some of the eleven disciples doubted; in Luke, all the disciples doubted and thought the women's story an idle tale; and in John, it is Thomas who represents all who doubt and fear to commit to belief.[28] Indeed, Thomas voices what many throughout the ages have thought: "Unless I can find historical proof that satisfies every question I can ask concerning the resurrection story; unless I can be convinced of the physical reality of Jesus and thrust my hand into his flesh; unless I can personally see and hear him, and touch the marks of the nails myself, I cannot believe that a crucified man could rise from the dead." In other words, "unless I see, I will not believe." But is seeing believing?

Some of the disciples must have convinced Thomas to be with them in the upper room on the following Sunday. Then, perhaps, Jesus would appear again and Thomas could see for himself if what they had said was true. Of course, no one knew for sure if Christ would return. Could the Lord be expected to come into their midst on demand?

> A week later his disciples were again in the house, and Thomas was with them. Although the doors were shut, Jesus came and stood among them and said, "Peace be with you." Then he said to Thomas, "Put your finger here and see my hands. Reach out your hand and put it in my side. Do not doubt but believe." (John 20:26–27)

One may only imagine the shock and wonderment with which Thomas beheld the risen Lord. He did not need to touch the wounds, as he had demanded he must do, because he could see for himself that Jesus was truly and physically alive and standing before him, speaking directly to him. A flood of emotion overcame Thomas. From the depths of his heart, he cried out: "My Lord and my God!" (John 20:28), perhaps falling to his knees and worshiping Jesus as the Christ, the Anointed One of God, the Messiah. John places these most succinct and sacred words of faith into the mouth of the former doubter. In doing so, he reassures everyone who doubts that a radical turnaround is always possible.

28. See Moloney, *The Gospel of John*, 516.

Seeing or Believing?

In reflecting on this scene, we might ask: Did Thomas believe that Jesus was truly God (and therefore could rise from the dead) because he *saw* him, or was he empowered to see who Jesus actually was because he came to *believe* in him? In answer to this question, one that must have been on the minds of many first-century Christians, the evangelist has Jesus say: "Have you believed because you have seen me? Blessed are those who have not seen and yet have come to believe" (John 20:29). Here, John adds a new beatitude. Henceforth, those who see Jesus with the eyes of faith are as blessed as those who once saw him with physical eyes. This applied to Christians in the Johannine community at the end of the first century as well as to every Christian who would come to faith in the future. The implication is that, since Thomas actually *saw* Jesus, he did not have to believe. He could be certain that Jesus had risen from the dead through his own personal, existential experience, as could the other disciples. Those who would come after would have to believe on the faith and testimony of those who *had* seen. That faith would transform their lives and spread throughout the world. Yet even the ability to recognize Jesus for who he was seems to have depended on more than merely physical sight.

Thomas's words reflect a profound understanding of Jesus' identity—as both Lord of the universe and Son of God—that developed in the early church. Though writing his Gospel during the late first century, John seems to have assumed that the faith of Thomas, however inchoate at the time, was already an intuitive understanding of who Jesus really was, granted by the Holy Spirit in the very moment of recognition. As such it was much like Peter's answer to Jesus' question: "But who do you say I am?" to which Simon Peter answered, "You are the Messiah, the Son of the living God." (Matt 16:15–16; Mark 8:29). Jesus attested that such a testimony of faith can only come from the Holy Spirit. It is a gift of God to any heart open and receptive to grace. From time to time, we also may be privileged to experience a profound sense of divine presence and these same words may arise in our hearts. The response is, like that of Thomas, awe and adoration.

John ends this dramatic episode with a formal statement of purpose that seems to draw his entire Gospel to a close.

> Now Jesus did many other signs in the presence of his disciples, which are not written in this book. But these are written so that

you may come to believe that Jesus is the Messiah, the Son of
God, and that through believing you may have life in his name.
(John 20:30–31)

As it was in the beginning, so it is in the end. John's Prologue had
proclaimed that "in the beginning" the Word was with God and the Word
was God. Through him, all creation came into being. This Word is life, a
life that became the light of all people. "The light shines in the darkness,
and the darkness did not overcome it" (John 1:5). Thus from the first
words of his Gospel, John announced who Jesus really was—the perfect
"expression" of the Father—and where he really came from, and that he
took on human flesh, and lived among human beings as one of us. Before
he told any stories about Jesus, the evangelist bore witness that the Law
came through Moses, but the "grace and truth" of salvation came through
Jesus Christ. "And the Word became flesh and lived among us and we
have seen his glory, the glory as of the Father's only Son, full of grace and
truth" (John 1:14). According to John, Jesus himself proclaimed that no
one has ever seen God. But John insists that "It is God the only Son, who
is close to the Father's heart, who has made him known" (John 1:18). In
other words, John bears witness that the glory of God was made fully
manifest in the life, death, and resurrection of the man Jesus.

At the first ending of his Gospel, John attests that Jesus appeared and
worked many signs and miracles, both before and after his resurrection,
that could not be included in this book. There were simply too many of
them. But those that the evangelist had included were chosen to bring the
reader and the listener to greater faith and "life in his name." They serve
one purpose: to enliven and strengthen the faith of the community of
Christians who were enduring great trials and who would continue to do
so throughout future time. These signs bear a message of light, hope, and
courage: no matter how dire things get, because Christ is resurrected, he
has overcome suffering, death, and everything else that could destroy us.
"I have said this to you, so that in me you may have peace. In the world
you face persecution. But take courage; I have conquered the world!"
(John 16:33).

John's Epilogue

Chapter 21 of John's Gospel presents another appearance of Jesus that
might seem like an epilogue added on by another writer. However, the

dramatic style, careful attention to character delineation, and layering of symbolism are all recognizable as the work of John. Nevertheless, there are verbal expressions and literary aspects in this section not found elsewhere in the Fourth Gospel. It may have been written and redacted at a later date when the evangelist's community came under increased persecution.[29]

There is also an internal problem presented by John's setting of the scene on Lake Tiberias (Sea of Galilee) with seven of the disciples having returned to their former occupations as fishermen, as if nothing had radically changed in their lives. And this, after all that had happened in Jerusalem: Christ's resurrection, his appearances, and the coming of the Holy Spirit in the upper room. It may be that Peter and the others had traveled north to Galilee, as indicated by Matthew, to await further directions. Perhaps they needed to provide for their families and so went back to fishing for fish instead of for people. They may also have lost heart that those in Galilee to whom they had spoken about the resurrection of Jesus would not believe them. They may have lost the initial urgency of their "eschatological task, to bring home the people of God," and the conviction that "this task does not allow the smallest delay."[30] It is also plausible that Peter still needed to experience *personal forgiveness* from the Lord for his denial as well as clarity about his role before he could begin his public ministry. Notably, in John's Gospel, we do not read that when the cock crowed and Peter realized that he had denied Jesus three times, that "he went out and wept bitterly," as we do in Matthew 26:75 and Luke 22:62. In John's version, until Peter was personally absolved of his sin of denial and formally empowered by Christ to carry on his work as shepherd, the other disciples were effectively without a leader.

Frustrated Fishermen

The epilogue to the Gospel of John begins with the announcement that "after these things" (presumably the episode with Thomas), Jesus "showed himself again" to the disciples by Lake Tiberias (John 21:1). Seven disciples—Simon Peter, Thomas the Twin, Nathanael of Cana in Galilee, the two sons of Zebedee (James and John), and two others (unnamed)— had been fishing all night long, but caught nothing. "Just after daybreak,

29. Moloney, *The Gospel of John*, 546.

30. Jeremias, *New Testament Theology*, 133.

Jesus stood on the beach; but the disciples did not know that it was Jesus" (John 21:4). As at the tomb, John set the scene at sunrise to suggest the dawning of light out of darkness and despair. This has been a familiar theme in John, ever since the Prologue when the evangelist characterized the Word of God as the light that shines in the darkness. Once again, as with Mary Magdalene, Jesus appeared out of nowhere but was not immediately recognized. He called to the men, using a familial greeting: "'Children, you have no fish, have you?' They answered him, 'No'" (John 21:5). Jesus knew they had not caught anything, so by this negative yet concerned question, he let the disciples know that he understood their frustration. (Perhaps the implication was that the fishermen had already tried repeatedly to preach the gospel and to baptize in Galilee, but they had failed utterly to make any new disciples.) Then Jesus told them to cast their net on the right side of the boat and they would find "some fish." They did as Jesus said and immediately "they were not able to haul it in because there were so many fish" (John 21:6).

This extraordinary catch signaled to "the disciple whom Jesus loved" that "It is the Lord!" (John 21:7). He was the only one of the seven to recognize Jesus. When Peter heard this, he immediately tucked his outer garment around himself so that he would not appear naked before the Lord and, with his usual impetuosity, jumped into the water to be the first to get to Jesus. He left the other disciples to bring in the boat, dragging the net full of fish. When Peter and the others after him arrived at the shore, there was already a charcoal fire, with fish on it, and bread. Jesus knew the disciples would be hungry and he planned to feed them himself. He asked them to bring some of the fish they had just caught and Simon Peter went back on the boat and helped haul the net in. The exceptional count of large fish was one hundred fifty three, yet the net was not torn. This may be a symbolic number or perhaps it signified the number of Christians who were eventually "caught" by the disciples and had been formed into the Johannine community. Unfortunately, the original meaning is impossible to decipher.

> Jesus said to them, "Come and have breakfast." Now none of the
> disciples dared to ask him, "Who are you?" because they knew it
> was the Lord. Jesus came and took the bread and gave it to them,
> and did the same with the fish. (John 21:12–13)

Jesus invited the exhausted fishermen to breakfast on the beach. They all knew by now who he was. They were close enough to recognize him.

But they dared not ask him where he had come from, how he had arrived there on the beach, or where he had gotten the fish and bread at such an early hour. Just as at the multiplication of the five barley loaves and two fish (John 6:1–15), which also took place at Lake Tiberias, Jesus *came* and *took* and *gave* the bread to the disciples, and he did the same with the fish. While some scholars associate Jesus' action with a eucharistic meal, others downplay the parallel.[31] Presumably Jesus and the disciples ate the meal together. One wonders whether it was consumed in silence, because the disciples were too afraid to start a conversation. Or did Jesus, as he always used to do, reveal himself verbally to them? Did they ask him questions about his death and resurrection? His transformed body? What he wanted them to do? In response to all the questions we would like to have answered, there is only silence.

John finished this seaside segment by saying, "This was now the third time that Jesus appeared to the disciples after he was raised from the dead" (John 21:14). Indeed, it was the third appearance to the male disciples, but actually the *fourth* appearance mentioned in John's Gospel. The first was to Mary Magdalene.

The Shepherd and the Beloved

After breakfast, Jesus and Simon Peter went for a walk along the pebbly beach by the sea. Presumably, they were alone and out of hearing of the others. Jesus asked Simon Peter:

> "Simon son of John, do you love me more than these?" He said to him, "Yes, Lord; you know that I love you." Jesus said to him, "Feed my lambs." A second time he said to him, "Simon son of John, do you love me?" He said to him, "Yes, Lord; you know that I love you." Jesus said to him, "Tend my sheep." He said to him the third time, "Simon son of John, do you love me?" Peter felt hurt because he said to him the third time, "Do you love me?" And he said to him, "Lord, you know everything; you know that I love you." Jesus said to him, "Feed my sheep." (John 21:15–17)

Three times Peter had denied even knowing Jesus. Now Jesus was giving his disciple a once-in-a-lifetime chance to tell the Lord how much he loved him, three times over. Peter must declare that he loves Jesus more

31. See Moloney, *The Gospel of John*, 553, n13.

than he loves any of his brethren or (alternatively) more than his brethren love Jesus. John's depiction of the scene is full of poignancy. Peter is at first hurt to be asked over and over again what the Lord knows so well; that is, that Peter loves him. But for Peter's sake, it is necessary that he repent each of his three denials and experience that he is completely forgiven in his threefold affirmation. Such repentance and forgiveness produces an eruption of *joy*—the joy of the lost soul returning home to its Father, being invited to a banquet with singing and dancing: "The return home is a resurrection from the dead, because there is life only in the sphere of the kingly reign of God. Anyone who belongs to it has even now attained the consummation of the world beyond the barrier of death."[32] After each affirmation of his love, Peter is given a heartfelt commission by Jesus: feed my lambs, tend my sheep, feed my sheep.

In John's Gospel, Jesus had described himself as the Good Shepherd: "I am the good shepherd. The good shepherd lays down his life for the sheep" (John 10:11). Now Jesus is entrusting that role of shepherding to Peter. The disciple must attend to the physical care and spiritual nourishment of all the disciples and continue Christ's own work of salvation. Peter would also need to love and forgive others just as Jesus had forgiven him. There would be no limit to this life of service. As a young man, Peter could buckle up his tunic and go "wherever he wished." But Jesus tells him that when he grows old, "you will stretch out your hands, and someone else will fasten a belt around you and take you where you do not wish to go" (John 21:18). Just as Jesus had stretched out his hands and been bound by the guards in the garden of Gethsemane, so one day Peter would be bound and led off to die like his Master. Peter's thrice-stated commitment to love would eventually demand everything of him: his wife, his children, his extended family, his fellow disciples. Finally, as Jesus had laid down his life for his sheep, so Peter would have to do so. He could not hold anything back. Now he must commit himself *unconditionally* to the work of the Lord. Jesus made this pointedly clear in just two words: "Follow me" (John 21:19).

At that moment, Peter realized that "the disciple whom Jesus loved" was close behind them. He, too, was "following" Jesus. When had he arrived? How much had he overheard? This was the Beloved Disciple who had reclined next to Jesus at the Last Supper and had been courageous enough to ask Jesus who would betray him. Was Peter perhaps a bit

---

32. Jeremias, *New Testament Theology*, 157.

jealous of the Beloved Disciple who had never betrayed or deserted Jesus? Who had stood at the foot of the cross with Mary the mother of Jesus and Mary Magdalene? Peter asked Jesus, "Lord, what about him?" In other words, would the Beloved Disciple also be bound, and led away, and suffer a violent death? "Jesus said to him, 'If it is my will that he remain until I come, what is that to you?'" (John 21:22). The Lord would not countenance Peter comparing himself to anyone else, nor would he answer such a question. Jesus merely reiterated the commission to Peter: "Follow me!" That is all Peter needed to know, both now and in the future.

Apparently, in the interim between the writing of chapter 20 and the writing of chapter 21, the Johannine community—no doubt familiar with this apparition story—had spread a rumor that the Beloved Disciple would not die until the Lord returned in person to take him to heaven. In John's Gospel, the Beloved Disciple had been the eyewitness to all that had happened at the Last Supper; he had gained Peter entry into the courtyard of the High Priest during the trial of Jesus; he was entrusted with the care of Jesus' mother at the crucifixion; he ran ahead of Peter to see the empty tomb. He was the first disciple who believed that something extraordinary had happened to Jesus on Easter morning, even before he had actually seen the risen Jesus. It is highly probable that this same Beloved Disciple had personally influenced, dictated, or actually written the Fourth Gospel. He may even have been the founder of the Johannine community.

Some scholars think that the Beloved Disciple had died before the writing of the Epilogue. His community had been thrown into confusion and doubt about Christ's seemingly failed prediction that the Beloved Disciple would *not* die before the Lord returned in glory to reveal his kingdom in the *parousia*. The delay of the expected second coming of Christ had proved a serious stumbling block for the early church communities. By the time the epilogue writer amended the gospel, disappointed expectations about the immediacy of the *parousia* had to be addressed; mistaken notions about the Beloved Disciple had to be corrected. It became necessary to add this last apparition account on the beach in order to issue a strong statement to the community that *Jesus never said* the Beloved Disciple would not die. The narrator of this passage writes unambiguously that "Jesus did not say to him that he would not die, but, 'If it is my will that he remain until I come, what is that to you?'" (John 21:23). Of course, by the time of the writing of John's Gospel near the end of the first century, James, Peter, and Paul had all been martyred for their faith, as had countless other Christians. It was all the more imperative to reassure the persecuted Johannine community that even though they could not see him, Jesus would always be with them in life and would personally come for them in death. Like the first generation of Christians, they were to follow and bear witness to the Savior unquestioningly, no matter where it might lead or how long it would take for the fullness of the kingdom to be revealed.

The Beloved Disciple

Who *was* the Beloved Disciple? At the end of the first century, it was commonly believed that he was John the Evangelist, one of the twelve apostles and a son of Zebedee. Alternately, he might have been James the Greater, the *other* son of Zebedee. Or perhaps he was James the Less, son of Alphaeus, "brother" of Jesus (Gal 1:19), also one of the twelve apostles. Or he might have been one of the "two others of his disciples" in the fishing boat at the Sea of Galilee (John 21:2).[33] Some scholars suggest Lazarus of Bethany, whom Jesus raised from the dead (John 11:1–44).

At the end of the second century, Bishop Polycrates (fl. c. 130–196 CE) wrote that the Beloved Disciple "was John, who was both a witness and a teacher, who reclined upon the bosom of the Lord, and, being a priest, wore the sacerdotal plate. He fell asleep at Ephesus."[34] Likewise, Bishop Irenaeus (c.130–202 CE) repeatedly identified John the Evangelist with the Beloved Disciple: "John, the disciple of the Lord, who also had leaned upon His breast, did himself publish a Gospel during his residence at Ephesus in Asia."[35] Augustine of Hippo (354–430 CE) also taught that John the Evangelist was the Beloved Disciple.[36]

Modern scholars, however, have generally rejected this attribution and suggested that "the disciple whom Jesus loved" might have been a minor disciple and not an apostle but nonetheless, *one who was an eyewitness* to key events in the life, death, and resurrection of Jesus. After the resurrection, a community of disciples may have formed around this disciple; the same community for which the Fourth Gospel was

33. Craig, *The Son Rises*, 81.

34. Eusebius, *Church History*, Book V, chapter 4.

35. Irenaeus, *Against the Heresies*, 3.1.1; see also, 1.8.5; 1.16.3; 2.2.5; 2.22.3; 2.22.5; 3.3.4; 5.33.3.

36. Augustine, *Tractates on the Gospel of John*, Tractate 119, 45–49.

eventually written. The community itself might have considered him the Beloved Disciple and so the evangelist placed him in the climactic gospel scenes. Another theory is that the Beloved Disciple might represent *every disciple* who is faithful to the teachings of Christ and who is willing to follow the Lord through suffering and death into a new life. Whoever it may have been, the editor of the last part of the Epilogue concluded the Gospel with the strong affirmation that it was the Beloved Disciple, a reliable eyewitness, who was responsible for this authentic account of the life, death, and resurrection of Jesus Christ. If not the direct author, the Beloved Disciple seems to have been the prime authority behind the witness and the text.[37]

> This is the disciple who is testifying to these things and has written them, and we know that his testimony is true. But there are also many other things that Jesus did; if every one of them were written down, I suppose that the world itself could not contain the books that would be written. (John 21:24–25)

It would have been impossible to record every story about what Jesus said and did during his lifetime and after his resurrection. It is also impossible to tell the stories of everything Jesus has accomplished in and through individuals throughout the ages. The multiplication of narratives continues, even in our own times. Jesus is always and everywhere at work: "My Father is still working, and I also am working" (John 5:17). We are creating new gospels with our own lives.

Allegory or Truth?

Some contemporary scholars have suggested that all of John's appearance stories were devised as allegories to describe what the disciples "came to feel" about Jesus' abiding presence within them and the power of the Holy Spirit working through them. But these vivid dramatic stories were not written merely as a feel-good panacea for a persecuted community of first-century Christians. These narratives concerned real, historical people with recognizable names, characteristics, fears, flaws, hopes, doubts, and faith. They were artistically crafted re-enactments of basic story lines that had been told and retold within the church community for decades before they were written down. They were recorded to bring the reader to believe what the disciples knew to be true: that the individual

37. Moloney, *The Gospel of John*, 561, n22–24.

the first witnesses saw was indeed Jesus, alive in a transformed body. Thomas (noticeably, not Peter) became the unlikely spokesperson for the whole group and for all the ages. With his pronouncement of "my Lord and my God" (John 20:28), Thomas bore witness that the man standing before him was the incarnation of the living God. For the evangelist writing these words on parchment, it was essential that the resurrection not be considered merely a "spiritual experience" of Christ's inner presence. Jesus really appeared. Jesus was really in a body. Therefore, the resurrection really happened.[38] Jeremias attests to the discernable validity of the textual accounts:

> The characteristic feature of the *earliest stratum of tradition* is that it still preserves a recollection of the overpowering, puzzling and mysterious nature of the events: eyes opened at the breaking of the bread, beams of heavenly light, a figure on the shore at the break of day, the unexpected appearance in a closed room, the outbreak of praise expressed in speaking with tongues, the sudden disappearance—all these are ways in which the earliest tradition is formulated. The same mysterious *chiaroscuro* surrounds the earliest accounts of the reactions of the witnesses: now they fail to recognize the Risen One, now the heavenly brightness blinds them, now they believe that they have seen a ghost. Fear and trembling, anxiety, uncertainty and doubt struggle with joy and worship.[39]

Of course, in John and in Luke, metaphorical meanings and symbolic signs have been layered on top of this eyewitness foundation, but that does not change the essential nature of the resurrection story from fact to fiction. If some scholars and theologians choose to characterize these accounts as mere allegories created to describe "spiritual feelings" of Christ's presence after his death, they inflict serious damage on the veridical weight of what the witnesses claimed had happened. Jesus did not simply send his disciples a consoling spiritual message that he had risen from the dead and gone straight back to heaven. He reappeared on earth precisely to be the physical proof of the resurrection event in real time. If we fail to honor the clear intention of all the evangelists—to tell stories based on their unswerving conviction about the reality of the appearances—then we reduce them to liars and deceivers.

---

38. Wright, *Resurrection*, 668.

39. Jeremias, *New Testament Theology*, 303, emphasis in original.

We are left with the conclusion that both the evangelists themselves, and the sources to which they had access, whether oral or written, which they have shaped to their own purpose but without destroying the underlying subject-matter, really did intend to refer to actual events which took place on the third day after Jesus' execution.[40]

On the foundation of these sacred writings, we base our faith—not only in Christ's bodily resurrection from the dead, but in our own.

> *Therefore we have been buried with him by baptism into death,*
> *so that, just as Christ was raised from the dead by the glory of the Father,*
> *so we too might walk in newness of life.*
> *For if we have been united with him in a death like his,*
> *we will certainly be united with him in a resurrection like his.*
> (Rom 6:4–5)

40. Wright, *Resurrection*, 680.

4

Questions, Doubts, and Faith

JUST AS WE DISCUSSED multiple theories disputing the empty tomb, so we must examine repeated attempts at alternative interpretations of the resurrection appearances. Most Christians probably do believe that Jesus really died, that his tomb was empty, and that he came back to life. However, some scholars consider that he returned in *exactly the same body* that he had before he was crucified. So in that case his rising would have been similar to that of Lazarus, whom Jesus raised from the dead after four days in the tomb (John 11:1–44); or to the raising of the son of the widow from Nain (Luke 7:11–17); or to the return from the sleep of death that had occurred for the daughter of Jairus (Mark 5:21–43; Matt 9:18–26). This theory maintains that Jesus was not actually resurrected, but merely *resuscitated*. Such an explanation would imply that Jesus, like those he restored to life during his earthly ministry, would have had to die again. He would not have conquered death forever.

Alternative theories propose that yes, Jesus died and was duly buried and returned to life, but not in a *bodily* resurrection. Rather, only his soul or spirit was raised from the dead. His decaying corpse remained inside the tomb. Jesus is alive, but as a pure spirit. Therefore, his was a "spiritual" resurrection and return to his Father in heaven and his appearances to the disciples were only visions or ghostly apparitions, not physical realities.

Alternatively, the tomb was empty, a physical body was raised, but this glorified body had *no continuity* with the physical body in which Jesus had lived and died. It was not the same Jesus.

Then there are the confirmed disbelievers who admit Jesus died but deny the empty tomb, the resurrection, and the appearances altogether.

They dismiss these stories as pious legends or prescientific myths.[1] The disciples merely *felt the interior presence* of the man Jesus whom they remembered as being still with them after his death and this feeling emboldened them to become courageous enough to preach and die for the gospel. Such revisionists go so far as to claim that even the disciples did not really believe that Jesus had conquered the finality of death once and for all; the evangelists and Paul did not really mean that Jesus rose from the dead and was glorified; the first Christians were not really convinced that Christ had risen. These skeptics refuse to grant to the New Testament language the right to mean what it actually says. Instead, they presume to construct new meanings according to what more "rational" postmodern minds can tolerate. They insist that they know better than the evangelists and Paul what really happened at the resurrection and what was really meant by "Jesus is risen."[2]

Additionally, there are scholars and theologians who do not focus on what happened to Jesus at all, but rather on what happened to the disciples. Theologian Gordon Kaufman affirms that "it was really *what Jesus' resurrection signified* for the disciples that was the crucial element of that event."[3] He considers that the resurrection event was all about the divine "breaking into history" through Jesus of Nazareth. Kaufman insists that the most important element for the early Christians was not belief that the Messiah rose from the dead, but rather, "the theologically important element in their new-found faith was their consciousness of the *continuing activity of 'the God and Father of [our Lord] Jesus Christ'* (Rom 15:6) *in their historical existence,* not the resuscitation of their former friend and leader."[4] According to this theory, resurrection was all about the divine activity of God the Father breaking into the history of human beings. It was not about what happened to the Son. For reductionist scholars and theologians, the real meaning of the resurrection is not that Jesus rose from the dead and appeared to his disciples. Their theories focus so heavily on what happened to Jesus' disciples (and what might happen to those who believe), that they fail to consider what might actually have happened to Jesus!

---

1. Davis, *Risen Indeed*, 35.

2. O'Collins, *Jesus Risen*, 105–6.

3. Kaufman, *Systematic Theology*, 428, emphasis in original.

4. Kaufman, *Systematic Theology*, 428–29, emphasis in original.

Taking another view, Rudolf Bultmann claims that "faith in the resurrection is nothing other than faith in the cross as the salvation event, as the cross of Christ."[5] Then he asks: "How do we come to believe in the cross as the salvation occurrence? Here there seems to be only one answer: because it is *proclaimed* as such, because it is proclaimed together with the resurrection."[6] He further declares that Easter does not affirm an actual bodily resurrection at all; rather, "faith in *the word of proclamation* is the genuine faith of Easter."[7] In other words, Jesus does not actually live in a glorified body, but only in the salvific proclamations (that is, the preaching) of the church.[8] According to this theory, the triumph of the cross or the hidden work of Jesus in human hearts is itself sufficient to explain the development and dissemination of Christianity throughout the world.

Inevitably, the question arises: But without a bodily resurrection, where is "the triumph of the cross"? Where is Christ's actual victory over the all-too-palpable power of evil, death, and bodily decay? And without a bodily resurrection, what is there to preach?

Feeling or Fact?

In these various theories, either the ancient faith in Christ's bodily resurrection becomes thoroughly spiritualized into an otherworldly arising to heaven, or the "something that happened" to Jesus gets minimized into something that happened to his disciples: a new self-awareness, a fresh feeling of hope, a spiritual sense of Christ's presence, or even a divine intervention of some sort.[9] As a direct result, the various appearances to the female and male disciples are sometimes considered to be illusory "Christophanies" emanating from heaven, similar to Old Testament stories of divine and angelic visitations. Either that, or they are dismissed as imaginative creations by the evangelists intended to support the faith of early Christian communities. But this is not how the story of the resurrection of Jesus was first told. Those who put the spotlight on the relevance of what happened to the disciples (no matter

5. Bultmann, *New Testament and Mythology*, 39.

6. Bultmann, *New Testament*, 39, emphasis added.

7. Bultmann, *New Testament*, 39, emphasis added.

8. Davis, *Risen Indeed*, 35.

9. O'Collins, *Jesus Risen*, 103–4.

how transformative), or suggest an out-of-body arising followed by later ghostly visions completely miss the point. If Christ had not risen *bodily* from the dead, there would have been no "divine breakthrough" to discuss and certainly no life-altering experience for the disciples.

While perhaps expressing a form of sincere devotion, such widely variant viewpoints do not do justice to what the four Gospels and the letters of Paul and the Acts of the Apostles tell us actually occurred. Unless Jesus had truly risen from death in the tomb and appeared in a recognizable (albeit gloriously transformed and immortal) human body, there would have been no sense of Christ rising in the hearts of his disciples; no hint of the "saving efficacy of the cross"; no church to proclaim that "Christ has died, Christ is risen, Christ will come again"; no experience of Christ as the source of "new life" without end; and certainly no possibility of a radical transformation in the minds and hearts of the disciples. On the contrary, these men and women would have remained scandalized, heartbroken, and deeply disillusioned human beings, hiding in a locked room in fear of being arrested as followers of a disgraced and crucified rabbi (John 20:19). Christianity would have been dead before it had begun, buried forever in the tomb with Jesus.

Reductionist theories overlook or undervalue the cataclysmic event that had to have actually happened in order to reveal such a "breaking in" of God the Father into human history to resurrect the Son. And it had to have happened in order for the disciples ever to have come to believe in such an unprecedented event—one for which, as we have seen, they had no grounding in religious expectations. To underestimate the fact of the resurrection is, slowly but surely, to water down what the New Testament proclaims: that Christ truly died, was buried, and rose again. To deny the original meaning of the words "he is risen!" or "he has been raised!" (Matt 28:6) is also to eviscerate the possibility of Christ's *radical transformation* of all reality within himself. To interpret the resurrection as a spiritual "going home to God" by Jesus is to nullify the very reality of Christ's *resurrection* from an earthly place within historical time. Likewise, to reduce the resurrection to a merely human event (something that happened to the disciples), rather than extol it as a divine event (something that happened to Jesus), is to label the New Testament witnesses and evangelists as either psychologically gullible, emotionally unbalanced, spiritually duped . . . or blatant liars.

In setting forth such alternative scenarios, the existential reality of the resurrection of Jesus Christ is simply equated with a new feeling about human freedom, a new insight into the value of life on earth, even a new self-consciousness. But is that all resurrection means? "He is risen!" was not written as a symbolic, metaphorical, or spiritual statement of how the disciples gradually came to feel after they got over the shock and shame of Jesus' death. It was not some sort of wishful thinking or total denial of his radical and glorious transformation following a brutal death. It was a resounding testimony to the truth of what the disciples knew for themselves had happened on the third day after Jesus was buried: he rose. The various forms of reductionism distort the evident intention of the evangelists to bear witness to Christ crucified and resurrected: "These writers portrayed the resurrection of Jesus as a surprising act of divine grace that actually occurred and not just as a mysterious or symbolic or mythological way of revealing some sort of message."[10] Furthermore:

> When Paul quotes an early Christian formulation about "Jesus Christ and God the Father, who raised him from the dead" (Gal 1:1), the ordinary conventions covering the use of language indicate that this confession primarily concerned Jesus and offered some factual information about what happened to Jesus himself after his death. A new event, distinct from and subsequent to the crucifixion, brought Jesus from the condition of death to that of a new and lasting life. To allege that the true primary referent in the proposition "the Father raised Jesus from the dead" was not Jesus but his disciples is to open up an extraordinary gap between what Paul (and other New Testament witnesses) wrote and what they meant.[11]

As we shall discuss in more detail in chapter 5, Paul vehemently defended Christ's bodily resurrection when he wrote to the skeptical Corinthians who doubted the resurrection of the body: "If there is no resurrection of the dead, then Christ has not been raised; and if Christ has not been raised, then our proclamation has been in vain and your faith has been in vain" (1 Cor 15:13–14). It could not be clearer than that.

Of course the disciples experienced a radical change of heart and a deepened consciousness that they expressed in their new communal faith. There is no doubt that the resurrection had profound transformative psychological and spiritual effects on the disciples, even as it continues to affect all those who believe in every age. But these effects could only have occurred as a result of something that had actually happened. "Unless

10. Davis, *Risen Indeed*, 40.

11. O'Collins, *Jesus Risen*, 105.

Jesus is bodily risen, i.e., unless he is alive in the full integrity of his humanity symbolized in his body, he is not present, either as the presence of humanity in God or as God's divinely human presence in us."[12] To give that event a more easily "acceptable" interpretation for postmodern readers is to rob the original profession of faith even of its denotative meaning. Biblical scholar Raymond Brown speaks for many:

> ... if a critical modern investigation shows that as far back as we can trace the NT evidence, resurrection from the dead was an intrinsic part of Jesus' victory over death, then the observation that modern man does not find bodily resurrection appealing or meaningful cannot be determinative. Nor . . . can we allow Christian theology to be shaped by contemporary distrust of the miraculous.[13]

We must remember that the disciples were willing to suffer and die for their conviction that Jesus was truly risen and bodily alive. Not one of the original witnesses to the resurrection was ever known to have recanted: "if the original disciples had not believed that they had seen the resurrected Jesus, their firm commitment to the Christian faith after the death of their leader is not easily explained."[14] It was only because of the persistent belief that Jesus was the Son of God who died and was resurrected from the dead that Christianity arose in the first century, survived hundreds of years of persecution, and spread throughout the world. It falls to skeptics to prove an alternate theory that would explain this two-thousand-year-old phenomenon.

The Early Creeds

Contrary to revisionist or reductionist reinterpretations, the earliest creedal formulas are luminously clear about what the disciples and the first Christians believed had happened to Jesus: "But in fact Christ has been raised from the dead, the first fruits of those who have died" (1 Cor 15:20); "For to this end Christ died and lived again, so that he might be Lord of both the dead and the living" (Rom 14:9); "The Lord has risen indeed and he has appeared to Simon!" (Luke 24:34); "this man, handed over to you according to the definite plan and foreknowledge of God, you

12. Schneiders, "The Resurrection (of the Body)," 171.

13. Brown, *The Virginal Conception and Bodily Resurrection of Jesus*, 72.

14. Licona, *Resurrection*, 371.

crucified and killed by the hands of those outside the law. But God raised him up, having freed him from death, because it was impossible for him to be held in its power" (Acts 2:23–24); "This Jesus God raised up, and of that all of us are witnesses" (Acts 2:32). The scriptural testimonies are numerous and without qualifications. Jesus was bodily and visibly *alive*.

Furthermore, Christ's resurrection became understood not as a fresh insight into our flawed human nature, but as a *total transformation of that nature at its very root*. From being sinful, suffering, merely mortal human beings, early Christians were convinced that their own lives had been radically and irrevocably altered by Christ's resurrection. They believed that they were destined to receive the same inheritance of immortality and freedom from suffering as had Jesus Christ himself. His bodily resurrection changed their whole outlook on life, death, and eternity.

> Blessed be the God and Father of our Lord Jesus Christ! By his great mercy he has given us a new birth into a living hope through the resurrection of Jesus Christ from the dead, and into an inheritance that is imperishable, undefiled, and unfading, kept in heaven for you, who are being protected by the power of God through faith for a salvation ready to be revealed in the last time. (1 Pet 1:3–5)

Throughout the New Testament, the resounding cry that "He has been raised from the dead" (Matt 28:7; Mark 16:6); or "the Lord has risen indeed" (Luke 24:34); or "God raised him up" (Acts 2:24); or "this Jesus God raised up" (Acts 2:32); or "he was raised on the third day" (1 Cor 15:4) forms the bedrock of everything else that is written about Jesus of Nazareth. It is the foundation for Christian faith that Jesus was truly the Son of God. Because he was the Son of God, he was conceived not by human means of reproduction but by the overshadowing of the Holy Spirit. Because he was the Messiah, everything he preached was focused on fulfilling the prophecies of Scripture and building the new kingdom of God; not a temporal kingdom like that of King David, but an everlasting one. Because he was divine, he could work countless miracles of healing, cast out demons, and resuscitate the dead. Because he was God, he could forgive sins. Finally, because he rose from the dead, Christ was understood as the new Adam, who overcame sin, suffering, and death in the name of all humanity. That is why *the fact* of his bodily resurrection matters so much. "In a profound sense, Christianity without the resurrection is not simply Christianity without its final chapter. It is not Christianity at all."[15]

Altered States?

Nevertheless, in addition to historical and theological objections to Jesus' bodily resurrection, there are persistent *psychological* theories as to just what the disciples actually saw. Some scholars have argued that even though the disciples *believed* they had seen Jesus in the flesh, these experiences must be categorized as visions, hallucinations, or self-delusions. The disciples merely experienced "an apparition" of Jesus while in an altered state of consciousness. They could not have been physical encounters with the real Jesus.

According to many psychologists, visions are usually uplifting experiences, accompanied by light and pleasant feelings, increased joy and love, sometimes even a euphoric trance. Visions may appear to an individual in an ordinary state of consciousness or as part of an altered consciousness, such as in out-of-body transportation, spiritual ecstasy, near death experience, or a mystical state of union. Throughout the Gospels, whenever a person experiences a dream, a vision, or a trance, the text itself clearly differentiates this altered state of consciousness from an ordinary state of consciousness. However, "such descriptions [of altered states] are *almost entirely absent* in the resurrection narratives with the lone exception of Luke 24:23, which refers to the women seeing a vision of angels at the tomb."[16] Quite deliberately, the evangelists depicted the resurrection events as occurring in everyday space-time when the recipients were in an *ordinary* state of consciousness.

A Vision?

As we have seen, all the canonical Gospels report clearly that the tomb was empty and the corpse was gone. Any stranger arriving on the scene could have attested to these basic facts. There was no need to portray the discovery of this observable situation as having occurred in an altered state of consciousness or in a vision. Notably, a vision "is not the same as an image or a fantasy, in which one 'sees' something in one's mind's

---

15. O'Collins, *The Easter Jesus*, 134.

16. Licona, *Resurrection*, 578, emphasis added.

eye, mentally. Visions are seen *outside* oneself."[17] Except for the sudden appearances and departures of Jesus on a road, in the upper room, or on the beach, the actual resurrection appearances seem less astonishing than one might expect from a visionary or ecstatic experience. Jesus does not make himself manifest in blazing light, does not levitate, does not work miracles or grant healings. And again, there is no indication in the texts that what the disciples saw was to be *understood* by anyone as a "vision." Quite the contrary. Matthew, Luke, and John all describe Jesus doing the very things he usually did, just as he had done them during his earthly ministry. He stands, walks, reclines, blesses, teaches, eats, cooks, and speaks in a familiar human voice. Only Luke describes Jesus as having been "carried up into heaven" (Luke 24:51) before the eyes of the assembled group in what seems like a supernatural experience. However, in context, it seems that in this passage Luke created a distinctly symbolic scene to indicate that Jesus had returned to the Father. (Notably, some ancient authorities do not include this phrase in the text.)

Hallucination?

Other contemporary scholars are convinced (and try to convince their readers) that the resurrection appearances were a clear case of "mass hallucination." Just what is a hallucination?

"A hallucination is the experience of a sight, sound, smell or taste in a situation in which there is no verifiable physical cause of or evidence for that experience."[18] A hallucination is further defined as a *false perception* produced by the senses that seems real to the observer, but lacks any external, verifiable reality. "A psychotic hallucination is a projection from one's unconscious mind into the outside world."[19] According to psychologists, hallucinations may involve one or more of the senses, are more common to certain personality types, seem to be more frequent in females than in males, and are more likely to appear to older, grieving adults.[20] Modern psychiatry has categorized hallucination as either "a disturbance of brain structure, a disturbance of neurotransmitters, or as

---

17. Gersten, *Are you Getting Enlightened?*, 191, emphasis added.

18. Gersten, *Getting Enlightened,* 191.

19. Gersten, *Getting Enlightened,* 193.

20. See Licona, *Resurrection,* 483–84.

an emergence of the unconscious into consciousness."[21] Furthermore, "visual hallucinations can be the result of all 3 processes, given the interplay among disturbances of brain anatomy, brain chemistry, prior experiences, and psychodynamic meaning."[22] It is essential to note that, like optical illusions, visions, or dreams, hallucinations are produced by the individual mind and brain of the perceiver; thus they are *nontransferable* from one person to another. Nonetheless, some scholars still insist that all the disciples, men and women alike, had the same hallucinatory experience of the risen Jesus at the same time and in the same place.

Based on modern scientific research, this is highly unlikely—in fact, totally improbable. Every one of the disciples in the upper room could not have experienced the same hallucination of Jesus in the same way and at the same time. These men and women were of different ages, backgrounds, personality types, and emotional susceptibilities. They all had different minds. Granted they had all suffered immense shock and grief at the death of Jesus, and felt fear for their own lives. Nevertheless, for each of them (and we have no idea how many were there in addition to the "eleven" mentioned) to have the same experience of Jesus in a mass hallucination—and on several occasions—stretches the limits of scientific credulity. One clinical psychologist who has studied the professional literature exhaustively writes that he has "yet to find a single documented case of a group hallucination, that is, an event for which more than one person purportedly shared in a visual or other sensory perception where there was clearly no external referent."[23]

Another possibility arises: Did each disciple have a *different* hallucination, occurring at precisely the same time and in the same place, and yet producing the same conviction that Jesus was standing there, risen from the dead? This contention is equally implausible:

> All of the resurrection narratives written shortly after the oral tradition suggest that this was not the case but that all of the disciples (as opposed to only some of those present) experienced *the same phenomenon* (as opposed to experiences of a different phenomenon). In other words, the experiences of the risen

---

21. Asaad and Shapiro, "Hallucinations," 143; 1088–97.

22. Teeple et al, "Visual Hallucinations," 11(1) 26–27.

23. As quoted in Licona, *Resurrection*, 484. See also n64.

Jesus were of such a nature that the disciples believed they had participated in *the same event*.[24]

Psychotic Delusion?

A most exotic explanation for the group appearances is based on the idea of Peter's having had a "psychotic" incident of seeing Jesus. One New Testament scholar, Gerd Lüdemann, contends that the apostle was so stricken by his betrayal of Jesus and then by Christ's scandalous death that he became a victim of severe "self-deception."[25] His emotional and mental anguish so completely disrupted his ability to judge the real from the imaginary that his mind became unbalanced. He hallucinated a vision of Jesus because he needed to believe the Lord had risen from the dead to forgive him for his sin in person and relieve his extreme state of guilt and mourning. Moreover, the power of Peter's self-delusion was so great that the other disciples, in a kind of chain reaction, shared his fantasy and saw Jesus, too. "By a bold if unconscious leap Peter entered the world of his wishes. As a result he 'saw' Jesus and thus made it possible for the other disciples to 'see' Jesus as well."[26] Thus, an individual hallucination became a mass hallucination.

Granted, many of us may have experienced extraordinary sensory phenomena as part of a grieving process associated with the death of a loved one. This is perfectly normal. We may have had vivid dreams in which the person appeared to us as real as in life. Even while awake, we may have "heard" the dead person speak to us in a recognizable voice. We may have "seen" a vision of the deceased standing before us as if truly present. However, in our normal state of awareness, we knew that what we had dreamed, imagined, or experienced as a spiritual presence was radically different from actually seeing our loved one bodily alive in the room, sitting down together with us to share a meal and engage in conversation. Nor did those around us experience the exact same dream, vision, or sense of spiritual presence.

Yet as the psychotic hallucination theory goes, because of the disciples' naturally superstitious inclination to believe in the appearance

---

24. Licona, *Resurrection*, 485, n64, emphasis added.

25. Lüdemann, *Resurrection*, 24.

26. Lüdemann, *Resurrection*, 166. See also Carmichael, *The Death of Jesus*, 210, 215–18.

of ghosts, angels, and demons, Peter's own conviction that he had really seen Jesus resulted in a "group fantasy" that had both audible and visual aspects. Such a shared hallucination "assured them of forgiveness for their desertion of [Jesus] in his time of need."[27] According to this theory, the appearance to James and the "more than five hundred brothers and sisters at one time" (1 Cor 15:6) was also a form of "mass ecstasy."[28] In addition, the later post-resurrection appearance of Jesus to Paul was another classic case of self-deception because of Paul's mental conflicts about his persecution of Jewish Christians. In short, this hypothesis states that *all the resurrection appearances* were merely "subjective delusions," arising in gullible disciples as a result of severe "psychological disorders." Is this plausible? Had grief and guilt rendered all the disciples psychotic and therefore completely "disconnected" from reality, unable to tell the ghostly from the bodily, the abnormal from the normal? In essence, were the appearances, whether to two women or to more than five hundred at a time, simply a form of "group fantasy" or "mass hysteria"?

Invalid Conjectures

In answer, we may quote scholar Dale C. Allison, who considers such conjectures "just that: conjectures. They do not constitute knowledge. In recent decades contemporary historians have been more leery than their predecessors of the viability of reconstructing and then analyzing the psycho-histories of men and women long dead."[29] In other words, we must beware of the pitfalls of psychoanalyzing people from another time and culture who have been dead for 2,000 years!

Moreover, the "wishful thinking" alluded to in this theory does not fit the mind-set of the women on their way to the tomb. As we have considered, from the scriptural account these women had *no expectation* that Jesus would or could rise from the dead, and no hope of seeing anything other than a corpse. It would not have occurred to any of them to engage in wishful thinking or to succumb to a dreamlike state of self-delusion that Jesus was alive. Neither did the two disciples on their way to Emmaus expect to meet a resurrected Jesus. Nor did Peter and the Beloved Disciple, or any of the other disciples, for that matter. After Jesus'

27. Licona, *Resurrection*, 498.
28. Lüdemann, *Resurrection*, 81.
29. Allison, *Resurrecting Jesus*, 242. Quoted in Licona, *Resurrection*, 505.

death, they were all simply devastated. They did not anticipate that they would ever see Jesus again. The disciples did not remember or else did not believe Jesus' predictions that he would rise from the dead. Even when they did see Jesus alive and in a transformed body, they had trouble believing it was truly he. They were full of fear and doubt that it was really Jesus. They themselves questioned what they saw precisely because they did not trust illusions, visions, or altered states of reality. These disciples do not seem like typical hypnotic subjects nor do we have any evidence that they were prone to self-delusion. The rough and rugged fishermen and the former tax collector, as well as the down-to-earth, determined women who had followed Jesus from Galilee, were not typical candidates to become ecstatic visionaries.[30] By all accounts, the disciples were much too naturally skeptical and yes, *disbelieving*, for that.

Finally, let us recall that no one in first-century Judaism—neither the original disciples, Saul, nor the later evangelists—had ever anticipated that any individual, even the Messiah, would rise from the dead before the last judgment at the end of the world.[31] If Jesus' closest followers had no expectation that Jesus would rise from the dead, how could their minds have concocted the kind of wishful thinking necessary to project such a "collective hallucination"?

> Hence hallucinating disciples projecting their prior beliefs could not have claimed that Jesus had been raised and glorified in anticipation of a universal resurrection of the dead which was still to come (for example, 1 Cor 15:20). There was no such prior belief to be projected.[32]

Appearance to Saul

The hallucination theory also does not explain the post-resurrection appearance to the man named Saul, on his way to Damascus, a few years after the appearances to the disciples in the upper room in Jerusalem, on a mountain in Galilee, or a beach by Lake Tiberias. At that time, Saul did not even know Peter and the other apostles. He could not have been part of a "chain reaction hysteria." Of all people, Saul had no mental predisposition for wanting to see a resurrected Jesus. In fact, by rounding

30. O'Collins, *Jesus Risen*, 108.

31. Perkins, *Resurrection*, 37–56.

32. O'Collins, *Jesus Risen*, 109.

up early disciples of Jesus and delivering them to the Sanhedrin to be put on trial and condemned to death, Saul showed himself to be an ardent persecutor of this man Jesus and all those associated with him. To Saul, Jesus was a blasphemer, an apostate from the Torah, and a threat to established Judaism who had deserved to die. So must his followers. Saul was convinced that such heresy must be stamped out. He certainly would not have projected a vision of Christ because he wanted forgiveness for persecuting Christ's disciples. He thought he was serving God by *killing* Christians!

Experiential Conviction

When we are considering the resurrection appearances, we are not talking about phenomena that can be examined in a systematic way from the perspective of historical, psychological, or biological investigation, at least as these disciplines are currently understood. These experiences were recounted precisely as unique and extra-ordinary events. They were at once shocking, exhilarating, overwhelming, and empowering. They produced fear, joy, doubt, and belief, all at once. They could not then and cannot now be "explained" by merely human methods of investigation, psychological or otherwise. They could only be *experienced* by those privileged to experience them. For us in the twenty-first century, they can only be pondered with a sense of wonder, humility, and awe.

It is well attested that the disciples were willing to suffer torture and die brutal deaths as a result of their personal conviction that Jesus had risen from the dead. They had no doubt that they had seen Jesus with their own eyes, heard him with their own ears. Indeed, "the disciples' conviction that they had seen the Risen Christ . . . [is part of] historical bedrock, facts known past doubting."[33] Those who witnessed the risen Jesus could not deny him because, in a profound way, they had been totally transformed by his resurrection and already become like him. By following in his footsteps through preaching, forgiving sins, working miracles, and bearing witness in public that the risen Jesus was Lord and Messiah, they knew perfectly well what the consequences were likely to be. They had no illusions, no delusions, *only convictions*. "The case is strong that they did not willfully lie about the appearances of the risen

33. Fredriksen, *Jesus of Nazareth*, 264.

Jesus. Liars make poor martyrs."[34] Everyone else who has ever believed, hoped, and endured persecution and death for the sake of Jesus Christ, has done so based on the convincing witness of these first disciples. Throughout the ages, Christians have not seen the risen Jesus, but they know in whom they have believed.

> Although you have not seen him, you love him; and even though you do not see him now, you believe in him and rejoice with an indescribable and glorious joy, for you are receiving the outcome of your faith, the salvation of your souls. (1 Pet 1:8–9)

What Can We Believe?

The following facts have been generally agreed upon by historical scholarship as well as by the majority of biblical and theological scholars as well. First, that Jesus was crucified, died, and was buried. Second, that soon after his death, certain followers of Jesus experienced bodily appearances of the same person they had known in his lifetime, and that these experiences convinced them that God had raised Jesus from the dead. Third, that the disciples who had been mournful, fearful, and doubtful after the crucifixion, became joyful, courageous, believing, and empowered to preach the gospel at whatever cost. And fourth, that within a few years of Jesus' death, Saul of Tarsus, a fanatical persecutor of Christians, had a post-resurrection experience of the risen Christ that led him to become the foremost preacher of the good news of the gospel. There is no explanation for such a radical transformation in the lives of these people other than a firm belief in the reality of Christ's resurrection. As philosopher Stephen T. Davis writes:

> The most plausible explanation of these facts, say those who believe in the resurrection, is that Jesus did indeed rise from the dead and show himself to the disciples. It does not seem sensible to claim that the Christian church, a spiritual movement with the vitality to change the world, was started by charlatans or dupes. If the disciples knew that Jesus was not really risen, they were charlatans. If they believed he was risen, when in fact he was not, they were dupes.[35]

---

34. Licona, *Resurrection*, 370.
35. Davis, *Risen Indeed*, 15.

Of course, we must acknowledge that it was not until *after* his death, when Christ showed himself to them as being resurrected from the dead, that the disciples finally "got" it; that they came to the realization of who Jesus really was. If God had revealed bodily resurrection in *this* man, then Jesus must indeed be the long-awaited Messiah. In that recognition, the disciples were radically changed, all of them. Even though they did not understand at first what had happened, the women who came to the tomb were empowered to tell the disciples what they had seen. Likewise, once the men were transformed by the descent of the Holy Spirit, they were emboldened to come out of their hiding place and bear witness to Jesus as the Messiah. They knew, given the political situation, that they would be arrested and condemned like Jesus, which eventually many of them were.

In conclusion, nothing in the Gospels makes any sense unless Jesus of Nazareth was resurrected and precisely *in that unexpected way* showed himself to be the long-awaited Messiah, the Anointed One of God. Even considering the authority of his preaching about the kingdom of God; his miraculous healings of the deaf, the dumb, the blind, the lame, the leprous; his power to forgive sins and transform lives; his willingness to suffer and die as a criminal to demonstrate the divine compassion that enters into the pain of all humankind: *unless Jesus had truly risen from the dead in a transformed body, the entire story might have been dramatic and inspiring, but ultimately, a tragic fiction.* Unless Jesus had risen from the dead, his extraordinary actions as a human being would still not have shown him to be divine. He would not have revealed what it means to be the Son of God incarnate. He would not have shown what it means to conquer completely the evil of sin and the finality of death. Without the resurrection, there is no climax and no metamorphosis to the story of salvation. Belief in the bodily resurrection of Jesus Christ is the most reasonable and finally, the *only* comprehensive explanation for everything written in the Gospels. It is also the only explanation for Christian hope that death is not the end of life.

> And this is the will of him who sent me,
> that I should lose nothing of all that he has given me,
> but raise it up on the last day
> This is indeed the will of my Father,
> that all who see the Son and believe in him may have eternal life;
> and I will raise them up on the last day. (John 6:39–40)

5

Paul and the Resurrected Body

WE KNOW THAT SAUL of Tarsus, the zealous Pharisee, was a violent persecutor of the followers of Jesus Christ, even to the point of overseeing the stoning of Stephen, the first Christian martyr. After that event, full of righteous indignation, Saul went to the high priest in Jerusalem and obtained letters to the synagogues in Damascus, Syria, which would allow him to arrest any Jewish followers and bring them back to Jerusalem to be tried and condemned to death. In his own words, Paul later described himself as "violently persecuting the church of God" in order to destroy it (Gal 1:13). However, on the road to Damascus, Saul had a transcendent experience that turned him from being the most fanatical hater of Jesus Christ to his most indefatigable apostle and outspoken defender: he saw the resurrected Lord appear to him.

Paul also heard a voice saying, "'Saul, Saul, why do you persecute me?' He asked, 'Who are you, Lord?' The reply came, 'I am Jesus, whom you are persecuting'" (Acts 9:4–5). Paul was temporarily struck blind, and led by his companions into the city. After three days, a devout Christianized Jew, Ananias, was told by the Lord in a vision to go to Saul, "for he is an instrument whom I have chosen to bring my name before Gentiles and kings and before the people of Israel; I myself will show him how much he must suffer for the sake of my name" (Acts 9:15–16). Ananias went to the house where Saul was staying and laid hands on him. Saul was filled with the Holy Spirit, his blindness fell from his eyes like scales, and thereafter he was baptized. Saul had to be struck blind before he could see. Then he spent several days with the disciples in Damascus, and soon "began to proclaim Jesus in the synagogues, saying, 'He is the

Son of God'" (Acts 9:20). All this happened a mere one to three years after the resurrection. Such was the spiritual rebirth of Paul, the apostle of Jesus Christ.

During the three decades that Paul proclaimed Jesus as the Messiah, from his initial conversion (c. 36 CE) to his probable martyrdom under Nero (c. 64 CE), the apostle visited at least fifty cities from Jerusalem to Rome. He may even have traveled as far as Spain (Rom 15:24, 28). Throughout his journeys, Paul had the difficult task of convincing both Jews and Greeks—even baptized Greek Christians—of the reality of a *physical* resurrection. In his letters to the Corinthians and Galatians, Paul dealt with issues concerning the resurrected body that are still being debated today: *Was Jesus resurrected bodily? Will our own bodies be resurrected? If so, what kind of body will it be: physical or spiritual?* As we shall discuss, Paul used both vigorous argument and evocative metaphor to make the concept of bodily resurrection abundantly clear for the newly converted Greeks, and indeed, for generations to come. However, like many postmodern people, these early Christians had serious resistance to belief in the resurrection of the body.

Paul on the Resurrection

Paul proclaimed his ardent expectation of the day of our resurrection in his first letter to the Thessalonians, most probably written from Corinth c. 51–52 CE:

> But we do not want you to be uninformed, brothers and sisters, about those who have died, so that you may not grieve as others do who have no hope. For since we believe that Jesus died and rose again, even so, through Jesus, God will bring with him those who have died. For this we declare to you by the word of the Lord, that we who are alive, who are left until the coming of the Lord, will by no means precede those who have died. For the Lord himself, with a cry of command, with the archangel's call and with the sound of God's trumpet, will descend from heaven, and the dead in Christ will rise first. Then we who are alive, who are left, will be caught up in the clouds together with them to meet the Lord in the air; and so we will be with the Lord forever. Therefore encourage one another with these words. (1 Thess 4:13–18)

Obviously, Paul expected that the Lord's return would be imminent. He warned the Thessalonians that "the day of the Lord will come like a thief in the night" (1 Thess 5:2) and thus they should "keep awake and be sober" (1 Thess 5:6). At this point in his correspondence, Paul did not feel the need to defend the fact of resurrection itself.

However, it is in Paul's first letter to the Corinthians, most likely written from Ephesus, that we find the apostle's most cogent arguments concerning Christ's bodily resurrection. Notably, these teachings were written before any of the Gospels were set to parchment. While Paul's first letter to the Corinthians has been dated to c. 53–55 CE, almost all scholars agree that it records the essential proclamation of Christian teaching that had already been well established *two decades earlier*, not long after the Lord's crucifixion. In this letter, Paul cites as the foundation of all his teaching the "good news" that he had learned directly from the apostles and then faithfully preached to the Corinthians:

> For I handed on to you as of first importance what I in turn had received: that Christ died for our sins in accordance with the scriptures, and that he was buried, and that he was raised on the third day in accordance with the scriptures, and that he appeared to Cephas [Peter], then to the twelve. (1 Cor 15:3–5)

Paul is very careful to affirm that this is *not* his own personal teaching. He is "handing on" or "delivering" what he had already "received"; it is the long-accepted apostolic tradition that is of primary importance. Joachim Jeremias has identified several distinct non-Pauline terms in this passage that support the contention that Paul was citing already-established kerygma and not his own formulations. For example, the phrase "for our sins" appears instead of "sin." Paul's usual mention of "sin" is in the singular (except in Gal 1:4), "because sin for Paul is a personified power."[1] Likewise, the exact phrase, "in accordance with the scriptures" is not found in any other Pauline works; normally, Paul writes: "according to the Scriptures."[2] Paul also does not use the perfect passive construction "was raised" except here and in direct reference to this confessional formula (1 Cor 15:12–14, 16–20, and in 2 Tim 2:8).[3] In addition, mention of "the twelve" is not a typically Pauline term; he usually

---

1. Jeremias, *Eucharistic Words*, 101–2.

2. Jeremias, *Eucharistic Words*, 102.

3. Jeremias, *Eucharistic Words*, 102.

refers to "the apostles."[4] Furthermore, "there are, if not strict proofs, at any rate signs that the core of the kerygma is a translation of a Semitic original. . . . These Semitisms show that the kerygma was formulated in a Jewish-Christian milieu."[5] Yet even though the kerygma as we now have it must have developed in a Greek-speaking environment, "it cannot have originated there. With Paul's closing assertion, 1 Cor 15:11, that his kerygma was identical with that of the first apostles . . . it is a safe conclusion that the core of the kerygma was not formulated by Paul, but comes from the Aramaic-speaking earliest community."[6]

"On the third day" requires more explanation. It is a Semitic formula that means "in a little while" and is employed by Paul only in this passage. Frequently in the Old Testament, God acted "on the third day" to show divine power and deliverance (Gen 22:4; Exod 19:11, 16; 1 Sam 30:1–2; 2 Kgs 20:5, 8; Esth 5:1; Hos 6:2).[7] In the New Testament, the phrase appears often, but mostly *prior* to the resurrection. At his trial, Jesus' opponents use the term to accuse him: "We heard him say, 'I will destroy this temple that is made with hands, and in three days I will build another, not made with hands'" (Mark 14:58). Those who taunt Jesus on the cross cry out: "Aha! You who would destroy the temple and build it in three days, save yourself, and come down from the cross!" (Mark 15:29). Jesus himself uses the term in describing the nature of his ministry to some Pharisees: "Listen, I am casting out demons and performing cures today and tomorrow, and on the third day I finish my work. Yet today, tomorrow, and the next day I must be on my way, because it is impossible for a prophet to be killed outside of Jerusalem" (Luke 13:32–33). Again Jesus employs a layered statement to indicate the short span of time that would lead to his passion: "A little while, and you will no longer see me, and again a little while, and you will see me" (John 16:16, 17, 19). However, Jeremias affirms: "In none of these passages can the phrase about the three days be derived from the three days from Good Friday to Easter."[8] He further explains that "Semitic languages have no word for 'several', 'a few', 'some', and use the expedient . . . of saying 'three' instead."[9]

---

4. Jeremias, *Eucharistic Words*, 102.

5. Jeremias, *Eucharistic Words*, 102–3.

6. Jeremias, *Eucharistic Words*, 103.

7. Craig, *The Son Rises*, 71.

8. Jeremias, *New Testament Theology*, 285.

9. Jeremias, *New Testament Theology*, 285.

Thus in both Old and New Testaments, "after three days" actually means "soon." Jewish theologian Pinchas Lapide elaborates: "'on the third day' has nothing to do with the date or with the counting of time but contains for ears which are educated biblically a clear reference to God's mercy and grace which is revealed after two days of affliction and death by way of redemption."[10]

From whom did Paul derive this early information about Jesus' death, burial, resurrection, and appearances? In his letter to the Galatians, as well as in numerous places in Acts, it is made clear that the original kerygma came from the apostles who were residing in Jerusalem during the very time that Paul had been persecuting the early church. Presumably, Saul the Pharisee had become outraged at hearing Peter proclaim the gospel of the risen Lord publicly and considered it a dangerous heresy that must be wiped out. Eventually, the Jerusalem apostles must have learned about Paul's sudden and dramatic conversion in Damascus. Paul tells us himself that after his life-transforming experience, "I did not confer with any human being, nor did I go up to Jerusalem to those who were already apostles before me, but I went away at once into Arabis, and afterwards I returned to Damascus" (Gal 1:16–17). Then, three years after his theophany, "I did go up to Jerusalem to visit Cephas and stayed with him fifteen days; but I did not see any other apostle except James the Lord's brother" (Gal 1:18–19). At that time, Paul must have inquired about Jesus' life and teachings from both Peter (Cephas) and James. He may even have discussed his own emerging christological understanding. Then again, fourteen years later, Paul revisited Jerusalem to defend himself to James, Peter, and John concerning his revelation that Greek converts to Christianity did not first have to be circumcised as Jews (Gal 2:1–10). Throughout his missionary journeys, Paul preached the gospel in close companionship with esteemed members of the Jerusalem community such as Barnabas, Judas (called Barsabbus), and Silas, all of whom were "leaders among the brothers" (Acts 15:22). We may deduce from these citations that Paul *personally* knew many of the disciples who had been close to Jesus during his lifetime and who had actually seen him resurrected from the dead. Paul preached the good news just as he had received it. Hence his faithfulness to the already-established wording of the kerygma.

10. Lapide, *The Resurrection of Jesus*, 92. For OT references to "the third day," see Gen 22:4; 42:18; Exod 19:16; Jonah 1:17; Esth 5:1; Hos 6:2.

Accordingly, although certainty eludes us, it is most reasonable to conclude that the tradition in 1 Corinthians 15:3–7 was formed in Jerusalem and that Paul either received it directly from the Jerusalem apostles or from someone he deemed very credible. . . . It is widely accepted today that the tradition goes back to the Jerusalem Church.[11]

Which Scriptures?

In Paul's proclamation, the statements that "Christ died for our sins" and that "he was raised" are both said to have been "in accordance with the scriptures." But which Scriptures? Paul does not give explicit references. In Luke's resurrection account, Christ had said "that everything written about me in the law of Moses, the prophets, and the psalms must be fulfilled" (Luke 24:44). At the beginning of Acts, as mentioned earlier, when Peter addresses the crowd at Pentecost, he references Psalm 16:10: "David spoke of the resurrection of the Messiah, saying, 'He was not abandoned to Hades, nor did his flesh experience corruption'" (Acts 2:31). In Acts 13, Luke reconstructs the type of scriptural support for Jesus' resurrection that Paul used in his speeches to Jews in the synagogues. Paul quotes from Psalm 2:7: "You are my Son; today I have begotten you"; from Deutero-Isaiah 55:3: "I will give you the holy promises made to David"; and also from Psalm 16:10: "You will not let your Holy One experience corruption." Then Paul concludes:

> For David, after he had served the purpose of God in his own generation, died, was laid beside his ancestors, and experienced corruption; but he whom God raised up experienced no corruption. Let it be known to you therefore, my brothers, that through this man forgiveness of sins is proclaimed to you; by this Jesus everyone who believes is set free from all those sins from which you could not be freed by the law of Moses. (Acts 13:36–39)

In Romans 15:3, Paul quotes Psalm 69, suggesting that Christ on the cross intentionally took upon himself the sins committed against the God of Israel: "The insults of those who insult you have fallen on me" (Ps 69:9). And in speaking of the end of the world, when Christ will hand over the kingdom to the Father, having first destroyed all other rulers,

11. Licona, *Resurrection*, 227–28.

authorities, and powers, including death itself (1 Cor 15:24–28), Paul references Psalm 110, beginning with: "Sit at my right hand until I make your enemies your footstool" (Ps 110:1).[12]

However, scanning Paul to find *explicit* quotations from the Hebrew Bible that predict the passion, death, and resurrection of the longed-for Messiah is not entirely productive. First of all, as we have seen, no prophet or psalmist ever expected that when the Messiah came to earth, he would be rejected by his own people, suffer persecution, and undergo a shameful death by crucifixion. As N. T. Wright tersely observed, "A crucified Messiah was a contradiction in terms."[13] According to the prophets, the coming of the Messiah would herald a new age of divine power and glory. God would not abandon his people forever. After a long period of chastisement, Deutero-Isaiah reassured the nation that the Lord would return to Israel and comfort her:

> See, the Lord God comes with might,
>   and his arm rules for him;
> his reward is with him,
>   and his recompense before him.
> He will feed his flock like a shepherd;
>   he will gather the lambs in his arms,
> and carry them in his bosom,
>   and gently lead the mother sheep. (Isa 40:10–11)

Ezekiel envisioned the glory of the God of Israel appearing in Israel from the east, re-entering and filling the whole Temple: "the sound was like the sound of mighty waters; and the earth shone with his glory" (Ezek 43:2). The Messiah would triumph over all earthly powers, redeem his people, and establish the reign of God in a new and all-powerful kingdom of Israel. Furthermore, all the nations would come to acknowledge this new king and kingdom.

> Break forth together into singing,
>   you ruins of Jerusalem;
> for the LORD has comforted his people,
>   he has redeemed Jerusalem.
> The LORD has bared his holy arm
>   before the eyes of all the nations;
> and all the ends of the earth shall see
>   the salvation of our God. (Isa 52:9–10)

12. Hays, *First Corinthians*, 256.

13. Wright, *Paul*, 213.

However, it did not happen as expected. No one could have anticipated that the Savior would have to die as a despised outcast before he would rise again as the triumphant Lord of creation—yet entirely beyond the scope of political power. In Deutero-Isaiah's Suffering Servant there was certainly a foreboding that a divinely appointed man would have to endure persecution to atone for the sins of many:

> By a perversion of justice he was taken away.
>   Who could have imagined his future?
> For he was cut off from the land of the living,
>   stricken for the transgression of my people.
> They made his grave with the wicked
>   and his tomb with the rich,
> although he had done no violence,
>   and there was no deceit in his mouth. (Isa 53: 8–9)

But this prophecy was generally believed to represent the suffering in captivity of *all* of Israel, not the ordeal of the single heaven-sent Messiah. And even though the prophet writes that after the Servant makes atonement for the sins of the nation, "he shall see his offspring, and shall prolong his days; through him the will of the Lord shall prosper" (Isa 53:10)—and furthermore that God will "allot him a portion with the great, and he shall divide the spoil with the strong" (Isa 53:12)—*there is still no explicit suggestion that the Servant would rise bodily from the dead in order to enter into his glory.*

Searching the Old Testament for precise prophecies of the resurrection does not do justice to the scriptural viewpoint of Paul or the early church. The apostle and the first Christianized Jews came to understand that *the entire history* of Israel—including Yahweh's promises to Abraham, the liberating exodus from Egypt, the giving of the Law to Moses and the establishment of the Covenant, the prophets' proclamations, and the inspired prayers of the psalmists—formed the divine preparation for the good news of the gospel. Indeed, the agonies of the Suffering Servant were considered by Paul and the church to be a direct prefiguration of the passion. Jesus was acknowledged as "the true son of David, announced as such in his resurrection, bringing to completion the purposes announced to Abraham and extended in the psalms to embrace the world."[14] It was more than enough proof for Paul that a great number of disciples had seen the Lord at specific times

---

14. Wright, *Paul*, 130.

and places; that their lives were forever changed by those experiences (including his own); and that as a result of the appearances, the early church emerged. "It is highly suggestive that for Paul the resurrection of Christ marks the moment in history at which the new age began, and the eschatological hope came true."[15]

Thus it was not always deemed necessary to quote particular lines of prophecy or verses from the psalms in order to justify the entire kerygma. So whenever Paul writes "in accordance with the scriptures," it seems he is alluding to *all* the Old Testament promises of salvation made to the patriarchs, revealed by the prophets, and sung by the psalmists, which were finally fulfilled in the new Davidic King, Christ the Lord.

What is Missing?

As concerned as Paul was in 1 Corinthians to preserve the traditional kerygma about the resurrection, it is noticeable that in his short, concise, formulaic list quoted above, there is no mention of the empty tomb. Based on such an omission, some scholars have leapt to the conclusion that since Paul did not mention the empty tomb, he must not have known about it. According to this hypothesis, the empty tomb must not have been part of the earliest tradition but rather a later addition, cooked up by the disciples as proof after the fact of Christ's bodily resurrection. However, if everything Paul left out of his letters was also later fabricated by the evangelists, then we might assume that Christ never told parables, never performed miracles of healing or exorcism, and that there is no record of where he suffered his passion and crucifixion. Simply because Paul does not mention parables, miracles, or many other aspects of Christ's public ministry, or details of his crucifixion and death in Jerusalem under Pontius Pilate, does not mean he did not know about them or that they did not happen.

Moreover, as we discussed in chapter 1, in the ancient Jewish and Greek world, "resurrection" meant one thing and one thing only: *bodily* rising from the dead. If it could have been proven that Christ's decaying corpse was still lying in the tomb in Palestine, how could any one of Paul's listeners have believed that Jesus had risen from the dead? If the tomb had not been certifiably empty, how could anyone ever be expected to believe Paul's claim that Christ's body had been physically raised? The

15. Dodd, *The Parables*, 76, n1.

Corinthians would have considered Paul out of his mind to make such a statement! As one scholar commented, the fact that Paul does not mention an empty tomb "shows nothing except that such stories were not a part of the traditional kerygma. It certainly does not mean that Paul or any other early Christian could have conceived of a 'resurrection from the dead' in which the body remained in the tomb."[16]

In his letter to the Romans, written from Corinth c. 55–57 CE, Paul speaks clearly of Christ having been *buried*: "Therefore we have been buried with him by baptism into death, so that, just as Christ was raised from the dead by the glory of the Father, so we too might walk in newness of life" (Rom 6:4). It stands to reason that whenever Paul wrote of the resurrection of Christ's body after burial, there was an implicit assumption that the same body was no longer in the tomb.[17] Paul's silence about the empty tomb does not prove his ignorance of it, nor his disbelief in it. On the contrary, Paul's conviction that Christ's resurrection involved a *radical physical transformation* necessitated that his corpse had not remained where it was buried.[18] It has even been suggested that to mention the empty tomb is a redundancy that would have spoiled the logic and symmetry of the original kerygma; that is, "death confirmed by burial; risen confirmed by appearance."[19] Paul, once an ardent Pharisee committed to preserving Jewish tradition, would have considered the Christian formulation of the apostles a sacred creed that was not to be altered.[20] His mission was to impart faithfully the Jerusalem death-burial-resurrection-appearance kerygma just as he had learned it.

Paul's letters were not meant to be complete narrative accounts of Christ's life. When writing to the Thessalonians, Galatians, Corinthians, and Philippians, the apostle was addressing those to whom he had previously preached the good news in person. He had no need to repeat in his letters whatever specifics he had already told them about Christ's story. Rather, the letters focused on how to *maintain belief* amidst a maelstrom of erroneous viewpoints, personal antagonisms, and communal divisions. These were what occupied Paul's mind. For example, we know from Galatians and 1 Corinthians (and also from the later Acts of the Apostles)

---

16. Hays, *First Corinthians*, 256.

17. Davis, *Risen Indeed*, 75–76.

18. See Licona, *Resurrection*, 334–35.

19. Licona, *Resurrection*, 336, referencing Waterman, *The Empty Tomb*, 203–4.

20. Licona, *Resurrection*, 224.

that early Gentile believers were being told by Jewish followers of Christ that they must first be circumcised as Jews before they could be baptized. Paul fought many a verbal battle against this kind of thinking: "Listen! I, Paul, am telling you that if you let yourselves be circumcised, Christ will be of no benefit to you" (Gal 5:2). Paul was also deeply concerned about the moral behavior (and misbehavior) of recent Gentile converts who were still surrounded by pagan cults and easily seduced by idolatrous and immoral practices.

Additionally, in many of Paul's writings, he had to confront bitter dissensions between Jewish and Gentile Christians that had developed within the house churches. He had to deal with problems arising from personality cults and flagrant abuses at the celebration of the Lord's Supper as well as outright opposition from those he had taught, trusted, and loved. Paul wrote passionately and persistently to bear witness to the gospel of "the Son of God, who loved me and gave himself for me" (Gal 2:20). The apostle insisted that, as a result of Christ's vanquishing of the forces of evil on the cross and his glorious resurrection as Lord and Savior of the whole world, the churches must come together in mutual love (Greek, *agape*) and fellowship (Greek, *koinonia*) to celebrate their new creation and their new equality. Amidst these much more pressing pastoral points, perhaps, for Paul, the empty tomb was simply not worth mentioning. It was self-evident. If Jesus the Messiah rose bodily from the dead, the tomb *had* to be empty. What need was there to state the obvious?

What About the Women?

Then, for those who complain that Paul never alludes to the women as the first witnesses to the resurrection, we must remember that when Paul was writing his letters there were, as yet, no Gospels testifying that the women were the first to discover the empty tomb. But even if Paul knew the oral tradition and deliberately excised the women from his list of the resurrection appearance stories—preferring to mention that Jesus appeared to Peter and the other disciples, and to James, and then to a crowd of five hundred—that still does not prove that he did not know and believe it. Paul might have recognized that the Gentiles would have had little or no interest in the testimony of a few "unreliable" Jewish women back in Palestine. So he may have used his discretion and decided not to mention this important point, at least in his letters, lest the embarrassment of referencing women as the primary witnesses might seriously undermine the strength of his preaching. For apologetic reasons, he may have considered it generally more compelling to his audiences to feature the culturally more reliable witnesses of men. We may fault him for this omission, but we may not then jump to the conclusion that simply because Paul does not mention women as the first witnesses to the resurrection, therefore the oral tradition was not already well established.

Addressing all these points, theologian Michael R. Licona writes:

> What is historically certain is that Paul knew the Jerusalem apostles and their teachings, that he claimed to preach the same thing as they did about Jesus' resurrection, that Paul taught that Jesus' corpse had been raised . . . that the tradition Paul cites in 1 Corinthians 15:3–7 very probably reflected the Jerusalem "tradition," that he was firm in his belief that such "tradition" must be adhered to strictly and that he believed he had no authority to alter or add content to the "tradition." The implication that the Jerusalem apostles were teaching the resurrection of Jesus' corpse is so strong that those making assertions to the contrary carry a heavy burden of proof.[21]

Paul's Additions

In order to further substantiate the historical fact of the resurrection of Jesus, Paul adds something else he knew to be part of the oral tradition, but that was perhaps not preached as core kerygma. After Christ appeared to Cephas and the Twelve, Paul attests:

> Then he appeared to more than five hundred brothers at one time,[22] most of whom are still alive, though some have died. Then he appeared to James, then to all the apostles. (1 Cor 15:6–7)

Paul tells the Corinthians that many of the hundreds of people who saw the risen Lord are still alive. They can be questioned as eyewitnesses. And they can be believed. James, the brother of the Lord, also saw him, although this appearance is not recorded in the later Gospels. Nevertheless, James

---

21. Licona, *Resurrection*, 336–37.

22. The NRSV adds "and sisters" but notes that this is not in the original Greek. It is the NRSV's choice to use inclusive language, but it would not have been Paul's way of addressing his readers.

was known as the esteemed leader of the church in Jerusalem.[23] Since we know that Paul met with James (Gal 1:19), Paul may well have heard from the apostle's own lips in what form Christ had appeared to him after the resurrection. Paul also refers to "all the apostles" to whom Jesus showed himself, suggesting a larger group than just the Twelve.[24] Finally, Paul reminds the Corinthians—who had dared to impugn his apostolic authority to preach—that he, himself, was an eyewitness to the risen Christ.[25] "Last of all, as to one untimely born, he appeared also to me" (1 Cor 15:8). Paul, too, can be questioned and believed. Throughout this section, Paul is making a strong case that the resurrection appearances did not occur as mystical experiences, in a dream, in a vision, as a hallucination, or in the clouds but, as it were, on the ground. They were real events that occurred in real times and places to known individuals. What Paul and all the eyewitnesses saw was a recognizable human being walking the earth in a transformed body risen from the dead.

What does Paul mean by characterizing himself "as one untimely born"? The Greek term, *ektroma*, usually refers to an aborted fetus; a miscarriage. Did Paul consider his life "aborted" or "miscarried" until he met the risen Lord on the road to Damascus? Had his former existence as a self-righteous Pharisee ended then and there so that he could be born into a new life in Christ? Some scholars have suggested that this epithet, *ektroma*, had been crudely applied to Paul by those Corinthians who disparaged his physical appearance as "weak" or criticized his powers of speech as "contemptible" (2 Cor 10:10).[26] Whatever the case, Paul turns the pejorative term into an asset. He admits that he was indeed the most unlikely and untimely man to be born of Christ, the most imperfect human being to be called to preach the good news, both on physical and spiritual grounds. "For I am the least of the apostles, unfit to be called an apostle, because I persecuted the church of God" (1 Cor 15:9). Paul speaks candidly of what he was before: an oppressor of Christians. Like the Corinthians, he, too, once did not believe that Jesus was the Anointed One of God. He, too, did not believe in the resurrection of this man from the dead. . . . until he was physically blinded after seeing the risen Jesus in person.

23. See Gal 1:19; 2:9, 12; Acts 15:13–21; 21:18.
24. Hays, *First Corinthians*, 257.
25. See 1 Cor 4:3–5; 9:3.
26. Hays, *First Corinthians*, 258. See also, Gal 4:13–14; 2 Cor 12:7–10.

"But by the grace of God I am what I am, and his grace toward me has not been in vain" (1 Cor 15:9–10). Paul boasts in the Lord that despite his former persecution of Christians and his stubborn unwillingness to believe, plus his personal shortcomings, he is what he is precisely because of divine grace. Without mincing words, Paul attests: "On the contrary, I worked harder than any of them—though it was not I, but the grace of God that is with me" (1 Cor 15:10). Paul uses his very weakness to prove that it is not himself speaking or writing, but the power of God working through him that has enabled him to preach and endure more than any other apostle. Despite his physical handicaps, and even if the Corinthians do not approve of his lack of eloquence or his blunt manner of reprimand, they must acknowledge that he has been appointed by God to spread the gospel. So have the other legitimate disciples who have brought the Corinthians to faith in Christ. "Whether then it was I or they, so we proclaim and so you have come to believe" (1 Cor 15:11). Once again, Paul affirms that he is reiterating *the same tradition* concerning Jesus Christ that other apostles and disciples have also proclaimed. In doing so, he strongly implies that since he was the last person to see the risen Jesus face to face, he was also the last apostle.

Paul's Debate

Yet in spite of the authoritative preaching they had received, it is clear from both of Paul's letters to the Corinthians that these Greek converts to Christianity were arguing *against* belief in the bodily resurrection of the dead. The philosophy of the Corinthians may well have been steeped in Platonic thought and filtered through "a common tradition of Hellenistic Jewish speculation."[27] If so, they would have considered the earthly and mortal body inferior to the rational and immortal soul that was destined to be liberated from the body forever. To them, the human body, with its unruly passions and base needs, was considered a major hindrance to the contemplation of pure wisdom (Greek, *sophia*). As we have seen, according to Hellenistic thought, in order to set the mind free for union with the divine, the body had to be discarded forever in death, not raised to new life.

It seems the Corinthians believed that their adoption of Christianity had given them access to a higher form of knowledge (Greek, *gnosis*) than

27. Perkins, *Resurrection*, 325, n35.

that of other Hellenists. Because they had been baptized and received the Holy Spirit, they saw themselves as the intellectual "elite." In their pride, they considered themselves to be *already spiritually realized*. Paul himself gave thanks at the beginning of his letter that because of the graces the Corinthians had received, they had been greatly enriched "in speech and knowledge of every kind"; indeed, they were "not lacking in any spiritual gift" as they waited "for the revealing of our Lord Jesus Christ" (1 Cor 1:5, 7). Later he acknowledged that some spoke in tongues (1 Cor 12:10); some had received the gift of prophecy (1 Cor 14:29–31); while others had special spiritual powers (1 Cor 14:37). However, Paul repeatedly warned the Corinthians about being "puffed up," "arrogant," or "boastful" because of these gifts (1 Cor 4:6; 4:18–19; 5:2; 8:1; 13:4). They failed to acknowledge the true source of their wisdom; namely, the grace of Jesus Christ crucified. In addition, they lacked any understanding of the afterlife and the reality of bodily resurrection.[28]

In effect, the Corinthians were making the same statement as ancient Greeks and modern skeptics: "Dead men don't rise!" They were convinced there was no such thing as a resurrected life of the body. As New Testament scholar Richard B. Hays puts it most graphically:

> The phrase translated "resurrection of the dead" (*anastasis nekron*) means literally "rising of the corpses." For the spiritually refined Corinthians, this was not the stuff of Christian hope; it was a scenario for a horror story. This would have been particularly true for those members of the community with greater education and philosophical sophistication—precisely the higher-status members of the church whose infatuation with wisdom, knowledge, and tongues was creating the problems with which Paul wrestles throughout the letter. His talk of a future "resurrection of the dead bodies" would have sounded to them like the superstitious foolishness of popular legends.[29]

Paul answers the objections of the Corinthians with a stinging deconstruction:

> Now if Christ is proclaimed as raised from the dead, how can some of you say there is no resurrection of the dead? If there is no resurrection of the dead, then Christ has not been raised; and if Christ has not been raised, then our proclamation has been in vain and your faith has been in vain. (1 Cor 15:12–14)

---

28. Hays, *First Corinthians*, 70.

29. Hays, *First Corinthians*, 253.

Paul does not mince words. If the Corinthians confess that they believe in Christ as the Son of God and risen from the dead, how can they insist that it is impossible for the dead to rise? Did they actually think that Christ only rose "spiritually" and that only his soul had ascended into heaven, to return to the Father? Did they consider "risen from the dead" to be a metaphor for the spiritual emancipation of Christ's soul from his mortal body? Was the resurrection merely a symbol for the power of the Spirit that the Corinthians experience in their wisdom and spiritual gifts?[30] Paul's argument *ad absurdum* continues: If the Corinthians believe that it is impossible for dead bodies to rise, then Christ has *not* been raised and their faith in Christ is utterly pointless.

Paul continues his reasoning by suggesting that if it is true that there is no possibility of bodily resurrection—and yet if he and other Christian disciples continue to maintain the resurrection of the body—then they could be accused of misrepresenting God, whom they testify as having raised Jesus. Indeed, taken to its extreme: "If Christ has not been raised, your faith is futile and you are still in your sins" (1 Cor 15:17). That must have come as a shock to the Corinthians who had already received severe admonishment from Paul in this letter for being boastful, arrogant, argumentative, sexually immoral, idolaters, and unspiritual people of the flesh (Greek, *sarx*).

Then Paul pushes his argument even further: if there is no resurrection, then all those who believed they had died in Christ and who expected to rise with him at the general resurrection, have instead perished forever. They are no more. Their hope was in vain. They are utterly lost. Paul also asserts that if we merely hope in Christ for "this life only," then "we are of all people most to be pitied" (1 Cor 15:19). Why is this? Because, if there is no bodily resurrection, we Christians are living a lie and deluding ourselves and others with false hope. In essence, Paul presents the Corinthians with a no-holds-barred argument that reduces the objections of the skeptics, both ancient and modern, to an absurd conclusion: How can you call yourself a Christian and deny bodily resurrection—whether of Jesus Christ or of humankind? The fact is: "There is no authentic Christian faith without fervent eschatological hope, and there is no authentic eschatological hope without the resurrection of the dead."[31]

---

30. Hays, *First Corinthians*, 260.

31. Hays, *First Corinthians*, 262.

Christ, "the First Fruits"

Paul then counters the skeptical Corinthians with an argument based on what he has experienced personally: "But in fact Christ *has* been raised from the dead, the first fruits of those who have died" (1 Cor 15:20, emphasis added). For Paul, this is the rock bottom foundation of Christianity. It is the promise of our salvation. Paul goes on to explain that "since death came through a human being, the resurrection of the dead has also come through a human being; for as all die in Adam, so all will be made alive in Christ" (1 Cor 15:21–22). Here Paul is referencing the biblical story of the creation of humankind, as typified by Adam, who was formed in the image of God (Gen 1:27). However, since Adam fell from grace through his disobedience to the divine commandment, so sin, and with it both suffering and death, came as a result of human actions (Gen 3:6–19). Paul then identifies Christ as the antitype of the prototype known as Adam. Christ is the *new* Adam, who redeemed humankind through his perfect obedience, even to the point of dying on a cross (Phil 2:8).

For those who might still question how the resurrection of Jesus would affect the rest of us, Paul further expressed his understanding in his letter to the Romans: "For if we have been united with him in a death like his, we will certainly be united with him in a resurrection like his" (Rom 6:5). And again: "But if we have died with Christ, we believe that we will also live with him" (Rom 6:8). Repeatedly, Paul insisted that "If the Spirit of him who raised Jesus from the dead dwells in you, he who raised Christ from the dead will give life to your mortal bodies also through his Spirit that dwells in you" (Rom 8:11). The point is that we shall be raised from death to new life by *the same Spirit of God* that raised Christ himself. The divine action made manifest in Jesus revealed for all time that it is indeed possible to overcome the curse of death, which was not inherent in human nature from the original creation. Because it had happened once in Christ, so every member of humankind could, in union with Christ, be "made alive" again in a way that would utterly transcend the possibility of dying again. Thus Christ became the "first fruits" of a new human nature, one that will be restored to—and greatly exceed—the fullness of what humanity was originally intended to be: no longer a fallible, limited, corruptible nature, but a perfect reflection of the very image of God.

It should be noted that, according to Torah, the first fruits of the harvest (wheat, barley, dates, figs, pomegranates, grapes as wine, and olives as oil) were designated to be offered in the Temple in thanksgiving to God from the festival of Shavuot to the festival of Sukkot.[32] These sacrificial offerings were a sign and a symbol of the abundant harvest; indeed, they represented the entire people of Israel. Likewise, early Christian theologians understood that in taking on human nature through the incarnation, the Son of God took on the essence of *all* humanity. In his death as in his life, Christ epitomizes all human beings. Therefore, if we are genuinely united in Christ's death, we are dead to sin; and if we are united by the Holy Spirit to his glorious resurrection, it becomes possible for each one of us to rise to new life. Thus, according to Paul, Christ is not the *only* fruit, the only human being to rise from the dead. He is the divine/human progenitor, the *first* fruits of the heavenly harvest to come. "He is also the one through whom the creator will accomplish this—because he is the one who, as 'life-giving Spirit', will perform the work of raising the dead."[33]

Paul continues: at the end of the world, when Christ will have destroyed every earthly ruler, authority, and demonic power, and put all his enemies under his feet, then "the last enemy to be destroyed is death" (1 Cor 15:26). According to Pauline theology, in order for a *new* creation to arise, the intruder that is death must be completely vanquished. Paul understands that God the Father has willed to place all created things (even death) in subjection "under the feet" of the Son, Jesus Christ (1 Cor 15:27). We must note that while Paul generally presents the Father and Son in a relationship of perfect equality (1 Cor 8:6; 12:4–6), on occasion the apostle seems to portray Jesus in his human nature as being *subordinate* to the Father (1 Cor 3:23; 11:3). Nevertheless, Paul's developing Christology strongly affirms that once Christ has gained mastery over the totality of creation, he will return all that exists as a final offering to the Father, "so that God may be all in all" (1 Cor 15:28).

Paul further questions an apparently common practice of baptism by proxy when he writes: "If the dead are not raised at all, why are people baptized on their behalf?" (1 Cor 15:29). Perhaps such a custom had developed for those who were prevented from being baptized because of severe illness, while in prison, or because they had died unbaptized as

32. See Exod 23:16–19; Lev 23:9–14; Deut 26:2.

33. Wright, *Resurrection*, 355.

martyrs to the faith. Paul asks: if there is no certain belief in resurrection to new life, why bother to be baptized in the name of loved ones if death either means complete termination, in which case there would be no one left to be helped anyway, or else automatic spiritual release of the soul, in which case baptism would be unnecessary? If baptism does not signify death to sin for a *whole person* who will be resurrected to new life, it would be a futile act based on a foolish superstition.

Then Paul asks a rhetorical question concerning himself and all those who preach the good news at great personal risk. If the Corinthians and others like them do not believe in resurrection, then Paul wonders: "why are we putting ourselves in danger every hour? I die every day!" (1 Cor 15:30–31). He uses the metaphor of martyrdom: "If with merely human hopes I fought with wild animals at Ephesus, what would I have gained by it?" (1 Cor 15:32). Here Paul implies the intense verbal battles (and quite possibly imprisonment and tortures) that he had to undergo against his detractors in order to preach the gospel in Ephesus. What point would there be in enduring such conflict and persecution if Jesus was not raised from the dead? Why risk one's life for a lie? Then he quotes Isaiah 22:13 to suggest, ironically: "If the dead are not raised, 'Let us eat, drink, for tomorrow we die'" (1 Cor 15:32). In essence, Paul is warning the Corinthians that wrongheaded thinking about the afterlife and indulgent behavior in this life form a slippery slope down which they may slide to their ruin. Those who insist that this life is the *only* life and flaunt God's law with impunity because they have no expectation of a future bodily life beyond the grave, have no compelling reason to live a moral life. Paul implores the Corinthians not to be so easily tempted and duped: "Come to a sober and right mind, and sin no more; for some people have no knowledge of God. I say this to your shame" (1 Cor 15:34).

The Resurrected Body

Now Paul takes on the very questions that many still pose today: "But someone will ask, 'How are the dead raised? With what kind of body do they come?'" (1 Cor 15:35). Instead of immediately giving answers to his own questions, he cries: "Fool! What you sow does not come to life unless it dies" (1 Cor 15:36). N. T. Wright insists that "resurrection does not refer to some part or aspect of the human being *not* dying but instead going on into a continuing life in a new mode; it refers to something that *does* die and is then given a *new* life."[34] Clearly, Paul is not talking about resuscitating corpses or reconstituting mummies. He is insisting on an entirely new kind of bodily existence. Theologian and New Testament scholar Hans Conzelmann commented: "At all events his exposition of the question shows that existence without a body is a thing he cannot conceive of at all."[35] Unlike Paul, the sophisticated Corinthians could not fathom everlasting life that was still somehow embodied. They considered everything corporeal to be a severe detriment to spiritual transcendence. How could a corpse rise again? Why would a soul liberated by death even *want* another body? Yet supposing it was possible, who could imagine what bodily form it might take?

To challenge their mental conditioning, Paul employs the metaphor of a seed. "And as for what you sow, you do not sow the body that is to be, but a bare seed, perhaps of wheat or of some other grain" (1 Cor 15:37). The human body, he explains, is like an encased seed of wheat or barley. It must be planted in the ground of suffering, death, and eventual decay. Unless it breaks open and dies to being what it was, a seed encased in a shell, it cannot become what it will be, a living plant. Here, Paul uses the same metaphor which, decades later, John the Evangelist will quote as coming from the collected sayings of Jesus: "Very truly, I tell you, unless a grain of wheat falls into the earth and dies, it remains just a single grain; but if it dies, it bears much fruit" (John 12:24). For Paul, the all-pervasive goodness of creation bears witness that the Creator is forever bringing new life out of death. Everything living must eventually die; but, with the hope of resurrection, nothing dies forever.

Paul continues his seed analogy. When we sow a seed, we do not sow the finished plant. (Anyone who has ever planted a seed can attest to this fact: it looks nothing like the picture on the seed package.) But we plant in faith and expectation that through the interaction of sunlight, water, soil, and time, the seed will sprout, put down roots, grow upward toward the light, and eventually produce the desired plant. Likewise, our bodies as they appear to us now must be planted in the ground and die every day to what they have been in order to become the transformed bodies they will be. "But God gives it a body as he has chosen, and to each kind of seed its own body" (1 Cor 15:38). Just as the Creator enables each seed that is sown to grow into its own kind of plant, so God gives to

34. Wright, *Resurrection*, 314, emphasis in original.
35. Conzelmann, *1 Corinthians*, 280.

each created person that lives, dies, and is buried in the ground a different resurrected body. Here Paul implies that the resurrection will be the gift of a wholly *new* body by God, one that is individual to each and every one created.[36] As at the beginning in the story of creation, when the Spirit of God mystically breathed "the breath of life" (Gen 2:7) into the man made from the dust of the earth so that humankind became alive, so will it be at the end when the Creator will breathe divine life into what has died so that it may become completely transformed in resurrection.

Kinds of Bodies

Paul draws out the comparison: "Not all flesh is alike, but there is one flesh for human beings, another for animals, another for birds, and another for fish" (1 Cor 15:39). There are heavenly bodies and earthly bodies, and they both have their own glory, but each is different. "There is one glory of the sun, and another glory of the moon, and another glory of the stars; indeed, star differs from star in glory" (1 Cor 15:41). In other words, just as there are countless forms of created things, so there are more possibilities of resurrected bodies than we can possibly imagine. Paul summarizes his seed analogy: "So it is with the resurrection of the dead" (1 Cor 15:42). As it is with earthly life, so it will be with heavenly life. At the resurrection of the dead, all things having died to their former bodies will be gifted with new bodies, each body receiving its own particular glory.

Now Paul addresses *how* this new body will differ from the old. "What is sown is perishable, what is raised is imperishable. It is sown in dishonor, it is raised in glory. It is sown in weakness, it is raised in power" (1 Cor 15:42–43). The earthly body is able to suffer and die; the resurrected body is not. The earthly body, while formed upon a model that God created as good, is liable to dishonor itself by sin; the resurrected body cannot sin once it is clothed in divine perfection. The earthly body is full of ignorance, blindness, and lack of power; the resurrected body will be gifted with wisdom, light, and an abundance of divine capabilities. "This sort of body is entirely outside our present experience (except insofar as we know something about it through the body of the risen Christ), but it is nonetheless *a body*. So Paul argues."[37]

36. See Conzelmann, *1 Corinthians*, 281.

37. Hays, *First Corinthians*, 271.

Natural and Spiritual Body

Following his list of contrasts, Paul concludes with an unequivocal statement: "It is sown a natural body [Greek, *soma psychikon*], it is raised a spiritual body [Greek, *soma pneumatikon*]. If there is a natural body, there is also a spiritual body" (1 Cor 15:44).[38] Here we must be very careful to understand the precise meaning of the Greek terms Paul is using or we may draw false conclusions. Various translations have muddied the waters and generated a great deal of controversy about what Paul meant by differentiating these two terms, natural and spiritual body.

In Paul's Greek, *soma* is the physical body, the flesh; *psychikon* derives from the Greek *psyche*, the "soul" that was understood to inform the physical body, animating the human person. Hence *soma psychikon* may be considered the "psychic body," the "soulish body," the "sensuous body," the "animated body"; or more commonly, as in the New English Translation quoted above, the "natural body." By this term Paul means the earthly, corporeal, corruptible human body animated by a living soul; a body that is completely natural to humankind yet is woefully subject to sin, suffering, and death. This is the less-than-perfect body/soul complex that produces our ordinary life, our experience of being a thinking, feeling, fleshly, and fallible human person here and now. Note that "the adjective [*psychikon*] describes, not what something is composed of, but *what it is animated by.*"[39]

In contrast, *soma pneumatikon* derives from the Greek *pneuma*, which means "breath," "soul," or "spirit," and is most often translated as "spiritual body." For Paul, this term (however seemingly self-contradictory) best describes the resurrected and transformed human body, liberated from the ravages of sin, death, and corruptibility because it is illuminated and enlivened from within by the life-giving Spirit of God. "By far the most graceful translation of verse 44 and the one that best conveys the meaning of Paul's sentence, is found in the *Jerusalem Bible*: 'When it is sown it embodies the soul, when it is raised it embodies the spirit. If the soul has its own embodiment, so does the spirit have its own embodiment.'"[40]

In juxtaposing these two designations of body—natural and spiritual—we must be very clear that Paul is *not* contrasting them as

38. NET Bible®, available at http://bible.org.

39. Wright, *Resurrection*, 352, emphasis added.

40. Hays, *First Corinthians*, 272.

physical versus spiritual, corporeal against non-corporeal, or material as opposed to immaterial, as we might understand these terms philosophically. Neither does he suggest that, unlike earthly bodies, spiritual bodies will be "ethereal" or "angelic" beings, floating in the heavens like artistic renditions of cherubs. Neither does he describe the spiritual body as a spark of divine being or an astral body shining in the sky. Nor does he imply that the earthly body with its passionate human nature must be forever discarded, as the philosophy of Plato would have it, in order to enjoy the immortality of a disembodied mind that contemplates pure wisdom.

For Paul, the resurrected body would be a spiritual body "not in the sense that it is somehow made out of spirit and vapors, but in the sense that it is determined by the spirit and gives the spirit form and local habitation."[41] To him, the idea of a transformed human mind or spirit existing for eternity *without* a resurrected body was not an option. It simply would not conform to the biblical concept of how God had originally created and intended the human being to be: *embodied spirit*. According to Jewish anthropology, a *dis*embodied spirit would not constitute a whole person. Most importantly, a disembodied spirit would not accord with the reality and model of Christ's own resurrection. Paul had seen the risen Lord in a glorified body. He had heard the testimonies of the apostles and other disciples who had seen, heard, and walked with the resurrected Christ. For Paul, as for Jews, resurrection required a transformed *body*. If Christ was truly resurrected, then both his human body and his human mind had been exalted in glory. Likewise, for Paul, *the whole human person* must and will be transformed into Christ. It is as radical as that.

An additional point: When Paul contrasts the natural with the spiritual body, at no time does he denigrate the human body. Rather, he is differentiating the body/mind that is earthly, blinded by ignorance and inclined to sin and death, from the body/mind that is enlivened by the Spirit of God and transformed in everlasting life. Even though Paul acknowledges that the sensory body must be purified of its disordered passions and ultimately recreated, he also affirms that the whole human person, as originally created by God, is *good*. Earlier in his letter, Paul had chided those Corinthians who considered themselves spiritually mature as being merely natural or sensual (Greek, *psychikos*) in their thinking. In

41. Hays, *First Corinthians*, 272.

fact, they were *unspiritual* beings due to their unwillingness to receive the gifts of God's Spirit, because these gifts seemed to them like "foolishness" (1 Cor 2:14). He acknowledged that such unspiritual or sensual people cannot understand the gifts of the Spirit precisely because these gifts can only be discerned spiritually. In contrast, Paul praises those filled with the Spirit of God (Greek, *pneumatikos*) as being truly spiritual and thus able to "discern all things" (1 Cor 2:15). Furthermore, he attests that spiritual persons are completely liberated and no longer subject to anyone else's scrutiny. Paul identifies himself with the *pneumatikos* and affirms: "we have the mind of Christ" (1 Cor 2:16).

Adam and Christ

> So also it is written, "*The first man, Adam, became a living person*"; the last Adam became a life-giving spirit. However, the spiritual did not come first, but the natural, and then the spiritual. The first man is from the earth, made of dust; the second man is from heaven. Like the one made of dust, so too are those made of dust, and like the one from heaven, so too those who are heavenly. And just as we have borne the image of the man of dust, let us also bear the image of the man of heaven. (1 Cor 15:45–49)[42]

Throughout his argument, Paul has been building his case based on the divine process of creation and re-creation. Now Paul directly evokes the creation story in which "the Lord God formed man from the dust of the ground, and breathed into his nostrils the breath of life; and the man became a living being" (Gen 2:7). Once again referencing Adam as the primordial archetype of a human being, Paul then juxtaposes Christ as the final perfection of a human person, designating him as the "last Adam." This implies that the culmination of what it means to be *human* is to become like Christ—and thus fully embody the Spirit of God that is the source of life itself. For Paul, the physical and mortal mode of being human (*soma psychikon*), which defines Adam and ordinary human existence as we know it, must necessarily precede the spiritual mode of being fully alive (*soma pneumatikon*), epitomized by the risen Christ. Continuing the archetypal analogy, Paul contrasts the "first man," Adam, who was formed from the dust of the earth, with the "second man," Jesus Christ, who comes directly from heaven. We might understand this as

42. NET Bible®, available at http://bible.org.

referring to the incomplete and imperfect relationship that we as human beings have with our material nature, since we are born into bodies and minds without yet understanding their nature: thus we emerge out of the dust of ignorance. Christ, in contrast, entered his human life directly "from heaven," without ever being stained by the darkness of ignorance or sin: he is the pure effulgence of divine Spirit taking on a body. Furthermore, since this Lord of heaven arose from human death to a fully perfected "spiritual body," then all those who are reborn in Christ can likewise be resurrected. Just as we humans have borne the mortal image of the earthly Adam, so Paul implores us to bear—even now!—the immortal image of "the man from heaven," the resurrected Christ.

Because of the triumph of Christ over death that has already occurred historically in the resurrection, all humankind may look forward to resurrected life as a real possibility. In the *parousia*, or second coming of the risen Lord, the original creation will not only be fully restored, but far surpassed. It will be utterly *transformed*. The human being originally made in the image and likeness of God—the awareness of which was lost through disobedience—will be *remade* in the image and likeness of the perfect human being, Jesus Christ. In his letter to the Philippians, Paul attests that this is the glorious life to which we are truly destined:

> But our citizenship is in heaven—and we also eagerly await a savior from there, the Lord Jesus Christ, who will transform these humble bodies of ours into the likeness of his glorious body by means of that power by which he is able to subject all things to himself. (Phil 3:20–21)[43]

What is the Spiritual Body?

As we have discussed, according to Plato the goal of life on earth was to escape the imprisonment of the body, with its corruption and decay, so that the human soul would be free to enjoy heavenly immortality. To do this, the divine essence within each individual needed to be "stripped naked" and the human body abandoned forever, along with its passionate nature and attachments to things of this world. For Paul, however, the goal of life is not to escape the physicality of the body insofar as it is *physical*, but rather to be liberated from the detrimental effects of our broken relationship with a physical world. Paul considers the unredeemed,

43. NET Bible®, available at http://bible.org.

unenlightened human soul, with its tendency to spiritual blindness and pride, to be the cause of the body's corruptibility. We might call this "unspiritual soul" the part of the person that is soaked in ignorance, the part of the mind that misunderstands its own nature. We simply do not see the immense complexity of factors that brings our precise array of experiences into being in each moment, nor do we comprehend the depth of divine creativity that enables anything to exist at all. Yet we continue to think and act as though everything were really just the way it appears to the senses and the conceptual mind. All these mistaken perceptions drive us to shore up a sense of autonomy. Such a mentality falsely conceives itself to be independent, able to exist and function on its own, without taking full responsibility for its actions in the face of the divine order. Inevitably, our deep ignorance leads to wrong thoughts and choices that manifest both in sinful actions and in the sufferings they engender. Ultimately it is our *misunderstanding of the very nature of our material and psychological existence* that impels the malign forces that gradually demean the body, cast it down, dishonor it, and cause it shame. Death is the final sign of our inability to engage with a material world from the divine perspective, for we have not yet been able to recognize it exactly as it is being created by God in each and every moment.

Paul "sees that the true solution to the human plight is to replace the 'soul' as the animating principle of the body with the 'spirit'—or rather, the Spirit."[44] That is, the Holy Spirit. Thus in order to be resurrected in a spiritual body, we must become *divinized* in our very core. The second letter of Peter speaks of Christ's divine power that has "given us everything needed for life and godliness" (2 Pet 1:3). Furthermore, we have received Christ's own "precious and very great promises" that we "may become participants of the divine nature" (2 Pet 1:4). The mind with which we think must be the *Spirit of Christ*, not a mere human mind. For Paul, this means that through baptism, our very nature must be "clothed" anew with Christ: "As many of you as were baptized into Christ have clothed yourselves with Christ" (Gal 3:27).

This radically new clothing will be, in effect, "the spiritual body." It defines the transformed human person who has died completely to sin and lives in the resurrected glory of Jesus Christ through the power of the Holy Spirit. Like Christ's resurrected body, which is the promise and model of our own, our spiritual body will be capable of knowing with

44. Wright, *Resurrection*, 346.

the mind of Christ; of loving with Christ's love; of envisioning God and all created things through the eyes of Christ; of hearing the Divine Word spoken in and through everything that exists; of conversing and acting from the perspective of authentic wisdom; of appearing and disappearing at will. Our spiritual body will be incorruptible, meaning that it cannot decay. It will be free of physical defects and immortal, meaning it can never die again. It will be filled with honors and rejoice in its vast powers. It will experience the new creation and engage with other resurrected bodies in exalted ways that cannot possibly be imagined now: "What no eye has seen, nor ear heard, nor the human heart conceived, what God has prepared for those who love him" (1 Cor 2:9). For Paul, the resurrected, divinized spiritual body is the *fully actualized human person*, clothed in a transformed physicality, animated through and through by the Spirit of God, the heart of divine love.

Who will attain a Spiritual Body?

Paul cautions that "flesh and blood cannot inherit the kingdom of God, nor does the perishable inherit the imperishable" (1 Cor 15:50). Contrary to what some scholars have suggested, Paul's use of the term "flesh and blood" here does *not* contradict what he has written about the transformed but physical resurrected body. The phrase "flesh and blood" is a common Semitic phrase designating the living human body, composed of flesh (Greek, *sarx*) and blood (Greek, *haima*), the latter thought to be the source of life. As such, the term suggests the *soma psychikon*, the fallible, sinful, suffering, mortal, corruptible, and eventually decaying human body. Of course such an imperfect body/mind cannot "inherit" the kingdom, any more than that which is perishable has any place beside that which is imperishable in timeless glory.

Another consideration: was Paul referring here to those who would be left still alive—in their "flesh and blood" bodies—at the *parousia*? Was he implying that they could not be resurrected and given spiritual bodies because they had not yet died? In his earlier letter to the Thessalonians, Paul had written that he fully expected to be alive when Christ returned: "Then we who are alive, who are left, will be caught up in the clouds together with them to meet the Lord in the air; and so we will be with the Lord forever" (1 Thess 4:17). How would the bodies of the living be resurrected along with those that had already died? Paul answered this conundrum by sharing a personal revelation concerning divine mystery. He was certain that "even the living will undergo transformation into a new form, receiving their resurrection bodies without having to pass through death."[45] Referencing the rapturous symbolism of both Jewish apocalyptic literature and the prediction by Jesus of "the Son of Man coming in the clouds" at the *parousia* (Mark 13:26),[46] Paul writes:

> Listen, I will tell you a mystery! We will not all die, but *we will all be changed*, in a moment, in the twinkling of an eye, at the last trumpet. For the trumpet will sound, and the dead will be raised imperishable, and we will be changed. For this perishable body must put on imperishability, and this mortal body must put on immortality. When this perishable body puts on imperishability, and this mortal body puts on immortality, then the saying that is written will be fulfilled:

> "Death has been swallowed up in victory."
> "Where, O death, is your victory?
>   Where, O death, is your sting?" (1 Cor 15:51–55, emphasis added)

With this summation, Paul imparts his vision of how it is that the bodies of those who are already dead and those who are still alive at the end of the world will be completely changed. In a moment of divine transformation, the mortal body will be clothed in immortality, the corruptible flesh will become incorruptible. Then both the living and the dead will rise to eternal life.

Paul's theology here is based upon his understanding of what caused human mortality in the first place. "The sting of death is sin" (1 Cor 15:56). Because it disobeys and works in contradiction to the perfection of God's law, sin is what produces all our suffering and eventually, our death. Under the old law, the twisted nature of sin condemned us all and as a result all of us will have to die. However, by willingly taking our sins onto himself in death, the Savior revealed how death could be an act of perfect divine compassion, purifying sins through the crucible of suffering while entering the apparent annihilation of death without fear. Surrendering his spirit completely to the Father without grasping either to his divinity or to his human identity, Christ unveiled the layer of our own existence in which the ultimate source of life can never be

---

45. Hays, *First Corinthians*, 274. Concerning Paul's revelations of divine mysteries, see also Rom 11:25, 16:25–26; 1 Cor 2:7; 4:1; 13:2; Eph 3:2–4; Col 1:25–27.

46. See Brown, *An Introduction to the New Testament*, 463–64.

lost. Arising from death into a new kind of body, his resurrection is the promise of what human nature *could* be, once completely purified of sin and all its causes, which are so deeply rooted in ignorance. In essence, Christ cancelled for us the ultimate cause of death. Why, then, do we still have to die? Because in order to experience what Christ enacted in his perfect death, we must follow his example in every way. If we imitate him in the limitless compassion and surrender of his death, then, like Christ, we, too, shall be able to rise in a transformed body.

Sowing and Reaping

Paul concludes with an impassioned plea to the Corinthians: "Therefore, my beloved, be steadfast, immovable, always excelling in the work of the Lord, because you know that in the Lord your labor is not in vain" (1 Cor 15:58). These are ringing words, entirely applicable to every Christian today. In a similar way, Paul had exhorted the Galatians to do good works:

> Do not be deceived; God is not mocked, for you reap whatever you sow. If you sow to your own flesh, you will reap corruption from the flesh; but if you sow to the Spirit, you will reap eternal life from the Spirit. So let us not grow weary in doing what is right, for we will reap at harvest time, if we do not give up. So then, whenever we have an opportunity, let us work for the good of all, and especially for those of the family of faith. (Gal 6:7–10)

In his letters to both the Corinthians and Galatians, Paul traces a continuum between the earthly life that Christians are living now with the resurrected life to come. The apostle is insistent that the work of the Lord we do every day will have a *direct correlation* to the eternal gifts we will receive in the consummation and recreation of the world. The manner in which we see, listen, and speak; the acts of devotion and service that we perform; the spiritually enlightened mind and compassionate heart that we endeavor to cultivate in this life—these are the *immediate preparation* for the seeing, hearing, speaking, serving, knowing, and loving that we will enact in a resurrected body at the end of time as we know it. That is why the way in which we choose to live our earthly lives is so important!

In spite of all current frustrations, obstacles, and even failures, believers continue to do "the work of the Lord" and trust that "in the Lord our labor is not in vain." We try not to "grow weary in doing what is right" and to "work for the good of all." Faith in the resurrection gives meaning—*eternal* meaning—to even the smallest of our efforts. We know that nothing will be forgotten. Everything, including tragedy, will be transformed. In 1 Corinthians, Paul presents a tour de force of resurrection theology to explain to Christians then and now through whose power the dead will be raised to new bodily life. "For nothing will be impossible with God" (Luke 1:37).

Second Corinthians

In his second letter to the Corinthians, which scholars believe was written in c. 55 or 56 CE, Paul again exhorts the faithful not to lose hope. Christians carry the treasure of belief in the risen Lord "in clay jars," their fallible and mortal bodies, "so that it may be made clear that this extraordinary power belongs to God and does not come from us" (2 Cor 4:7). In addition, the faithful must also be keenly aware that they bear within themselves the cross of Christ.

> We are afflicted in every way, but not crushed; perplexed, but not driven to despair; persecuted, but not forsaken; struck down, but not destroyed; always carrying in the body the death of Jesus, so that the life of Jesus may also be made visible in our bodies. For while we live, we are always being given up to death for Jesus' sake, so that the life of Jesus may be made visible in our mortal flesh. (2 Cor 4:8–11)

The striking oppositions of death and life are of the utmost importance to Paul's theological vision. Furthermore, Paul acknowledges that he personally has "taken on" suffering for the sake of the Corinthians, so that they might be filled with the Spirit of life: "So death is at work in us, but life in you" (2 Cor 4:12). He identifies himself with all those who have gone through terrible suffering, even to the point of death, yet not lost faith in God's power at work: "I believed, and so I spoke" (2 Cor 4:13). This affirmation echoes the cry of the psalmist: "I kept my faith, even when I said, 'I am greatly afflicted'" (Ps 116:10). Like the psalmist, Paul had been plunged into physical and spiritual torment during his decades of missionary work, most especially during his more than three years in Ephesus (53–56 CE). He must have prayed often: "The snares of death encompassed me; the pangs of Sheol laid hold on me; I suffered distress and anguish" (Ps 116:3). But in referencing this psalm, Paul also affirms that God "delivered my soul from death, my eyes from tears, my feet from stumbling" (Ps 116:8).[47] For Paul, the sufferings of the present life bear witness to a very physical "dying with Christ" that is essential in order for us to rise with him in glory: "because we know that the one who raised the Lord Jesus will raise us also with Jesus, and will bring us with you into his presence" (2 Cor 4:14).

Thus Paul writes: "So we do not lose heart. Even though our outer nature is wasting away, our inner nature is being renewed day by day" (2 Cor 4:16). Paul implies that through willing endurance of our bodily pains and the mental agonies that wear us down—without grasping to them or feeling sorry for ourselves about them—our spiritual nature is growing more and more Christ-like. Every time we suffer with faith, abandoning any identification with our sufferings as the real "me," we can die a little more with Christ, and also rise a little more into union with him, even in this life and in this body. While in our mortal bodies, these two aspects of dying and rising in Christ are inseparable. No one knows this better than Paul. Later in this letter, he will even boast, like a fool, in what he has suffered for Christ (2 Cor 11:23–33). Nevertheless, Paul is convinced that everything he and we have endured in our mortal flesh for the sake of Christ will be rewarded in our immortal body. He concludes this section with a soaring act of hope in resurrection as the goal, not only of his life, but of *all* life.

> For this slight momentary affliction is preparing us for an eternal weight of glory beyond all measure, because we look not at what can be seen but at what cannot be seen; for what can be seen is temporary, but what cannot be seen is eternal. (2 Cor 4:17–18)

Our Eternal Dwelling

Then Paul switches from the metaphor of the body as a clay jar to that of a temporary and disposable covering, such as a tent or clothing. He assures us that even though our earthly tent is being dissolved, day by day, yet "we have a building from God, a house not made with hands, eternal in the heavens" (2 Cor 5:1). This new "house" will be our resurrected body, fashioned for us by God. Nevertheless, considering the human condition, Paul is ever the realist. He admits that even though we live in daily hope of attaining this resurrected body, still we suffer and complain while housed in this perishable tent of our earthly body. "For in this tent

47. For further analysis of this psalm, see Wright, *Resurrection*, 363–64.

we groan, longing to be clothed with our heavenly dwelling—if indeed, when we have taken it off we will not be found naked" (2 Cor 5:2–3). That is, when our mortal body has been cast off in death, we do not want to be left unclothed, without a body at all! We do not wish to become *dis*embodied souls.[48] Rather, we want to be "*further* clothed, so that what is mortal may be swallowed up by life" (2 Cor 5:4, emphasis added). This further clothing is the resurrected body. Paul assures his readers that God has prepared us "for this very thing," and "given us the Spirit as a guarantee. So we are always confident; even though we know that while we are at home in the body we are away from the Lord—for we walk by faith, not by sight" (2 Cor 5:5–7). This is how Paul wants us to anticipate the resurrected life, even in our present predicament.

Here Paul introduces a note of poignancy. By this time, it seems clear that he has become reconciled with the distinct possibility that he will die *before* the *parousia*, the expected return of the risen Lord in glory. Yet he feels a holy impatience, an overwhelming longing for eternal life. He implies that our very confidence in resurrection means we would rather be "away from the [earthly] body and at home with the Lord" (2 Cor 5:8). In this he does not denigrate living in the natural body; it is only that our current, exiled, *un*spiritual embodiment keeps us from being "at home with the Lord." However, he counsels that whether we are away from the Lord in our mortal body or at home with the Lord once we receive our immortal body, "we make it our aim to please him" (2 Cor 5:9). This is because we will all appear before the Lord at the judgment to receive just recompense for whatever we have done *in the body*, "whether good or evil" (2 Cor 5:10).

Some scholars have suggested that here Paul is abandoning his insistence on a resurrected body and revealing a hidden Platonic desire to escape the earthly body, in order to become a disembodied soul "at home" with God. Indeed, the apostle's previous distinctions between the seen and the unseen, the temporary and the eternal, the earthly body and the heavenly body, the present evil age and the age to come could be interpreted as espousing a Platonic dualism. However, Paul only

48. Note that some ancient mss. have an alternate reading for 2 Cor 5:3: "For in this tent we groan, longing to be clothed with our heavenly dwelling—if indeed, when we have put it on we will not be found naked." In this case, Paul would be implying that we long to put on (like new clothing) the incorruptible body of resurrection over our corrupted body, so that we will no longer be found naked in the grave. This version suggests that Paul might be thinking of an interim state of disembodied consciousness following death, before the resurrected body is given at the last judgment.

uses these terms in an eschatological, not an ontological, sense. He is reiterating the same dichotomy that he highlighted in First Corinthians: between the sinful, suffering, and decaying *mortal* body and the redeemed, impassible, and glorified *immortal* body.[49] For Paul, the concept of the "spiritual" body was still and always a *body*; a human person, a unity of physicality and consciousness, completely transformed by the Spirit of God. The corruptible body must be left behind only in order that the incorruptible body might replace it. For Paul, the sting of sin and the curse of death were the intruders between the human and the divine, not the physical body. As we read in his 1 Corinthians: "When this perishable body puts on imperishability, and this mortal body puts on immortality, then the saying that is written will be fulfilled: 'Death has been swallowed up in victory'" (1 Cor 15:54).

Furthermore, this body that we shall be given will be fully incorporated into Christ's mystical body. Earlier, in the first letter to the Corinthians, Paul had characterized those baptized into Christ and who receive him in Eucharist as becoming united to his own body:

> The cup of blessing that we bless, is it not a sharing in the blood of Christ? The bread that we break, is it not a sharing in the body of Christ? Because there is one bread, we who are many are one body, for we all partake of the one bread. (1 Cor 10:16–17)

Paul further elaborates the intimate nature of this divine/human union:

> For just as the body is one and has many members, and all the members of the body, though many, are one body, so it is with Christ. For in the one Spirit we were all baptized into one body—Jews or Greeks, slaves or free—and we were all made to drink of one Spirit. (1 Cor 12:12–13)

Thus Paul thought of the church and all who believe as being "the body of Christ and individually members of it" (1 Cor 12:27). We "drink of one Spirit" in Christ. It courses through our veins; it informs everything we are. Paul viewed the spiritual life we live in Christ right now as the sublime foretaste of the spiritual body that will be fully actualized in the resurrection. Then each one of us will see our self as the embodiment of a unique aspect of Christ's mystical body that only we as individuals are able to express; and this as a result of the unique lives we have lived, the good works we have done, the sufferings we have endured, the hope we

---

49. Wright, *Resurrection*, 366.

have held onto, the love we have poured out. Finally, it will be *by love* that we will look into the mirror of eternity and view ourselves as images of Christ.

Paul was convinced that the ultimate victory of divine love over sin and death would re-establish the original goodness of "materiality," most especially in the way that matter manifests as a purified and glorified human body, beyond our current experience of what it means to be physical. Moreover, this victory would mean liberation—not only for human beings, but for all living creatures; indeed, for the whole cosmos. "So if anyone is in Christ, there is a new creation: everything old has passed away; see, everything has become new!" (2 Cor 5:17). In Christ Jesus, the entire creation, heaven and earth, will be radically transformed, "that God may be all in all." This was Paul's comprehensive and sublime eschatology.

> *So if you have been raised with Christ,*
> *seek the things that are above, where Christ is,*
> *seated at the right hand of God.*
> *Set your minds on things that are above,*
> *not on things that are on earth,*
> *for you have died, and your life is hidden with Christ in God.*
> *When Christ who is your life is revealed,*
> *then you also will be revealed with him in glory.* (Col 3:1–4)

6

Dust, Bones, and Identity

PAUL LEFT US WITH an apparent paradox we are still trying to understand; that of the "spiritual body." As we have discussed, he provided a vivid metaphor for how the mortal body would rise to new life: like a seed buried in the ground that grows into a living plant. He stated by what agency this transformation would take place: by the power of the Creator who brings forth and sustains life in all its forms. He defined what kind of body it would be: not the resuscitated corpse or glorified mummy that so scandalized the Hellenists, but a new spiritual body. He asserted that every person would be raised at the last judgment and given a different kind of body. He acknowledged that there would be a radical *discontinuity* with the previous body: from perishable to imperishable, passible to impassible, mortal to immortal, weak to divinely empowered. Yet, there would also be a most definite *continuity* of identity in the resurrected body. That is, the same person who had died would rise in his or her own transcendent body. In short, Paul focused on resurrection as the fundamental transformation of a mortal, suffering, corruptible, natural body into an immortal, impassible, and incorruptible spiritual body (while still being a body). To some, it might have seemed that Paul had answered all the essential questions on the matter.

However, Paul's idea of a transformed spiritual body did not address whether *every single atom* of the corrupted corpse would have to be reassembled by God to form such a resurrected body. Nor did Paul discuss how the soul might continue to exist while separated from the body during the interim period after death and before resurrection. Furthermore, Paul did not specifically define *where the singular identity* of the human person lay: Was it inherent in the putrefied flesh? The liberated soul? The infused spirit? Or the resurrected body/soul/spirit unity of the whole person?

These are problems that plagued Church Fathers and foundational theologians over many centuries of Christian history. In order to understand how ancient and medieval Christians thought about these issues, we will first have to consider some ideas that may seem quite bizarre to us. Yet if we are to fathom why contemporary Christian teaching on the resurrection often looks and sounds the way it does, we must make the necessary effort to comprehend the cultural and philosophical contexts from which such teachings arose. In order to be able to separate, gently and with discernment, the core teaching of Christian revelation from the complex theories of resurrection that were developed in answer to particular questions and controversies through the course of history, we must examine that history, however briefly. Then, grounded in a richer context, we may more confidently explore new ways of thinking about the resurrection that might make more sense to us in our current cultural environments. These may also resonate more meaningfully with our own innermost spiritual longing and desire for transcendence.

Resurrection of the Flesh

Over the centuries following Paul's teaching on the spiritual body, new theories arose concerning the precise physical nature of the resurrected body. The topic of many an episcopal letter or theological treatise focused on how God would reassemble the dust and bones of the buried, burned, decomposed, or cannibalized flesh into a resurrected body. A great concern emerged to present the resurrection of the flesh as *the minute preservation of distinct particles of decayed physical matter*, rather than to focus on Paul's vision of radical transformation into a glorified body, like that of Christ. This reassembling of the precise material composition of the rotted corpse was considered necessary in order for the resurrected body to be truly the *same* body of flesh that the person had inhabited on earth. It seems that identity was considered synonymous with physicality.

Irenaeus of Lyons

Bishop Irenaeus of Lyons (c. 130–200 CE), perhaps the greatest apologist and theologian of the second century, insisted that resurrected bodies would incorporate all the same particles of matter in order to be precisely the same bodies of the persons who had died. For him, numerical identity could only be sustained in and through the actual flesh and bones of the individual body. If the material particles were not the same, then the personal identity would no longer be the same. Therefore the scattered, devoured, or putrefied bits of all the deceased would have to be gathered by God at the end of the world, and the same bits sorted out to remake the resurrected bodies. Irenaeus argued that if the flesh that had been martyred for Christ or the flesh that had sinned in this life was not the *very same flesh* that was resurrected, then that very same flesh would not be glorified for its faithfulness or punished for its sins in the afterlife. He strongly refuted the Gnostic argument that the dead, "since they claim to be spiritual, having put off their souls and become intellectual spirits, will be the spouses of spiritual angels."[1] Irenaeus declared that if souls attain the place of bliss merely because by nature they are *souls* (and not made of matter), "then it is useless to have faith, and the descent of the Savior was useless."[2]

Interpreting Paul's teachings on the resurrected body, Irenaeus explained that the term "spiritual body" does not mean the soul or spirit *without* a body, but a material body infused with the life of God's own Spirit, "so that by the Spirit they possess a perpetual life."[3] The bishop quoted Paul to prove that it is the complete body/soul/spirit complex (not only the soul) that is the temple of the Spirit here on earth (1 Cor 3:16). Furthermore, even though we do not yet see God face to face as we will in the spiritual body, Irenaeus affirmed that we are already being transformed; that is, divinized. The seal of the Holy Spirit "renders us spiritual even now, and the mortal is swallowed up by immortality."[4] Irenaeus held that there will be a *particular* judgment for each person at the moment of death. Thereafter, until the resurrection of their bodies, they will exist in an interim state:

> It has most clearly been said that the souls continue to exist: that they do not transmigrate from body to body; that they have the form of a human being so that they might also be recognized, and they remember the things that happened on earth . . . and

1. Irenaeus, *Against the Heresies*, 2.29.1.
2. Irenaeus, *Against the Heresies*, 2.29.1.
3. Irenaeus, *Adversus Haereses*, 5.7.2.
4. Irenaeus, *Against the Heresies*, 5.8.1.

that each soul receives, *even before the judgment*, the dwelling it deserves.[5]

The bishop refuted the Gnostics' claim that Paul's statement, "flesh and blood cannot inherit God's kingdom" (1 Cor 15:50), implied that created matter had *not* been saved by Christ on the cross. Irenaeus argued that only those who do not possess the life-giving Spirit are to be called mere flesh and blood, for these are the ones who do not have the Spirit of God within themselves.[6] Even though the flesh is weak and often casts the soul down with it, those who are sustained by the Spirit grow strong and become brave enough to bear witness to Christ by surrendering their lives as martyrs. He maintained that since the Word of God took on human flesh and by so doing redeemed it, then our flesh, too, will experience salvation: "If flesh did not have to be saved, the Word of God would never have been made flesh. And if the blood of the just had not been sought after, the Lord would never have had blood."[7] Thus, for Irenaeus, the incarnation is itself proof of the resurrection, "since if the Word assumed flesh He must have done so in order to save it."[8]

Tertullian of Carthage

Another brilliant apologist, Tertullian of Carthage (c.160–225 CE), has been called the father of Latin Christianity. Tertullian based his resurrection theology on the idea that human flesh created from mere clay is God's own handiwork, destined to become co-heir of eternal life along with the human soul. He affirmed that God *loves* human flesh (even though it is infirm, weak, disordered, and even sinful), precisely because it is divine creation. Tertullian even ventured to declare that "if flesh had not had these disabilities, God's kindness, grace, mercy, every beneficent function of God's would have remained inoperative."[9]

Tertullian clearly defined "resurrection of the dead" as referring to that which falls down into death—that is, the *flesh* of the body—and then rises up again, "since nothing will expect to rise again except that which

5. Irenaeus, *Against the Heresies,* 2.34.1, emphasis added.

6. Irenaeus, *Adversus Haereses,* 5.9.1.

7. Irenaeus, *Against the Heresies,* 5.14.1.

8. Kelly, *Early Christian Doctrines,* 468, referencing Irenaeus, *Against the Heresies,* 5.14.

9. Tertullian, *Treatise on the Resurrection,* 9, 29.

has previously succumbed."[10] In other words, something must die before it can rise and that can be true *only* of the body, since he considered the soul to have been created immortal. Tertullian vehemently disagreed with those Christians who claimed that the term "resurrection of the flesh" was a metaphorical figure of speech to describe a person who, "having come to the truth, has been reanimated and revivified by God, and the death of ignorance being dispelled, has as it were burst forth from the tomb of the old man."[11] (We may recognize such a spiritualized view as representative of some scholars and theologians in our own age who assert that the early disciples only believed in the Lord's abiding "spiritual presence" in the church, not his actual bodily resurrection.) Tertullian termed such erroneous views heresy.

For Tertullian, resurrection was not a metaphor or a figure of speech to describe *something else*; it was a literal truth. He referenced Scripture to establish that the resurrection of the dead had not already happened, nor was it taking place right now, nor would it occur immediately upon death. Tertullian clarified that when Paul wrote "we have been raised in Christ" (Col 3:1)—implying that resurrection had already occurred—he actually meant "a resurrection *in mind*, by which alone as yet we are able to reach up to heavenly things, things which we should neither be seeking nor setting our thoughts on if we were now in possession of them."[12] In other words, in our present life, it is only *in our mind* that we may rise with Christ. But for Tertullian, the spiritual transformation *must* happen in the mind before it can be fulfilled in the actual resurrection of the body. Nevertheless, what takes place in the mind is not yet the same as the complete bodily resurrection.

Like Paul and Irenaeus, Tertullian acknowledged that the body itself must also change drastically in order to be resurrected. However, that did not mean that the substance or essence of the material body would be destroyed or cease to exist altogether.

> But change must be distinguished from everything that argues destruction: for change is one thing, and destruction is another . . . And, for a proof that a thing can be changed and nonetheless be itself, the man as a whole does during his life in substance remain himself, yet changes in various ways, in outward aspect and in the very constitution of his body, in health and

10. Tertullian, *Resurrection*, 18, 49.

11. Tertullian, *Resurrection*, 19, 53.

12. Tertullian, *Resurrection*, 23, 63.

circumstances and honour and age, in occupation, business, craft, in means, abode, laws, and morals, yet loses nothing of his manhood, nor is so made into someone else as to cease to be himself: in fact he is not made into someone else but into something else.[13]

Thus, according to Tertullian, the fundamental transition from corruptibility to incorruptibility in the material composition of the resurrected body would still not eradicate the continuity of personal identity. This was considered to be of the utmost importance because, as his predecessors had also insisted, the final judgment cannot take place or be considered valid unless there is *complete identity* between the risen body and the previous one. We will only be judged based on the good or bad deeds performed in our particular body. For Tertullian, it was simply unbelievable that "either the mind or the memory or the conscience of the man" who exists today should be "abolished by reason of that festal garment of immortality and incorruption, since in that case . . . the stability of divine judgment upon both substances would be ineffective."[14] Tertullian argued further: "If I do not remember that it is *I* whose the deserts are, how shall I give glory to God? . . . But if the soul too is not to be changed, then there is no resurrection of the soul either"[15] for the soul could not be given the credit for having risen again, if it has not become different once it has risen.

But what of physical deformities, severe injuries to the body, even amputations? Shall these be restored in resurrection? Tertullian replied:

> What is belief in the resurrection, unless believing it entire? For if the flesh is to be restored from dissolution, much more will it be recalled from discomfort. Greater things prescribe the rule of the lesser. Is not the amputation or the crippling of any member the death of that member? If general death is rescinded by resurrection, what of partial death? If we are changed into glory, how much more into health. The defects that accrue to bodies are an accident: their integrity is a property.[16]

Tertullian was certain that the complete human body of the saved would be transformed into a state of perfect integrity and joy forever. Human

13. Tertullian, *Resurrection*, 55, 165–67.

14. Tertullian, *Resurrection*, 56, 169.

15. Tertullian, *Resurrection*, 56, 169, emphasis added.

16. Tertullian, *Resurrection*, 57, 169.

flesh would still be the same flesh that could potentially suffer, but by resurrection, it will have become *impassible*; that is, unable to suffer "in that it has received its freedom from its Lord, with the express intent that it should not be capable of suffering any more."[17] This transformation is not only possible, it is *guaranteed* because even in the natural order, divine power constantly renews all that is:

> To put it in one word, the whole creation is recurrent. Whatsoever you are to meet with has been: whatsoever you are to lose will be. Nothing exists for the first time. All things return to their estate after having departed: all things begin again when they have ceased. They come to an end simply that they may come to be: nothing perishes except with a view to salvation. Therefore, this whole revolving scheme of things is an attestation of the resurrection of the dead.[18]

Again, even though resurrection will involve radical change, Tertullian reiterated that all our physical characteristics—eyes, ears, nose, mouth, limbs, sexual organs, etc.—would be preserved in their unique material identity. However, he stated that their previous functions such as eating, digesting, copulating, and bearing children, would no longer be necessary. We will become like angels, but not the *same* as angels, because we will be fully and more perfectly *human*.

> So then the flesh will rise again, all of it indeed, itself, entire. Wherever it is, it is on deposit with God through the faithful trustee of God and men, Jesus Christ, who will pay back both God to man and man to God, spirit to flesh and flesh to spirit. He has already made an alliance of both in himself, has brought the bride to the bridegroom, and the bridegroom to the bride.[19]

Continuity and Discontinuity

This persistent concern with theorizing how the particular atoms of physical matter would be reassembled in order to reconstruct a numerically identical human body at resurrection may strike us as proceeding from a perspective of extreme materialism; one that situates the very locus of personal identity within the physicality of the body. When interpreting

17. Tertullian, *Resurrection*, 57, 173.

18. Tertullian, *Resurrection*, 12, 33–35.

19. Tertullian, *Resurrection*, 63, 183–85.

Paul's metaphor of the bare seed, some Church Fathers may have become so concerned with the particular atoms that make up the individual seed that they did not allow for the radical transformation of matter that has to take place every time a seed sprouts! It seems that the early Christian apologists believed that every particle of matter was created by God with a permanent identity tag and therefore held its own unique individuality that would endure through time. Thus one can imagine how it might have made sense for them to hold that God's power should eventually intervene to reassemble the material components of the body in exactly the right way to bring about the resurrection. Nevertheless, we may question if such an attempt to understand resurrection at the granular level does not, in a sense, lead to the notion of a God who is compelled to search out and reassemble the decomposed, digested, and widely scattered remains of the dead—recycled many times over millennia—in order to produce resurrected bodies identical in atomic structure to those that had died.

Given our contemporary understanding of biology and physics, some ideas that may have worked for the Church Fathers simply do not seem plausible to us any more: for example, the idea of unchanging atomic particles that could be reconstituted as the self-same flesh millions of years later, even by divine decree. Thus, in our own worldview, so deeply influenced by scientific modes of inquiry, we may be averse to thinking about the act of creation and recreation in concrete, physical terms. If God once formed (and continuously forms) everything out of nothingness, would divine power not be able to create our resurrected bodies anew as well? In order to grant us our future spiritual bodies, does God really need to gather up every one of our former material atoms? Yet the question of identity still hangs in the air: If God were to create our bodies entirely anew, by what criterion would we still be the same person? Strictly speaking, could a newly made body still be considered a *resurrection* of the body? Wherein does identity lie?

According to the traditional theories, further problems arise. *Which* body would be raised to eternal life: the one we had at birth, at seven, at seventeen, thirty-seven, sixty-seven, or perhaps ninety-seven? Would it be a body that somehow encompassed all its various ages? All its various talents, acquired capabilities, and achievements? Would this body include a physical brain that functioned as it had on earth and retained all the synapses from its former life? Would it recall a lifetime of sensory, emotional, and spiritual memories as well as the ties of personal relationships? Needless to say, when considering personal identity in narrowly defined terms, such questions only breed more problems rather than answers.

Material Identity

Overly concrete solutions to the conundrum of how God might resurrect and reunite the individual mind-body-spirit unity may seem repugnant or even shocking to some of us. But the complex problem of physical identity was of immense importance to the early theologians. It may be summed up in four points that were held in constant tension: How could one retain a *material continuity* of atoms, the *structural integrity* of organs, while at the same time admitting a degree of *transformation*, yet maintaining the blueprint of *identity*, like an abstract "Idea" associated with each individual human body? The fact that churchmen became so fixated on reclaiming the identical matter of eyes, ears, nose, teeth, limbs, torso, and inner organs, may indicate the degree to which they—conditioned by their culture—actually did identify with these parts of their bodies, which had to die in order to become something else.

Strange as it may appear to us, this obsession with material identity is not so far removed from those modern materialistic assertions that reduce the conscious mind to being nothing more than a function of the human brain—a complex array of nerve cells and electrical impulses. Although early theologians believed that the mind or soul as well as the spirit were distinct from coarse physical matter, at some level their thinking about the identity of the person in purely physical terms may not differ so much from what many in our scientific culture hold to be true. In fact, such materially limited notions of personal identity in a theological context may still resemble a kind of *biological reductionism*— one that defines the human person as no more or less than a physical network of atoms and molecules. While we may discount as naïve certain ancient theories about what happens to the disintegrated corpse in resurrection, do we postmoderns not have a similar obsession with the survival of the human body postmortem? Do we not experience many of the same trepidations that ancient Christians had concerning the treatment of cadavers and body parts? Should they be buried and allowed to rot naturally in the ground? Should they be cremated, blessed, and scattered in a place especially meaningful to the deceased or their survivors? Should they be composted? Even frozen? Will such choices affect the possibility of a successful resurrection?

In addition, we have new concerns that would have seemed inconceivable to the early apologists. What happens to personal identity in living bone marrow transplants, when core components of a particular body's cell manufacturing system, with its own unique DNA, are transferred to another person's body, and if successful, start producing new bone marrow with their own DNA in another human being? Whose bone marrow is it? Whose red and white blood cells? Given such organic transformation, whose blood is circulating through the brain, the heart, the torso, the limbs: that of the donor or the receiver? And if a deceased donor's organ is implanted in my body, is it still part of "him" or "her," or has it now become part of "me"? Yet who among us, in the twenty-first century, would insist that "I" am my hand, or my foot, or my breast, or my kidney, or my liver, or my heart, or even my bone marrow? What happens if I lose a limb in an accident or in war, or a breast to cancer? Do "I" then cease to exist? Of course not. But what am I?

Taking the reverse perspective: What if we designate our organs for donation at death—does that mean the eyes or heart or kidney or liver become part of another person's body and cease to be part of our own? Will the missing parts ever be returned to us? Whose organs will they be among the bodies of the resurrection? Indeed, we, too, tend to think of the body not only as the medium of expression for the soul or mind, but as the essential locus of our personhood. We, too, identify our *selves* with our physical bodies. Thus when our body dies, we think some essential aspect of our identity must die, too.

So the question that plagued the ancients remains: What *is* the person I call my "self"? We might consider that the appellation "person," functions as a way of describing all the facets that make up a human being on a day-to-day basis. People identify us by our name as well as by other aspects: gender, race, age, nationality, domestic status, academic degree, profession, occupation, even a social security number. But is any one of these aspects equivalent to what we mean when we think of my *self*? That is a moot point. Some of us may so identify with any one of these IDs, that when we suffer a change in that facet of our identity system, it seems some part of us has died. If we lose an artistic, professional, marital, or parental identification, we may think we have ceased being what we once were. Yet all these aspects of personal identity (and many other aspects as well) are mere names. They still do not identify the whole person.

Instability of Matter

Early theologians recognized that matter was unstable, changeable, and corruptible. Yet while they marveled at some mysteries of life, such as conception, birth, and growth, they were appalled by other natural processes, such as digestion, illness, aging, loss of physical and mental faculties, dying, and most especially, putrefaction. They knew only too well that everything born must eventually die. From the moment it was conceived, the body was destined to become a cadaver. Thus earthly life was considered both gift and liability. The organic activity of decay and dissolution of material particles was not appreciated as part of a dynamic life cycle, but denounced as the constant reminder that the wages of sin lead to death. Yet at the granular level, the inexorable change witnessed in the material stuff of the universe was only dimly understood; therefore, it not only disgusted but terrified many in the ancient world. For them, coming to perfection lay not in growing, changing, and evolving, but in reaching *stasis*—precisely because the threat of change over time implied incompleteness, imperfection, and eventual destruction. Only God was unchangeable and therefore perfect; fallen human beings were not.

It is interesting that concerns about death and dissolution do not disappear with contemporary scientific understanding of just how thoroughly matter is in a state of constant flux; they only intensify. First of all, quantum physicists know with ever greater clarity that the precise state of matter cannot be known in the abstract, in isolation from the influence and participation of an observer. They are certain, however, that at the subatomic level, particles of matter are not at all the solids we think they are. In a sense, based on the insights of quantum physics, we must begin to recognize that even what we thought was "matter" *cannot be found* apart from the perspective of a particular act of measurement. Atoms are described as fields of energy and potentiality; elementary particles cannot simultaneously be determined as having a definite location and momentum. So until they are measured according to a specific frame of reference, it does not even make sense to say that elementary particles "have" a precise location or momentum. When every atom is discovered to be a teeming storehouse of energy and motility, we realize that even our ordinary notion of "physicality" might be brought into question. As the Nobel laureate Steven Weinberg has said, "In the physicist's recipe for the world, the list of ingredients no longer includes particles. Matter thus loses its central role in physics: All that is left are principles of symmetry."[20]

Not only is so-called matter in a state of constant flux; at the most infinitesimal level, according to string theory, it may better be described in noncorporeal terms—more along the lines of vibration. For many physicists, the possibilities for how space, time, matter, and energy can be understood stretch far beyond the limits of our ordinary perceptions. The particle physicist Nima Arkani-Hamed comments:

> Many, many separate arguments, all very strong individually, suggest that the very notion of space-time is not a fundamental one. Space-time is doomed. There is no such thing as space-time, fundamentally in the actual, underlying description of the laws of physics.[21]

So dare we limit our own conception of the physical matter from which our resurrected bodies might be composed, if we can no longer presume there are any final definitions for *matter* or *energy*?[22]

What we do not know about the forms of material bodies, from the tiniest ant to the most immense black hole, is still far greater than what we do know. The prize-winning physicist Marcelo Gleiser describes the conundrum perfectly: "as the Island of Knowledge grows, so do the shores of our ignorance—the boundary between the known and unknown."[23] Inevitably, the more we learn about the vastness and instability of the cosmos, the greater becomes our fear of oblivion and the more impossible it seems that we could ever receive back any semblance of our earthly bodies as they were in this life. But does that mean we need doubt resurrection? Not at all. It does suggest, however, that we must seek a more nuanced understanding of *how the body will rise* and *what kind of body* it will be. As Paul wrote, the reality of resurrection is "a mystery" (1 Cor 15:51). However, what is mystery but divine revelation whose depths we are invited to plumb throughout our lives?

It seems that we have many of the same questions about the doctrine of resurrection as did early Christians: If the material continuity of the

20. Cited in Cole, "In Patterns, Not Particles, Physicists Trust."

21. Arkani-Hamed, "Messenger Lecture 1."

22. See Richard Feynman's famous statement: "It is important to realize that in physics today, we have no knowledge of what energy *is.*" *The Feynman Lectures on Physics*, Vol. I, 4–1.

23. Gleiser, *The Island of Knowledge*, xxii.

flesh is lost through death and putrefaction, how can personal identity be retained? If the reassembled bits of matter are transformed into a *new* "spiritual body," will that still be the same person? Or, as medieval scholar Caroline Walker Bynum explained, alluding to Paul's metaphor, "if we rise as a sheaf of wheat sprouts up from a seed buried in the earth, in what sense is the sheaf (new in its matter and in its structure) the same as and therefore a redemption of the seed?"[24] Physical change, even to glory, implies loss of continuity and therefore suggests loss of identity.

> There must be something that rises; there is no resurrection without identity. We know we are body; therefore body must rise. But there must be process and transformation as well, because the risen body must be radically changed. Unless something can change and still be the same thing, there can be no rising to glory of the corpse that has gone down into the grave.[25]

Change *and* Identity

In the first half of the third century of the Christian era, perhaps the most innovative of all ecclesiastical writers offered a striking alternative to the concept of the resurrected body as the identical reconstitution of dust and bones. This Alexandrian philosopher, biblical scholar, and theologian, was Origen Adamantius (c.185–254 CE). The appellation after his name meant "diamond" or "invincible" and as a philosopher, he was certainly a brilliant and sometimes impregnable mind. He confronted the philosophical paradox of the resurrection body as encompassing *both* change *and* identity. He argued that the resurrected body will be radically changed yet still retain its singular identity. How could this be? Origen understood that if personal identity was located in the physical continuity of minute bits of matter, then indeed, that identity could not survive the process of death, decay, and even transformation. However, if personal identity did not reside in the physical body, but rather *in the soul*, then (since, as he believed, the soul is immortal) identity could survive the destruction of death, even though the material elements of the body did not. It was a matter of where one located identity.

24. Bynum, *The Resurrection of the Body*, 60.

25. Bynum, *Resurrection*, 62.

The resolution Origen offered was based on his concept of the body as a flowing river, in a constant state of flux.[26] He acknowledged that the physical body lacked constancy; its substratum of matter did not remain the same for even two days.

> Yet the real Paul or Peter, so to speak, is always the same . . . because the form (*eidos*) characterizing the body is the same, just as the features constituting the corporeal quality of Peter and Paul remain the same.[27]

The one constant factor for Origen was the Platonic rational "form" (Greek, *eidos*), or "idea" of the body, that remains unchanging and preserves personal identity within matter. According to Origen, our resurrected bodies will have the same rational form they do now, although they will be radically changed for the better.[28] "It will be flesh no more."[29] By introducing the Platonic idea of form into the equation, Origen solved the problem of chain consumption; that is, to whom did the flesh belong if the same human flesh had been eaten by animals and thereafter consumed by other humans?[30] (This parallels the modern question: To whom would the transplanted heart belong?) For Origen, the *form* of each person was unique and would be retained, no matter what permutations had occurred with the physical matter of the body.

Most daringly, Origen intuited that resurrected bodies would become like the bodies of angels: "then shall the righteous having become one light of the sun shine in the kingdom of their Father."[31] While theological intuitions like this seem to have formed the basis of later attacks on the orthodoxy of Origen's theology,[32] it may be argued that the master was merely interpreting Paul's assertion that "flesh and blood" cannot enter eternal life. The old "fleshly" body of sin, mortality, and corruptibility (*soma psychikon*) must be transformed before it could become a purified spiritual body (*soma pneumatikon*) made full of light by the Holy Spirit. Thus the glorious and luminous resurrected body will be both the same and yet different from the former natural body.

26. Origen, "Commentary on Psalms," 1.5.

27. Origen, "Commentary on Psalms," 1.5.

28. Schmisek, *Resurrection of the Flesh*, 13.

29. Origen, "Commentary on Psalms," 1.5.

30. Schmisek, *Resurrection*, 14.

31. Origen, *Commentary on Matthew*, 415.

32. Schmisek, *Resurrection*, 15.

Like Paul, Origen affirmed that once the soul puts off its earthly body, "it puts a body on top of that which it possessed formerly because it needs a better garment for the purer, ethereal, and heavenly regions."[33] And just as Paul had indicated that such a radical transformation would occur without loss of identity (1 Cor 15:42–44), so Origen argued that this new body will be incorruptible and immortal; *but it will still be a body*. This teaching, of course, is thoroughly orthodox.

Alluding to Paul's analogy of the seed in the ground, Origen wrote of a "germ which is always safe in the substance of the body," which raises the dead from the earth, restores and repairs them, just like the power in the grain of wheat, "after its corruption and death, repairs and restores the grain into a body having stalk and ear."[34]

> We, therefore, do not maintain that the body which has undergone corruption resumes its original nature, any more than the grain of wheat which has decayed returns to its former condition. But we do maintain, that as above the grain of wheat there arises a stalk, so a certain power is implanted in the body, which is not destroyed, and from which the body is raised up in incorruption.[35]

Augustine and the Resurrected Body

One hundred and fifty years after Origen, in the late fourth to early fifth centuries, Augustine of Hippo (354–430 CE)—famous convert to Christianity, author of the *Confessions*, philosopher, theologian, and bishop—continued to preach the ancient tradition that the resurrected body would be very physical but still *transformed* human flesh. In his catechism, the *Enchiridion*, Augustine still insisted that every bit of the physical matter of the decayed corpse would be gathered up at the resurrection to be reunited with the soul:

> Nor does the earthly material from which mortal flesh is created perish in the sight of God, but whatever dust or ashes it may dissolve into, into whatever vapors or winds it may vanish, whatever other bodies or even elements it may be turned into, by whatever animals or even men it may have been eaten as food

33. Origen, *Contra Celsum*, 7.32, 420.

34. Origen, *De Principiis*, 2.10.3, 141.

35. Origen, *Contra Celsum*, 5.23, 281.

and so turned into flesh, in an instant of time it returns to the human soul that first gave it life so that it might become human, grow, and live.[36]

However, Augustine did not insist that all the hair and nails that had been removed by frequent cutting and paring would be restored to the body, for that would result in "a deformity." He used the analogy of a statue: just as a melted down statue can be restored using the same quantity of material, it does not matter which part of the material is used for which part of the statue, as long as "all the material of which the statue was originally made is used in the restoration." He attributed to God, the omnipotent and master craftsman, the ability to "remake our flesh with wonderful and indescribable speed *from all the material that had constituted it*."[37] "For if God made man who was not, can He not re-fashion that which was?"[38] Augustine suggested that resurrected bodies may no longer be of different heights, or thin or fat, as in earthly life. There will be no deformity resulting from lack of perfect proportion: all that is wanting to an emaciated body will be added and all that is excessive from a corpulent body will be removed "without destroying the integrity of the substance."[39] If the Creator wishes each person to retain his or her "distinctive and discernible appearance," then the matter that belonged to the person would be suitably modified "so that none of it perishes and any deficiency will be supplied by the one who was able to make what he willed even out of nothing."[40] Furthermore, he affirmed that the bodies of saints will rise "with no defect, no deformity, no corruption, burden, or difficulty, and their facility in living will be equal to their felicity. That is why they are called spiritual, although there is no doubt that they will be bodies, not spirits."[41]

Augustine also discussed thorny issues that had been raised repeatedly by pagans to repudiate and ridicule Christian belief in resurrection. Many of them had been dealt with by earlier apologists,

---

36. Augustine, *Enchiridion*, #88, 107.

37. Augustine, *Enchiridion*, #89, 107–8, emphasis added.

38. Augustine, *Sermons on Selected Lessons of the New Testament*, 77:14, 277.

39. Augustine, *City of God*, 22.19, 759.

40. Augustine, *Enchiridion*, #90, 108.

41. Augustine, *Enchiridion*, #91, 108.

such as Origen.[42] These issues included: Would miscarriages or aborted fetuses be raised? According to Augustine, they would:

> But who would dare to deny, even though he may not dare to affirm it, that resurrection will supply anything the fetus lacks in form and so that perfection that was destined to come with time will not be lacking . . . but what was not yet complete will be completed, and what had been spoiled will be restored?[43]

Would seriously deformed babies who only live a short while be raised whole and intact? Augustine believed they would "be restored to a normal human form by the resurrection so that each soul will have its own body."[44] He also suggested that resurrected bodies will have a most pleasant color: "how conspicuous shall it be where the just shall shine forth as the sun in the kingdom of their Father!"[45] The bishop even faced the controversial question: Would women remain women or must they become men in order to be "conformed to the image of the *Son* of God?" (Rom 8:29, emphasis added). Augustine was certain that "both sexes shall rise,"[46] but that there will be no marrying, quoting Christ's words to the Sadducees: "In the resurrection they neither marry nor are given in marriage" (Matt 22:30). Will parts of the body mutilated or lost in martyrdom be healed? Augustine affirmed that the marks will not appear as deformities, but as marks of honor "and will add luster to their appearance, and a spiritual, if not a bodily beauty."[47] He thought it seemly that in the new kingdom of heaven, no bodily member that had been severed would be lost, although the scars would be retained, even as Christ's own wounds were transformed into glory.

Then Augustine addressed the most difficult question of all, that of cannibalism: "To whom, in the resurrection, will belong the flesh of a dead man which has become the flesh of a living man?"[48] He contended "that flesh, therefore, shall be restored to the man in whom it first

---

42. Origen, *De Principiis* 1.6.4 and *Contra Celsum* 5.18. See Harmless, ed., *Augustine in His Own Words*, 363, n72.

43. Augustine, *Enchiridion*, #85, 105–6.

44. Augustine, *Enchiridion*, #87, 106–7.

45. Augustine, *City of God*, 22.19, 759 (citing Matt 13:43).

46. Augustine, *City of God*, 22.17, 756.

47. Augustine, *City of God*, 22.19, 760.

48. Augustine, *City of God*, 22.20, 760–61.

became human flesh."[49] It seems that Augustine, like Irenaeus, Tertullian, and many other apologists before and after them, felt compelled to deal extensively with the gross aspects of a fleshly resurrection. These arguments were fueled by historical circumstances such as the devouring of bodies by animals or the deliberate scattering of bodies after martyrdom as well as by bitter attacks from pagans, disbelievers, and Gnostics outside the church who questioned the goodness of matter and decried a bodily resurrection. Yet Augustine held firm that even though a corpse has been "ground to powder by some severe accident, or by the ruthlessness of enemies, and though it has been so diligently scattered to the winds, or into the water that there is no trace of it left, yet it shall not be beyond the omnipotence of the Creator—no, not a hair of its head shall perish."[50] Nevertheless, Augustine warned against excessive speculation: "But what this spiritual body shall be and how great its grace, I fear it were but rash to pronounce, seeing that we have as yet no experience of it."[51]

Inevitably, because of the wide dissemination of Augustine's writings, his staunchly *physical* interpretation of Paul's "spiritual body" became the standard Western view of eschatology. The Augustinian doctrine of resurrection that focused on final judgment and the continuity of body parts, rather than the Pauline metaphor of the seed that centered on radical transformation, greatly influenced Christian theological discourse throughout the medieval period and continues to do so into our own twenty-first century.[52] However, while some modern theologians still maintain that the corpse and the risen body must consist of the same physical matter, others hold that "in order to ensure the continuity of the resurrected person with him who was alive, the identity of the substantial form, i.e. the soul, is sufficient."[53] It is important to note that church teaching does not fully endorse any one view concerning the nature of the link between the earthly and the risen bodies.

In spite of Augustine's preoccupation with material continuity, he did follow Paul's teaching that the resurrected body would be a *spiritual* body, and that "the flesh shall then be spiritual, and subject to the spirit,

49. Augustine, *City of God*, 22.20, 761.

50. Augustine, *City of God*, 22.21, 761–62.

51. Augustine, *City of God*, 22.21, 762.

52. Bynum, *Resurrection*, 113.

53. Léon-Dufour, *Resurrection*, 320, n38.

but still flesh, not spirit . . ."[54] Near the end of the *City of God*, Augustine eulogized the innate beauties of the human body and tried to envision how it would be made even more magnificent by God when raised to glory. Considering the promise of resurrected life, Augustine asked:

> When this promise is fulfilled what will we be? What blessings shall we receive in that kingdom, since already we have received as a pledge of them Christ's dying? In what condition shall the spirit of man be, when it has no longer any vice at all: when it neither yields to any, nor is in bondage to any, nor has to make war against any, but is perfected, and enjoys undisturbed peace with itself? Shall it not then know all things with certainty, and without any labor or error, when unhindered and joyfully it drinks the wisdom of God at the fountainhead? What shall the body be when it is in every respect subject to the spirit, from which it shall draw life so sufficient as to stand in need of no other nutriment? For it shall no longer be animal, but spiritual, having indeed the substance of flesh, but without any fleshly corruption.[55]

In a soaring meditation, Augustine imagined that in our resurrected bodies, we might see God face to face with transfigured eyes. We would also see God in the faces of one another:

> Wherefore it may very well be, and it is thoroughly credible, that we shall in the future world see the material forms of the new heavens and new earth in such a way that we shall most distinctly recognize God everywhere present and governing all things, material as well as spiritual, and shall see Him, not as now we understand the invisible things of God, by the things which are made and see him darkly, as in a mirror, and in part, and rather by faith than by bodily vision of material appearances, but *by means of the bodies we shall wear and which we shall see wherever we turn our eyes.* As we do not believe, but *see* that the living men around us who are exercising vital functions are alive, though we cannot see them without their bodies, but see it most distinctly by means of their bodies, so, wherever we shall look with those spiritual eyes of our future bodies, we shall then, too, by means of bodily substances behold God, though a spirit, ruling all things. . . . God will be so known by us, and shall be so much before us, that we shall see Him by the spirit

54. Augustine, *City of God*, 22.21, 762.
55. Augustine, *City of God*, 22.24, 770.

in ourselves, in one another, in Himself, in the new heaven and
new earth, in every created thing which shall then exist; and
also by the body we shall see Him in every body which the keen
vision of the eye of the spiritual body shall reach.[56]

Aquinas and Personal Identity

The most renowned theologian of the medieval period was undoubtedly
Thomas Aquinas (1225–1274), a Dominican priest, influential teacher,
preacher, and voluminous writer, also known as the "angelic doctor." While
he did not live to complete his consummate work, the *Summa Theologica*
(especially the final section on resurrection), it was probably finished
after Aquinas's death by his secretary, Reginald of Piperno, working from
notes and commentaries that the Doctor had made on the writings of
Peter Lombard (c. 1100–1160). Lombard, in turn, had borrowed heavily
from Augustine to write his lengthy theological textbook, the *Sentences*.
Thus the tradition of teachings on bodily resurrection in the twelfth and
thirteenth centuries was directly connected to Augustine's own teachings
in the fourth century and to those of the Church Fathers before him.

As we have seen, generations of apologists had linked personal
identity with the "material bits" of the body; but they could not explain
how the unique person could survive when the body was corrupted
by death and decay. There remained the fear that if all the matter of
an individual corpse were not resurrected intact, the identity of the
person would be irrevocably lost. The enemy was not only death and
the separation of the soul from the body, but the disgusting process of
putrefaction. Employing Aristotle's metaphysical view that every being
is a composite of two principles—primary matter and substantial form—
Aquinas broke with tradition. Even though the Angelic Doctor believed
that God would reassemble all the particles of the body in resurrection,
he did not ascribe personal identity to the physical matter of the body.
Rather, Aquinas located identity in the substantial form of the body: that
is, in the *rational soul*. It was the soul that made a being to be what it is.
This approach was an important breakthrough. According to Thomistic
philosophy, since the soul is the seat of rationality in the human being,
personal identity can never be lost, even when the soul is separated from
the material elements of the body at death and the corpse decomposes:

56. Augustine, *City of God*, 22.29, 777–78, emphasis added.

Therefore since the rational soul remains, no substantial form of the human body falls away into complete nonentity. And the variation of accidental forms does not make a difference of identity. Therefore, the selfsame body will rise again, since the selfsame matter is resumed . . ."[57]

We may still ask, if there is a radical change of bodily matter in resurrection—from corruptible to incorruptible, from mortal to immortal—how can it be numerically *the same person* that rises again? For, according to Aristotle, "whatsoever things are changed in the corruptible substance are not repeated identically."[58] Would not the resurrected body/soul complex be, in effect, a *new* person, if the matter *in*formed by the substantial form has so thoroughly changed? No, said Aquinas:

> For we cannot call it resurrection unless the soul returns to the same body, since a resurrection is a second rising, and the same thing rises that falls: wherefore resurrection regards the body which after death falls rather than the soul which after death lives. And consequently if it be not the same body which the soul resumes, it will not be a resurrection, but rather the assuming of a new body.[59]

Aquinas quoted Augustine that "to rise again is naught else but to live again."[60] Unless the same identical person who died returns to life, he or she could not be said to live *again*, which would be "contrary to faith."[61]

Aquinas further argued that the body would have to be identical, because if it were not, the person could not obtain his or her final goal and would seem to have been created in vain. Thus, "it is necessary for the selfsame [person] to rise again; and this is effected by the selfsame soul being united to the selfsame body."[62] Aquinas assumed that all organs, entrails, and essential parts of the body would rise, as well as the "humors" (cold, hot, moist, and dry) that affect the behavior of the human body, and "accidental parts" like hair and nails; however, their

---

57. Thomas Aquinas, *Summa Theologica Supplement*, Vol. 5, Part III, Q. 79, article 2, reply to objection 4.

58. Aquinas, *ST Supplement*, Q 79, article 2, objection 1.

59. Aquinas, *ST Supplement*, Q 79 article 1, respondeo.

60. Augustine, *On the Trinity*, Books 8–15, viii, 5.2.13.

61. Aquinas, *ST Supplement*, Q 79. article 2, respondeo.

62. Aquinas, *ST Supplement*, Q 79, article 2, respondeo.

bodily functions would be changed. Merely accidental qualities such as sweat, urine, semen, and breast milk would no longer be necessary in the resurrected body. Neither would the resurrected body perform actions of the natural or "animal" life: "And since to eat, drink, sleep, beget, pertain to the animal life, being directed to the primary perfection of nature, it follows that they will not be in the resurrection."[63]

Aquinas also affirmed that "the soul stands in relation to the body not only as its form and end, but also as efficient cause."[64] He compared the soul and its relationship to the body "as art to a thing made of art . . . and whatever is shown forth explicitly in the product of art is all contained implicitly and originally in the art. In like manner whatever appears in the parts of the body is all contained originally and, in a way, implicitly in the soul."[65] Thus the body is the artistic "expression" of the soul. Furthermore, just as a work of art is not perfect if it lacks any of the aspects contained in the art, so human beings cannot be made perfect unless and until "the whole that is contained enfolded in the soul be outwardly unfolded in the body, nor would the body correspond in full proportion to the soul."[66] Therefore, he argued, all the members that make up the human body now must be restored at the resurrection.

The Interim State

It should be mentioned that Aquinas did not consider the soul to be immortal according to its nature in the classic Platonic sense—in which a soul was considered able to attain perfection *without* a body. Rather, Aquinas held that after death, God's incomparable goodness will grant the soul immortality as a *supernatural* gift and continue to maintain it in ongoing life.[67] During this interim state, when the soul/mind is temporarily separated from the body in a disembodied existence while awaiting resurrection, Aquinas argued that the soul will retain all its mental powers and functions, and thus maintain its individual identity. The already-purified soul that had been assured of its salvation at the particular judgment (immediately following death) will even be able to

63. Aquinas, *ST* Supplement, Q 81, article 4, respondeo.

64. Aquinas, *ST* Supplement, Q 80. article 1, respondeo.

65. Aquinas, *ST* Supplement, Q 80, article 1, respondeo.

66. Aquinas, *ST* Supplement, Q 80, article 1, respondeo.

67. Dahl, *The Resurrection of the Body*, 49.

enter into the vision of God: "For the separation of the soul from the body makes it capable of the divine vision, and it was unable to arrive at this so long as it was united to the corruptible body. Now, in the vision of God consists man's ultimate beatitude, which is the 'reward of virtue.'"[68] In other words, the disembodied soul that joins the communion of saints will be incorruptible, immortal, and able to rejoice in the vision of God.

However, since the soul will lack a body, Aquinas wrote that it will still be incomplete, without corporeal means of expression, and therefore, *deficient*.

> But the soul separated from the body is in a way imperfect, as is every part existing outside of its whole, for the soul is naturally a part of human nature. Therefore, man cannot achieve his ultimate happiness unless the soul be once again united to the body.[69]

In this disembodied state, Aquinas suggested that the soul will be unable to experience the supreme happiness of the unified person: "My soul is not I, and if only souls are saved, I am not saved, nor is any man."[70] The fullness of life will only be possible when the soul finally receives its resurrected body and assumes a new and definitive identity.

Qualities of the Glorified Body

In addition to immortality, incorruptibility, and the sublime capacity to envision God, Aquinas addressed other supernatural qualities that the glorified body (once reunited to the soul) would possess. First of all, it would be *impassible*; that is, unable to suffer from the extremes of passion—namely, pride, anger, greed, jealousy, revenge, and lust. Therefore the saints would not suffer physically the effects of sin, nor from heat, cold, pain, or any inconvenience.

> The human body and all that it contains will be perfectly subject to the rational soul, even as the soul will be perfectly subject to God. Wherefore it will be impossible for the glorified body to be subject to any change contrary to the disposition whereby it

---

68. Aquinas, *Summa Contra Gentiles*, 4.91.2.

69. Aquinas, *Contra Gentiles*, 4.79.11.

70. Aquinas, quoted by Geach in *God and the Soul*, 22.

is perfected by the soul; and consequently those bodies will be impassible.[71]

Next, the glorified body would be blessed with *subtlety*. Aquinas explained that "subtlety takes its name from the power to penetrate"; therefore, "a subtle thing is said to be penetrative, for the reason that it reaches to the inmost part of a thing, so is an intellect said to be subtle because it reaches to the insight of the intrinsic principles and the hidden natural properties of a thing."[72] Subtlety does *not* mean, as heretics had proclaimed, that the glorified body would become a rarified, spiritual substance: "so that human bodies in rising again will be like the air or the wind."[73] Aquinas argued that this is impossible because a body cannot become a spirit and the complete human person is composed of both body *and* spirit. In addition:

> Our Lord had a palpable body after the Resurrection, as appears from the last chapter of Luke, and we must believe that His body was supremely subtle. Moreover the human body will rise again with flesh and bones, as did the body of our Lord, according to Luke 24:39, "A spirit hath not flesh and bones as you see Me to have," and Job 19:26, "In my flesh I shall see God," my Saviour: and the nature of flesh and bone is incompatible with the aforesaid rarity.[74]

Further, the glorified body would be graced with *agility*, by which it would become perfectly subjected to the glorified soul, "so that not only will there be nothing in it to resist the will of the spirit . . . but also from the glorified soul there will flow into the body a certain perfection, whereby it will become adapted to that subjection."[75] This perfection is called "the gift of the glorified body." Just as by the gift of subtlety the body becomes completely subjected to the soul as its form, from which it derives its specific being, "so by the gift of agility it is subject to the soul as its mover, so that it is prompt and apt to obey the spirit in all the movements and actions of the soul."[76] Thus the gift of agility will

71. Aquinas, *ST* Supplement, Q 82, article 1, respondeo.

72. Aquinas, *ST* Supplement, Q 83, article 1, respondeo.

73. Aquinas, *ST* Supplement, Q 83, article 1, respondeo.

74. Aquinas, *ST* Supplement, Q 83, article 1, respondeo.

75. Aquinas, *ST* Supplement, Q 84, article 1, respondeo. Compare *Summa Contra Gentiles*, 4.86.3.

76. Aquinas, *ST* Supplement, Q 84, article 1, respondeo.

enable the glorified body to be wherever the mind/soul wishes it to be instantaneously, without any effort or labor.

Finally, Aquinas asserted that the body of the righteous would be radiant with luminous *clarity* because it was written: "The just shall shine as the sun in the kingdom of their Father," (Matt 13:43) and "The just shall shine, and shall run to and fro like sparks among the reeds" (Wis 3:7). As with the other aspects of the glorified body, Aquinas affirmed that "this clarity will result from the overflow of the soul's glory into the body"[77] and "so again it will overflow into each part of the soul according to the mode of that part."[78]

These four qualities—impassibility, subtlety, agility, and clarity—were known in the medieval period as the *dotes*, that is, the bridal dowries or gifts given to the resurrected body by the glorified soul. They became extremely important components of the discussion on the resurrected body throughout the ensuing centuries.

The Resurrected Body

A spiritual body does not imply a floating spirit, a ghost of sorts, even an angelic presence (although it was said that we shall be "like" the angels in our capacity for wisdom and in our ability to see God). As distinct from the theological debates that persisted over the ensuing centuries, Paul's conviction seems to have been that, at the resurrection, we will *not* receive back the exact same bits of earthly matter that we had before. "And as for what you sow, you do not sow the body that is to be, but a bare seed, perhaps of wheat or of some other grain" (1 Cor 15:37). Even as the seed in the ground must break open before it can put out roots, and struggle upward through the soil toward the light before it can sprout, so our body-mind complex must die to what it has been, before it can ever become something else. Indeed Paul called the Corinthians "fools" for thinking the same body that had died would rise again in exactly the same way, presumably reconstituted from the exact same particles of matter. The seed is nothing like the stalk of wheat; the grape bears no resemblance to the gnarly vine. Yet there *is* a continuity of identification,

77. Aquinas, *ST* Supplement, Q 85, article 1, respondeo.

78. Aquinas, *ST* Supplement, Q 85, article 1, reply to objection 4. Compare *Summa Contra Gentiles*, 4.86.4.

just as there is continuity of the person who is born, lives, dies, and is resurrected.

As we discussed in chapter 5, Paul also used the analogy of the body becoming covered or clothed with a new body, inhabited by Christ's own Spirit. As soon as we are baptized, this process of transformation begins: "As many of you as were baptized into Christ have clothed yourselves with Christ" (Gal 3:27). Paul exhorted Christians to "put on the Lord Jesus Christ" (Rom 13:14). This "putting on" of Christ is a lifelong process of loving, serving, suffering, and eventually dying with Christ so that we may be divinized by the very power of his resurrection. And we are promised that this glorious metamorphosis from one earthly kind of body to another resurrected kind of body will be part of a magnificent "new creation" by God.

Like the evangelists, the Church Fathers and medieval theologians did not venture to describe what the resurrection body might actually *look like*. How could they? Except for a select group of apostles and early disciples, no one had seen Christ risen from the dead in a transformed body. Though Paul tried to convey what had happened on the road to Damascus, namely the life-altering experience of encountering Jesus Christ in his resurrected body, even Paul never detailed Jesus' appearance. Nor did he deal—apart from metaphors—with exactly *how* our bodies will rise and how they might appear.

Why can we not envision our future existence? Perhaps our inability to conceive of a spiritual body is due not only to our difficulty in imagining life beyond death, but to our ignorance of the true nature of physical matter itself. The forms of material entities that we can see, touch, and posit are strictly limited. We cannot directly perceive the scale of material reality that stretches from the smallest quarks to the densest black holes. Likewise, the spectrum of light that appears to the visible eye is infinitesimally narrow relative to the vast scope of the range of electromagnetic waves. Similarly, the variety of corporeal and spiritual bodies that might inhabit our own world, much less the entire cosmos, is also *terra incognita* to us. If we cannot even see the full spectrum of earthly bodies that exist all around us, how can we expect to envision a heavenly body? At present, we are simply unable to comprehend what a transformed spiritual body might "look" or "feel" like. Neither can we imagine what kind of body would be a perfect image and likeness of Christ's own resurrected body, because we cannot yet perceive Christ's glorified body. We are far from knowing the transfigured radiance of the body that awaits those who die and rise in Christ, even when we try to envision a different dimension of "embodied being" beyond our present powers.

The Resurrected Mind

If we can hardly imagine the resurrected body, how are we to conceive of the resurrected *mind*? Just as we have little idea of the full potentiality of matter, so we have little idea of the true capability of mind. Again, we must first acknowledge that we are currently experiencing our physical bodies by means of minds that are fundamentally ignorant about the ultimate nature of matter, that have great difficulty in reasoning without flaws, that are full of moral conflicts, and that often make choices blindly. The mind that engages with our bodily self every day—and from which our needs, cravings, and feelings arise—is not yet a perfected mind. It is a limited, suffering mind that interacts with its world through a limited, suffering body. Only as the mind becomes purified will we be able to imagine more clearly a refined type of body—a form of sanctified matter. Yet as our minds do learn to perceive matter itself differently, we might indeed begin to anticipate what Paul termed the "spiritual body."

Generally speaking, Church Fathers, apologists, and theologians did not ask what sort of radical transformations might take place in the mind or soul as persistently as they argued about the physical matter of the resurrected body. Perhaps that is because they considered the reunification of body and soul so essential to the identity of the individual person that they assumed that if the body was transformed by resurrection, then the mind or soul would be, too. The *whole person* would become inspirited by God. Nevertheless, it might be beneficial to explore some ways in which our resurrected mind will have to be changed; that is, we know it must become very different from the imperfect mind with which we function now. It cannot remain blind, ignorant, conflicted, burdened, and inclined to sinful thoughts if it is to enjoy the vision of God! Our limited mind must be illuminated through and through by the mind and spirit of Christ. Only a *divinized* mind would enable us to be fully suffused with the light of the Trinity and thus experience ourselves in a glorified, resurrected body.

Will such a "resurrected" mind retain continuity with the mind of the person who died? Indeed, at some level logic demands that it must be the same mind but, like the body, radically changed. Every aspect of our being must function differently, especially our mental capacity. There will be no obstacles to our seeing whatever God graces us to see, to hearing the Word spoken from the mouth of Christ, to speaking praise of the Blessed Trinity with our whole being. Our mind will expand to contemplate reality with divine wisdom; our love and compassion will become limitless. Our personal history, too, will be transformed. All the wholesome, creative works of the mind in this life will be made glorious in the next; our emotional and spiritual wounds will be healed; our precious memories will be preserved; our talents will be magnified; our soul's beauty will shine in radiance.

But if there is so much change, what ensures continuity? Perhaps continuity lies simply in the fact that we will remain within the same *continuum of mind*. In a philosophical context less focused on the material world and more on the indubitable experience of consciousness, it is easier to posit that the continuity of a person primarily means continuity of mind. Mind is always the organizing principle that enables our bodies to *appear* in a certain way in relation to the current state of our spirit, emotions, habitual perspectives, and conceptual constructs. Yet insofar as the mind continues beyond death and transforms beyond its current ordinary habits, the resurrected body that is accorded to it must appear as a visible, viable *reflection* of the purified nature of that resurrected mind—now freed of its limited perspectives and afflictions.

How do we know this? Because Paul wrote: "What is sown is perishable, what is raised is imperishable. It is sown in dishonor, it is raised in glory. It is sown in weakness, it is raised in power" (1 Cor 15:42–43). Like the body, the structure and functioning of the mind must be completely altered. Extending Paul's analogy, we might venture to add: What was blindness will become light; what was ignorance, wisdom; what was selfishness, unbounded love. Furthermore, what was failure will put on fulfillment; what was loss will become gain; what was mourning will be rejoicing; what was restriction will be liberated. We will be the same person but in an utterly new existence. And in this transformed spiritual mind/body we will be able to contemplate God-in-Trinity: "when he is revealed, we will be like him, for we will see him as he is" (1 John 3:2). In this "new creation" we will experience all creation through the mind of Christ. We will exist in the divine dimension of reality where God is all in all.

Illumination by Wisdom

In 2 Corinthians, Paul wrote that the same Creator God who said "Let light shine out of darkness" (Gen 1:3), shines in our hearts "to give the light of the knowledge of the glory of God in the face of Jesus Christ" (2 Cor 4:6). Ever since the dawn of light at the creation of the world was darkened by our fall into ignorance and sin, the deity has worked to dispel the inner darkness of our minds and to illuminate the heart of human beings with divine light. Paul tells the Corinthians that Moses, ablaze with the light of Yahweh, had to put a veil over his face "to keep the people of Israel from gazing at the end of the glory that was being set aside" because "their minds were hardened" (2 Cor 3:13–14). But "when one turns to the Lord, the veil is removed" (2 Cor 3:16). The potential for human perfection was made fully manifest in the mind of Jesus Christ, in whom we are able to recognize the radiance of the glory of God. Now we are emboldened by hope that "all of us, with unveiled faces" may contemplate "the glory of the Lord as though reflected in a mirror" (2 Cor 3:18). Through the arduous process of purification and growth that is the spiritual path we may be transformed into the true image of God that is Jesus Christ. Paul affirms that we can glimpse the meaning of divine revelation *even now*, by the light of the Holy Spirit.

The book of Wisdom lists twenty-one qualities associated with the Spirit of Wisdom (Greek, *sophia*):

> There is in her a spirit that is intelligent, holy,
> unique, manifold, subtle,
> mobile, clear, unpolluted,
> distinct, invulnerable, loving the good, keen,
> irresistible, beneficent, humane,
> steadfast, sure, free from anxiety,
> all-powerful, overseeing all,
> and penetrating through all spirits
> that are intelligent, pure, and altogether subtle. (Wis 7:22–23).

What could more perfectly describe the transformed *mind* that would correspond to a resurrected body! There is more:

> For wisdom is more mobile than any motion;
> because of her pureness she pervades and penetrates all things.
> For she is a breath of the power of God,
> and a pure emanation of the glory of the Almighty;
> therefore nothing defiled gains entrance into her.

For she is a reflection of eternal light,
a spotless mirror of the working of God,
and an image of his goodness. (Wis 7:24-26)

When we are fully infused with this divine wisdom, our mind will become illuminated by Christ's own mind, plunging ever more deeply into the nature of his own understanding and unconditional love. To quote Paul more fully:

And all of us, with unveiled faces, seeing the glory of the Lord as though reflected in a mirror, are being *transformed into the same image* from one degree of glory to another; for this comes from the Lord, the Spirit. (2 Cor 3:18, emphasis added)

Divinization

The entire process by which we are purified and then transformed by the energies of the Holy Spirit is, in both the Eastern Orthodox and Western Christian traditions, called *divinization* (Greek, *theosis*)—that is, "becoming divine." Through our initiation at baptism, in the celebration of Eucharist and through all the sacraments, as well as by the revelations of sacred Scripture, we receive a boundless outpouring of love and grace from the cross and resurrection of Jesus Christ. This is what effects our transformation. We are given new eyes of wisdom and new hearts of compassionate love. Of course our divinization does not happen all at once. It is an ongoing process, both on earth and in the life to come. Here and now, we experience it as a dual energy: a planting and a pruning; a seizing and a surrendering; a building up and a stripping down of all we think we are, want to be, or wish to accomplish. It is creative and exhilarating as well as full of frustration and failure. It is the burning of the wick of our heart's desire and the melting of the firm wax in which it is encased, until there is only the single flame of Christ the light. "He must increase but I must decrease" (John 3:30).

Divinization is the work of Christ's own Spirit within us. As the great Byzantine monk, St. Symeon the New Theologian (949–1022), wrote:

Even now the same power of the most Holy Spirit will come upon you . . . Your mind will see him in the form of a spiritual light with deep calm and joy. This light is the prelude of the eternal and primordial light; it is the reflected brightness of everlasting blessedness *(cf. Heb 1:3)*. When this appears every passionate thought will vanish and every passion of the soul be dispelled, and every bodily disease healed. Then the eyes of the heart are purified and see that which is written in the Beatitudes (cf. Mt. 5:8).... As [the soul] perceives the greatness of the glory it is filled with all joy and gladness; it is struck with amazement at this wonder beyond all hope and flows with tears as from fountains.[79]

Through the medium of sustained contemplative practice, such sublime illumination will reveal that which creates *the very possibility* for our everyday consciousness and existence to arise. Mystically speaking, this has often been termed the "ground of being," or the God who is closer to us than we are to ourselves. As Augustine testified in his *Confessions*: "Thou wast more inward to me than the most inward part of me; and higher than my highest reach."[80]

Even though the surface layers of our mental consciousness will collapse when our body dies and even though we will no longer be able to formulate a single thought, yet the divine mind of pure light—that subtlest illumination which dwells as the source of our existence and grounds our very ability to be *aware*—will carry our identity from this life into the next. This suggests that, when the time is fulfilled, *it would only be the very subtle wisdom of God within us that can generate our ever-so-subtle body of the resurrection.*

Ultimately, as fully transformed human beings who have passed from the dark corridor of death into the blazing light of new life, suffused by divine grace, we will receive a "spiritual body." This resurrected body will not be anything like the coarse body that corresponds to our coarse and limited states of mind in this present life. Wherever we are on the spiritual path of purification, illumination, and union at the moment of our death (and once our mind becomes completely beatified through the ongoing purifying process of our transition after death), the body accorded to us in resurrection will indeed have a kind of form that we cannot imagine now. But we can trust that this transformed body must be a *precise reflection of our transformed mind*—recreated by the light of God within us. Christ's resurrected body was in total continuity with the incarnate body of Jesus of Nazareth, yet it was also the perfect expression of his completed union with and exaltation by his Father. And just as Christ's resurrected body reflects the incomparable glory of the Trinity, so

79. Symeon the New Theologian, *The Discourses*, 236.

80. Augustine, *The Confessions*, 38.

our resurrected body will become the *visible* expression of our invisible, intangible union with God. Furthermore, even though the resurrected body will reach a state of perfection, unable to suffer, decay, or die, it will not be static. On the contrary, as Paul indicated, it will be eternally *dynamic*, moving "from one degree of glory to another" (2 Cor 3:18).

Matter as Shaped by Mind

Where do such contemplations leave us concerning the ancient questions of continuity and identity? It is clear by now that according to the principles of contemporary quantum physics, we can no longer suppose that individual particles of matter carry inherent "identity tags" in the way that the early theologians believed. Rather, as we have seen, particles cannot be precisely identified—whether in location or momentum—until they have been questioned, measured, or interrogated from a particular perspective. Whether or not it is yet acknowledged by some scientists in other fields, to engage in a process of measurement requires *consciousness*. Furthermore, quantum physics has begun to recognize the integral role that the consciousness of an observer plays, not only in identifying, but in *determining* the nature of the matter it observes. As the theoretical physicist Andrei Linde writes, "Without introducing an observer, we have a dead universe, which does not evolve in time. Does this mean that an observer is simultaneously a creator?"[81]

Taking such logic into our present context, we may consider: Does the continuity of identity required for a resurrected body to be the resurrection of *the same body* actually require a continuity of the "exact same atoms" that were present in the corpse—if atoms themselves are now understood to be such a fleeting and uncertain category of existence? Is it really so much a question of the identity of the atoms? Or rather is it a question of what continues within consciousness that observes, configures, and identifies those throbbing fields of energy as being "mine"?

Carrying the notion of quantum uncertainty to a spiritual level, might we not begin to envision how it is that the many variant states of mind that arise throughout our lifetime have always played an integral role in shaping and configuring the array of merely labeled "atoms" we experience and identify as "my body"? From our own experience,

81. Linde, "The Universe, Life, and Consciousness," 198.

we know how significantly our state of mind affects the way our physical organs function. Then all the more, how would a mind utterly transformed by the death process and infused by the divine grace that purifies us of all that blocks us from a divine kind of seeing, become capable of experiencing the infinite and subtle potentialities of matter in a new body? How might such a body accurately reflect the glorification of that transformed mind? Thinking in this way, we might accept that such a resurrected body will indeed be "our" spiritual body, intimately connected to the personal continuum of our mind, but now forming and shaping the infinite potentiality of matter into a subtle and extraordinary kind of body—one that is a perfectly suitable correlate to the twenty-one qualities of divine wisdom described above.

Paul's understanding of the spiritual body both preserves and transforms identity through our putting on "the mind of Christ." We become "emptied" of the false sense of ego and of grasping to the illusion of an "I" that exists independently of its Creator. We realize—and this is true wisdom—that we were never separated from the core reality of divine mind in the first place. Only our ignorance and stubborn ego made us think we were. By the light of divine wisdom we begin to comprehend how intimately we are always enclosed and enfolded in Trinity. The mind of pure light empowers us to love in and through its own divine love. Dwelling there more and more we become manifestations of Christ: true Christians.

The Doorway of Contemplation

Is it possible to experience a foretaste of this divine luminosity, this pure wisdom, this light of resurrection? Most certainly. From many different contemplative traditions, we may learn the art of entering into the silence and stillness that can expand the capacity of our mind. Some may immerse themselves in the "prayer of the heart," a teaching traced to the Desert Fathers, or else in the "Jesus Prayer" of Orthodox Christianity. Others may practice centering prayer, or focus single-pointedly on a visualized image of the Savior, or gain inner stillness by observing the fluctuations of the breath, or cut through the barrage of mental activity by reciting a sacred word or mantra in order to dwell ever more deeply within the intentions of the heart. In refined practices of contemplation we may sit silently in awe at the wonder of the divine knowing that encompasses all things in all times and places at once; that is the source and wellspring of all that lives, without itself experiencing change or alteration; that pours out the abundance of life with no loss to its own completeness. Under the guidance of knowledgeable and experienced teachers, we may explore different approaches to contemplative prayer until we find one that is most meaningful for us. Whatever form of practice we choose, we must first learn how to *still the mind* so that we may drop down into a sustainable silence and experience the divine presence with an ever more vivid and unshakable quality of awareness. Then it is essential that we gain *stability* in such a form of interior prayer.

Through the daily practice of contemplation, we may begin to see for ourselves that the continuity of our identity is not dependent on the material atoms of our flesh and bones or on the electrical impulses charging the synapses of our brain; nor is it bound up in the constant fluctuation of our emotions; nor is it contingent upon our sense of individuality, our accomplishments, or our failures. As we learn to meditate in ever greater silence and stillness, we become better able to watch our mind changing right before our "inner eye." Then we may grow more acutely aware of the supreme gift of simply *being aware*.

The Christic Mind

Over a long period of time, as we penetrate more deeply into the wonder of awareness, we may intuit the inescapable truth that God is creating us and all that we experience, moment by moment, breath by breath, heartbeat by heartbeat. We may realize that at the most profound level our personal identity comes from the Holy Spirit that sustains us in life, just as the same Spirit will carry us through our death and divinization process. Ultimately, our identity is the imprint of God's image and likeness on a mind and body. Thus the person we are at root is *God's* dynamic life in us. Nothing less. We are more than the sum of all our mental and physical parts: we are defined by the indwelling of the Spirit, the all-pervading presence of divine light, the still point within, the Christ-life in our souls. Eventually, we may be graced to recognize these sublime mysteries as the very ground and wellspring of our whole being. We may be led into an understanding of the inner light of wisdom, which has its origin in the mind of the Creator. We may also become capable of experiencing directly the *divine* awareness that is pure love. This is the love that reveals to us who we are. There and only there will our true identity be discovered—"hidden with Christ in God" (Col 3:3).

What our resurrected identity will actually look and feel like in the new heaven and the new earth, is, as we have acknowledged, beyond our mind's capacity to conceive right now. However, even according to accepted theological traditions, we need not think that our resurrected body has to be pieced back together bit by bit from the scattered remains left on earth or from trillions upon trillions of atoms circulating in the universe. Rather we can believe with confidence that it must proceed from the source of pure wisdom who has always dwelt within us, who alone knows the person we are and always have been, what our deepest identity is, and how our resurrected body will appear. This is the Christic mind and it is the *only* mind that will enable us to see God.

> *For now we see in a mirror, dimly,*
> *but then we will see face to face.*
> *Now I know only in part; then I will know fully,*
> *even as I have been fully known.* (1 Cor 13:12)

7

Living Resurrected Lives

ONE DAY WE WILL be hit with the stark realization that we are going to die. A medical diagnosis, a near-fatal accident, the passing of someone we love: any one of these may bring home the full reality of our own death. We experience anger, fear, and a sense of irreparable loss. We are forced to acknowledge our own mortality and it always comes as a shock. We are never quite prepared.

What may be even more shocking is the realization that we are going to live forever. When that existential reality opens up before us, we encounter a gaping void, a sudden plummeting into a vast unknown. It is strange, mysterious, full of questions and doubts; yet also deeply intriguing. In that moment of expanded awareness, we know that everything is different. We recognize that we must cease living as if there were no tomorrow or *only* tomorrow, and begin living as if we were going to live forever . . . because we are. We feel a new desire to let go of extraneous things, activities, even dreams that once seemed so imperative to our temporary happiness. We understand that unless the full scope of what it means to be resurrected among the saints becomes the primary focal point of our life as Christians, the idea of eternal life as supremely blissful will remain only a faint and even foolhardy wish. We must dare to embark on living now in anticipation of the reality that we hope awaits us.

The Divine Dimension

At the same time, we may wonder how we can begin to inhabit a divine dimension—that of the resurrected life—when we can barely cope with this mortal life. We realize all the more keenly how plagued we are by mental and emotional demons, complex family relationships, and personal problems. We struggle with work, health, financial, and social issues; plus the everyday distractions that prevent us from asking the big questions about ultimate meaning and destiny. Why not simply take it on faith that death is not the last word, give lip service to the idea of resurrection, and then go about our business as if nothing has changed?

We cannot afford that course of inaction. That would be tantamount to saying that Christ might not really have risen from the dead and so we have little hope of rising ourselves. On the contrary, if we do believe that Christ conquered death—not only his but our own death as well—and if we believe that he rose to new life for us, we can trust that whoever truly dies with him will also rise with him. Rather than leaving us complacent, such faith demands that in every day of our present life, *we must prepare for our future life*. It is what we were created for and what we were redeemed for at such great cost by Christ. To fail to be ready for the divine "wedding banquet" to which we are called would be the ultimate tragedy. To put off becoming clothed in the wedding garment of Christ's forgiveness and the cloak of eternal salvation would be utterly foolish (Matt 22:11–13). Jesus has warned us again and again in his parables of the kingdom that we must always be on the watch, fully aware, attentive, expectant, and ready for his sudden arrival: "Therefore, keep awake—for you do not know when the master of the house will come, in the evening, or at midnight, or at cockcrow, or at dawn, or else he may find you asleep when he comes suddenly. And what I say to you I say to all: Keep awake." (Mark 13:35–37)

We must be ever willing to be taken, ready to surrender everything we are and all those we love in order to become re-created in Christ: "Be dressed for action and have your lamps lit; be like those who are waiting for their master to return from the wedding banquet, so that they may open the door for him as soon as he comes and knocks" (Luke 12:35–36). And in times of great suffering or temptation, Christ urged his disciples in the garden of Gethsemane: "Stay awake and pray that you may not come into the time of trial; the spirit indeed is willing, but the flesh is weak" (Matt 26:41).

The exhortation to be watchful for death is an ancient Hebrew idea, common in the time of Jesus and beyond. At the end of the first century CE, a Palestinian theologian, Rabbi Eliezer, challenged his students:

> Repent one day before your death. His scholars asked him: How can a man know the day of his death? He answered them: Since he may die tomorrow, it is all the more necessary to repent today; thus all through his life he will be found in a state of penitence. Moreover, Solomon in his wisdom has said: "let thy garments be always white; and let not thy head lack ointment" (Eccles 9:8).[1]

The white garment is repentance; the ointment is the oil of salvation. We must put them on the day *before* our death, the day *before* we could ever expect to be called home to God. That means every single day. This is not a morbid way to live. On the contrary, it is liberating. Confessing our shortcomings and seeking divine mercy on a daily basis assures us of the fact that we are already forgiven everything (long before we even asked!). We are already God's beloved, in whom God rejoices every time we repent. We are already members of God's kingdom, which is present within and among us. Indeed, an awareness of the reality of death is a passport to the fullness of life. It frees us from focusing on so many petty concerns and conflicts over which we have no control. It enlarges the horizon of our minds and hearts to contemplate the big picture: that we are forever being created from the heart of divine love, learning how to love God and each other, that we may be utterly transformed and divinized by eternal love. Such an attitude grounds all our endeavors and animates all our energies. Only if we set our minds on being prepared for death can the hope and joy of a new resurrected life become a way of living. As mentioned earlier, Paul urges us to realize "that just as Christ was raised from the dead by the glory of the Father, so we too might walk in newness of life" (Rom 6:4). Paul directly links this foretaste of our own resurrection to the vibrant reality of Christ's resurrection.[2] But we do not have to wait until death to experience this "newness of life." We can do it every day! In truth, only if we begin living resurrected lives *here and now* will our faith in resurrection grow more certain and more empowering than ever before. The more we practice believing, the more we will believe.

1. See Jeremias, *The Parables*, 188.
2. Brown, *An Introduction to the New Testament*, 613, n29.

Does this mean we have to give up focusing on our work and striving to realize our very human dreams? Of course not. While we are on this earth, we must be fully committed to creating, exploring, and experiencing every aspect of our God-given life. We must be completely dedicated to the human effort and to bringing some measure of God's kingdom of justice, peace, mercy, and love to this earth in our own lifetime. We must also be totally involved in nurturing and supporting one another. No one lives, dies, or is saved alone. The fact is that by seeking to live a risen life in Christ more and more deeply each day, we may also find ourselves able to bring greater compassion and determination to the full range of our *earthly* commitments. We may become wiser, calmer, more centered, more balanced, and more hope-filled in handling the ups and downs and even the tragedies of our existence. We may grow more accustomed to seeing everything that has happened in our life story, that is happening right now, and that does *not* happen, *from a divine perspective.* This is because we believe—with a conviction that no one and nothing can shake—that every precious memory, every joy, every love, everything beautiful that fades or young that grows old, is constantly being revivified by the power of Christ's own resurrection. Indeed, the whole creation will be renewed and transformed by the resurrection. That is the promise. Believing this is the foundation for living in a resurrection mentality.

Preparing for Heaven

How can we actively prepare for a resurrected life in heaven through the life we live now on earth? Paul has assured us that those who believe in Jesus Christ have received his own Spirit:

> Now we have received not the spirit of the world, but the Spirit that is from God, so that we may understand the gifts bestowed on us by God. And we speak of these things in words not taught by human wisdom but taught by the Spirit, interpreting spiritual things to those who are spiritual. Those who are unspiritual do not receive the gifts of God's Spirit, for they are foolishness to them, and they are unable to understand them because they are spiritually discerned. Those who are spiritual discern all things, and they are themselves subject to no one else's scrutiny. "For who has known the mind of the Lord so as to instruct him?" But we have the mind of Christ. (1 Cor 2:12–16)

Reading these words, we may wonder: How can we be sure that we act from "the Spirit that is from God" and that we understand and speak of God's gifts "in words not taught by human wisdom"? How can we be certain that we are not unspiritual or foolish, but are able to discern things that are spiritual and not of this world? In short, how do we gain this "mind of Christ"? Paul taught that it is through the practice of the virtues of faith, hope, and love—along with total trust in divine grace and devotion to service—that we may come to know the mind of Christ and thus begin even now to live our lives as a resurrected people. Then we may say with Paul: "it is no longer I who live, but it is Christ who lives in me" (Gal 2:20).

Living Faith

First of all, we must feed on *faith*—not the kind of faith that is professed glibly, without thinking, or that does not involve a daily commitment and sometimes, great risk; not the kind of faith that is worn as a badge of belonging to a certain community or that represents a way of thinking that fits nicely into one's own preexistent mind-set; not the kind of faith that incessantly debates pros and cons of belief, as if faith could ever be proven by rational deductions; not the kind of faith that is easily swayed by current trends toward alternative versions of Christ's bodily resurrection as though it were merely a fictional metaphor for the "spiritual rejuvenation" that takes place in our hearts and makes us feel good to be Christians; not even the kind of faith that resides solely in creedal pronouncements and strictly adheres to prescribed traditions; and finally, not the kind of faith that easily believes when things go just as we like but falls apart when trials and tribulations occur.

Paul wrote that "we have come to believe in Christ Jesus, so that we might be justified by faith in Christ" (Gal 2:16). This faith is a vibrant, demanding, and down-to-earth faith that is *lived*; one that is rooted so deeply in our inmost being that it informs and transforms every aspect of our daily existence. This is the faith that relies on the wisdom of the heart more than the reasoning of the mind. This is the faith that is expectant and attentive, that listens for and to the inspiration of the Spirit. This is the faith that in times of accomplishment and celebration, loving and sharing, creativity and success attributes it all to Christ as the source of divine ebullience—certain beyond doubt that such experience will never be forgotten and never end because *joy* is a sign and a promise of the bliss that springs eternal. This is the faith that is not afraid of challenge, of change, even of being severely tested, because it relies solely on the strength of the Spirit. This is the faith that prays for everything, for nothing is deemed too small or too great to ask for help with, or guidance about, or forgiveness for, or divine presence at, or a blessing on.

This is the faith that God is the very *ground* of one's being; that therefore the Holy Spirit must be existentially present within the soul or mind. This is the faith that trusts God cares about everything and everyone we care about immeasurably more than we ever could. This is the faith we hold onto in the sleepless dark night of fear and worry and that we finally drop into out of sheer exhaustion and childlike trust. This is the faith we cling to in the numbness of terror when someone we love is delirious and near death and we pray that God—closer to us than our own fears—will help us through the desperation of the situation. This is the faith that believes every adversity can be turned around and transformed, even and especially when all the odds are against it, because "nothing will be impossible with God" (Luke 1:37). This is the faith that never gives up pleading and that offers abundant thanksgiving in advance for whatever the outcome of prayer will be, trusting that God will reveal a solution or bring about a resolution in the best way possible. This is the faith that moves mountains of worry because it is confident that the Holy Spirit operates within all the unsolved mysteries of our lives.

This is the faith that knows that if only we could see the world through the eyes of Jesus Christ, we would understand that by his cross and resurrection, he has *already* initiated the new kingdom of God; it is already a reality and fully operative. This is the faith that is fed by Scripture and sacrament, that is continually nourished by meditation on Christ's declaration that *even now*, "the kingdom of God has come to you" (Matt 12:28; Luke 11:20). This is the unshakable faith that no matter how dire facts may appear on the ground, the reign of God is breaking into our lives in visible and invisible ways; the victory of God over sin and suffering is very near. As Jesus bore witness to the disciples of John of Baptist: "the blind receive their sight, the lame walk, the lepers are cleansed, the deaf hear, the dead are raised, the poor have good news brought to them" (Luke 7:22). In reference to this passage, it is worth recognizing that:

According to the thinking of the time, the situation of such men was no longer worth calling life: in effect, they were dead. But now help is extended to those in the depths of despair, now those who were as good as dead are raised to life. The water of life flows, the time of the curse is at an end, paradise is opened. Even now, *the consummation of the world is dawning.*[3]

This is the faith that believes that all debts have been cancelled and former sinners are called into the eternal banquet of salvation; the bridegroom is eager to share his table fellowship; the darkness of the house has been dispelled by the light of the divine lamp; the new wine is being poured out; the finest robe, ring, and sandals are being put on prodigal sons and daughters; the fields are ripe for the harvest; the fig tree puts forth new shoots signaling the eternal springtime; prisoners are being set free, the lost are being found, the mistreated are receiving comfort; the bread and water of eternal life are being given to children; justice is being granted to the poor and downtrodden; and the peace-filled reign of God has already begun.[4]

This is the faith that *sees through* times of darkness, doubt, and discouragement with the firm conviction that the light will break in eventually, the heavy stone that covers our hearts will be rolled away, and divine presence will reveal itself—because no darkness, no tragedy, no death, and no tomb can ever withstand the radiant and transformative light of the risen Lord. This is the vibrant certainty that the time for living Christ's resurrected life is here and now. This is faith on fire.

John the Evangelist attested that "to all who received him, who *believed* in his name, he gave power to become children of God" (John 1:12, emphasis added). Those who are fully committed to faith in Christ's life, death, resurrection, and ongoing mission in the world, are granted wisdom to perceive the good and grace to choose it. Paul exhorted the Christians in Rome, "Do not be conformed to this world, but be transformed by the renewing of your minds, so that you may discern what is the will of God—what is good and acceptable and perfect" (Rom 12:2). Every act of faith we make helps to transform and conform us more and more to the mind of Christ, his single-pointed intentionality, which is to accomplish the loving will of his Father. For us, it is an ongoing process that will be completed only in eternity.

3. Jeremias, *New Testament Theology*, 104–5, emphasis in original.

4. Jeremias, *New Testament Theology*, 105–7, 113–14.

Just as the courageous faith of the first disciples and martyrs was the best proof of the reality of Christ's resurrection from the dead, so the way in which we live our lives now is the most convincing testimony in our own age that "the Lord is risen." Our personal transformation from doubt to faith and from fear to fearlessness testifies that the Spirit of the risen Lord is truly alive within us. Yet there is even more at stake than our own transformation: *there is the future of faith itself.* Unless we believe and are willing to bear witness to that belief with passionate commitment, who will testify to the reality of Christ's resurrection? Unless we believe, who will commemorate the Last Supper and receive the body and blood of Christ in Eucharist? Who will follow Jesus to Calvary and stand at the foot of his cross? Who will venture out in the morning darkness to discover that the tomb is empty? Who will run to tell the other disciples? Who will walk on the road to Emmaus? Who will await his appearance in the upper room? Who will recognize the Lord on the shore of the lake? Who will forgive sins and bear the good news of salvation to the whole world? Who will stand up to our detractors and pray for our persecutors? The fact is that *unless we believe*, the story of Christ as revealed in the Gospels will become irrelevant words written on ancient papyrus. His life, death, and resurrection will carry no salvific meaning to our generation and the next.

However, *when we believe*, there is no limit to what our faith can accomplish. That is why living resurrected lives on fire with faith matters so much, not only to us and to our families, but to the whole world. Pierre Teilhard de Chardin wrote of this transformative faith:

> If we do not believe, the waves engulf us, the winds blow, nourishment fails, sickness lays us low or kills us, the divine power is impotent or remote. If, on the other hand, we believe, the waters are welcoming and sweet, the bread is multiplied, our eyes open, the dead rise again, the power of God is, as it were, drawn from Him by force and spreads throughout all nature. One must either arbitrarily minimize or explain away the Gospel, or one must admit the reality of these effects not as transient and past, but as perennial and actually true.[5]

In the fullness of faith lies the core of our faithfulness.

---

5. Teilhard de Chardin, *The Divine Milieu*, 115.

Daring Hope

A hopeful heart springs directly from a living faith. This is not the hope that everything we wish for will turn out as we would like; nor is it the hope that we will be spared times of trial and suffering, or that we will not be hurt, rejected, or left alone. It is the hope that the person we believe in, Jesus Christ, loved us enough to humble himself and become a human being; lived to teach us how to live and died to show us how to surrender our own lives obediently in death. In so doing, Christ overcame the deadliness of death and turned it into the passage to new life. This is the confident hope that the same Christ will keep his promise to be with us until the end of time, never to leave us orphans, and to give us his own peace that the world cannot give. It is the hope that we really will see him in his resurrected glory.

This certain hope for the future informs everything that happens, good or bad, in our lives right now. Because we live in the Spirit, Christ can be known, loved, and experienced in every situation; in the elation of every joy, in the depths of every sorrow, in the crisis of every need. This is the outrageous hope that defies human logic and anticipates the possibility of dire events being utterly transformed by divine compassion. If Christ overcame death, he can conquer anything! This is the hope that dares us to live for what we cannot yet envision: a future existence without sin, suffering, sadness, or death, when God will wipe every tear from our eyes, and "death will be no more; mourning and crying and pain will be no more" (Rev 21:4). Paul was convinced that the whole of creation "waits with eager longing the revealing of the children of God" (Rom 8:19). There is hope-filled expectation in the sprouting of a seed, the growth of a plant, and the rising of a tree. Likewise, there is hopefulness in the commitment to love, in the act of reproduction, in artistic creativity, in a life of dedication, in a moment of inspiration.

Yet we must be realistic. We are only too aware that everything we undertake has its element of frustration, disillusionment, and sometimes, failure. This is because creation was "subjected to futility" (Rom 8:20) as a result of human sinfulness. Whatever we create will deteriorate; whatever we enjoy does not last; whoever we love must pass away. And all around us, we see signs of destruction and dissolution. What are we to make of this? Jesus warned his disciples (and us) that the kingdom would only become reality through suffering. There would be "wars and rumors of wars"; "nation will rise against nation, and kingdom against kingdom;

there will be earthquakes in various places; there will be famines. This is but the beginning of the birth pangs" (Mark 13:5–8). Even though we hope in salvation, we must expect persecution, being handed over to our enemies, even being betrayed by those we have loved and trusted. But Jesus reassured us that "the one who endures to the end will be saved" (Mark 13:13).

No matter how dangerous our personal or world situation might become, there is always hope in the ground, both of the earthly soil and the human heart: "hope that the creation itself will be set free from its bondage to decay and will obtain the freedom of the glory of the children of God" (Rom 8:20–21). We must always hope for the end of our suffering mortality; we must always hope to be liberated from the stranglehold of evil. And we must always hope that there is a divine purpose working within and through the events of our lives. Paul intuited that the entire cosmos is like a woman in labor, suffering not as a helpless victim, but *in order to give birth:*

> We know that the whole creation has been groaning in labor pains until now; and not only the creation, but we ourselves, who have the first fruits of the Spirit, groan inwardly while we wait for adoption, the redemption of our bodies. (Rom 8:22–23)

All creation is changing, evolving, striving endlessly to reach its completion in the fullness of divine intention. Those who live in the Spirit ache to be adopted into Christ's resurrection and to witness the transformation of their mortal bodies. We may be certain that hope will be fulfilled, "for in hope we were saved" (Rom 8:24). Christ himself hoped for our salvation and it was his hope for us that inspired him to give his life to realize this hope.

Too often, maintaining hope seems hard; sometimes even impossible. Too often, we wait, we suffer, we hope, and we do not see any results from our hoping. Yet Paul reminds us that "hope that is seen is not hope. For who hopes for what is seen?" (Rom 8:24). If we already possessed all that we hope for, if we were already *in* our resurrected bodies, and if we were already fully living our resurrected life in Christ, we would not have to hope for it. "But if we hope for what we do not see, we wait for it with patience" (Rom 8:25). Hope must strive in faith toward what cannot be seen. And for this we must develop enduring patience; not in what *we* can accomplish, but in what God and God alone can and will accomplish in us, through us, and for us. No hardship, no sin, no suffering, no defeat, and no death are too great for Christ's triumphant power and abiding love to overcome:

> For I am convinced that neither death, nor life, nor angels, nor rulers, nor things present, nor things to come, nor powers, nor height, nor depth, nor anything else in all creation, will be able to separate us from the love of God in Christ Jesus our Lord. (Rom 8:38–39)

Radical Love

Sometimes, in spite of a living faith and daring hope, we feel plunged into darkness. What keeps us going? Love, a radical love. What is such a love like? In his panegyric to love, Paul tells us:

> Love is patient; love is kind; love is not envious or boastful or arrogant or rude. It does not insist on its own way; it is not irritable or resentful; it does not rejoice in wrongdoing, but rejoices in the truth. It bears all things, believes all things, hopes all things, endures all things. (1 Cor 13:4–7)

This love does not come from mere physical attraction, intellectual admiration, or human emotion. This is the love inspired by divine love itself. That is why such love learns to be patient and kind. That is why it can let go of envious thoughts or boasting about one's own accomplishments. On the contrary, such expansive love looks for ways to encourage and bolster the *other* person. It eschews arrogance or rudeness. It seeks only to serve, empower, and spread more love. It is outgoing, creative, and joyous. It is collaborative and works well with others for the common good. It is not set in its ways but always willing to be challenged, to learn, to grow. It is not short-tempered or easily angered. It allows irritating situations to pass over and, by its calm and centered disposition, imparts peacefulness in a crisis. Such love does not feed on gossip nor does it enjoy seeing other people fail, even those who have been obstructive. It prays for their healing, their reconciliation, their transformation. This love does not tell lies or flatter or use people for its own advancement. It rejoices in the truth, always and everywhere.

Such love may be gentle and meek, but it is strong and has been tested by fire. Thus it has learned to bear all things (however difficult this may be) because it believes firmly that divine love will eventually make all things well. Such love is impartial; it does not associate only with people it prefers, people who are similar, but reaches out to embrace the "other," the stranger, those on the margins of society. Such love is not easily dismayed by harsh words, rejection, even betrayal, implying a readiness to forgive both friend and foe without discrimination. This love hopes and prays that God's "will be done" in all circumstances, because it is absolutely certain that divine will is pure love. This love even extends to forgiving enemies and praying for persecutors, because they, too, are children of God. This love is able to bear whatever hardships and tragedies may occur, again because love comes from the grace of God and, like the ocean itself, it is the reality that sustains the human heart through every storm.

Paul goes on to say that this love will never end. Prophecies will end; special gifts such as speaking in tongues will cease; even our hard-won knowledge will end. This is because now we only know a part of the whole truth; we prophesy a part; "when the complete comes, the partial will come to an end" (1 Cor 13:10). When we were children, we babbled like a child, thought like a child, and reasoned like a child (and thought we knew so much as a child!). But when we came into adulthood, we had to put an end to our childish and self-centered ways of seeing and understanding. Nevertheless, insofar as we are ignorant of the divine dimension that is the ground of reality, we see the world through the cloudy, stained mirror of our own mind. We assume that everything and everyone exists, acts, and reacts exactly as we perceive them. But we are only seeing the world and the people in it according to the way our mind is able to perceive and judge at any given moment. Most of the time, because of our limited understanding and our past history of selfishness, we perceive wrongly; we are sorely mistaken, we make poor judgments. Thus even the wisest person among us is merely a child in terms of true wisdom. We have no idea what will be revealed to us—first through the path of mystical contemplation in this life and finally in the resurrection. It will only be in the blazing light of God that we will know the truth of all things, especially ourselves. Then we will perceive the divine radiance in which we were created, in which we lived, died, and are destined to live forever. We will finally understand how much we have always been known, forgiven, and loved by God. In that is our salvation.

Paul concludes his hymn of praise to love with the words: "And now faith, hope, and love abide, these three; and the greatest of these is love" (1 Cor 13:13). Why is love the greatest? Because it is a reflection of God who is divine love. We need to fall in love with God and rejoice that God's love is boundless and unconditional. Divine love is not dependent on how good we are; rather, we are good because divine love makes us so. This is all we may bring with us into eternity: our love. It is the only reality that lasts.

Total Trust

Throughout the Gospels, Christ tells his disciples: "Do not be afraid," "Do not worry," "Fear not," and "Peace to you." Next to faith, hope, and love, it seems that trust is what Christ wanted most for us: trust that he was taking care of us so that we could be at peace in our hearts. It sounds so easy . . . until it is hard. Why is this? Because we want to hold on to what we love at the human level and we want to be sure here and now, without having to trust. Yet, at its foundation, trust demands the total surrender to God of everything we are, everyone we love, everything we have ever worked for in our lives. To be relieved of the fear of losing everything, we have to give up everything, both in prayer and in action. We also have to loosen our grip and renounce "being in control" of what happens in our lives and the lives of our loved ones. We may have to endure long periods of doubt and near-despair, repeatedly letting go in trust that the "dark uncertain" is pulsating with divine presence. We may have to learn that walking in blind trust is, in fact, the *only* way to see. No matter how bad the crisis, we must trust with all our might that Christ *is* at work: "From the beginning I have not spoken in secret, from the time it came to be I have been there" (Isa 48:16). Like the disciples in the storm-tossed boat at sea, we may have to hang on for dear life until we experience Christ walking towards us on the very waves of our fear, telling us, "Take heart, it is I; do not be afraid" (Matt 14:27; Mark 6:50; John 6:20).

Trust is not something we do once and for all. With each new situation, we must learn to trust all over again. We throw ourselves on the mercy of God; we trust that our sins are forgiven, that our efforts are of value, and that our life has a deeper and everlasting meaning, no matter how many times we are dealt an unexpected blow or our temporary dreams fall apart. As with every virtue, we recognize that, in order to trust, we need a fresh infusion of grace from the Holy Spirit. We cannot even trust on our own! Yet the more we practice trusting in little things and large, the more we will experience the joy of having trusted in the depths of darkness when the light returns. We will also begin to understand that those we love so dearly and surrender in trust to God can never be taken away, for everyone and everything has been given to us by divine love in the first place. All our loves are sustained in God's love and they will be restored in God's love. When we are at home in eternity, we will no longer need to trust, for we shall see all our loves glorified in the consummate love of God. Then we may be sure that we will receive abundant thanks from Christ for having trusted when we could not see.

Devotion to Service

In the Gospel of Mark, Jesus is quoted as saying: "For the Son of Man came not to be served but to serve, and to give his life [as] a ransom for many" (Mark 10:45; Matt 20:28). Throughout his ministry, Jesus not only talked about the kingdom of God, he made that kingdom a reality. He cast out demons and performed countless miracles of healing; he comforted, he forgave, he reassured. Christ's unconditional love blazed out from the depths of his being; whether blessing little children, touching lepers, or eating with the rich, the poor, and the outcast. There was no one he would not stop and listen to; no one he would not go out of his way to help or heal. His entire life was one of devoted service to God's children, his own sisters and brothers. At the Last Supper, Jesus got down on his knees and washed the feet of his disciples, including the very man who had already betrayed him, the one who would deny knowing him, as well as the others who would abandon him that same night. When he had finished, he told them:

> "Do you know what I have done to you? You call me Teacher and Lord—and you are right, for that is what I am. So if I, your Lord and Teacher, have washed your feet, you also ought to wash one another's feet. For I have set you an example, that you also should do as I have done to you. Very truly, I tell you, servants are not greater than their master, nor are messengers greater than the one who sent them. If you know these things, you are blessed if you do them. (John 13:12–17)

To live a resurrected life here and now means choosing a life of service in imitation of Christ. We follow his example when we care for our families, friends, and larger communities; when we support and encourage those with whom we work and play; when we go out of our way to serve the poor, the hungry, the sick; and when we console the brokenhearted. We do not differentiate between those who will thank us and those who will thwart us. There should be no one we refuse to serve by our love and acts of kindness, patience, and caring. Of course, we cannot be of service unless we are guided and strengthened by the grace of God. Unfortunately, there are some whose current actions are so harmful that it would be wrong for our service to aid and abet them in accomplishing those deeds. Such a situation must be discerned carefully. Still we can always serve them at a deeper level through our prayer that their hearts may be transformed, and that their evil intentions might be reversed and vanish altogether. And when we face inevitable obstacles in our efforts to serve at many different levels, Paul assures us that "suffering produces endurance, and endurance produces character, and character produces hope, and hope does not disappoint us, because God's love has been poured into our hearts through the Holy Spirit that has been given to us" (Rom 5:3–5). In serving others, even in limited ways, we anticipate our life-after-death when we will become of incomparable benefit to those still on earth. And when the fullness of resurrection is realized, then we will see that every little thing that we did in service for someone else, we did for Christ (Matt 25:40). And every little thing that someone else ever did for us in service was Christ serving us. Finally, when we are transformed into the resurrected body, we will be fully Christ for one another.

Eucharistic Transformation

Yet we may ask: how are we to gain the graces we need to make Christ's resurrection—as well as the promise of our own—the vibrant reality of our lives? Through the liturgy of the Eucharist. Every time we celebrate the eucharistic banquet, we remember and re-enact the sacrifice of Christ's death on the cross and rejoice in his glorious resurrection. We bring our simple but heartfelt offerings of bread and wine—"fruit of the earth and work of human hands . . . fruit of the vine and work of human hands"[6]— to place on the altar. These gifts are the material representations of each one of *us*; the love, the work, and the service we pour out each day, as well as the frustrations, exhaustion, and sufferings we endure in the process.

6. From the Liturgy of the Eucharist, available at: www.catholic-resources.org/ChurchDocs/Mass.htm#Eucharist.

By the hands of the priest, we offer these precious and costly symbols of ourselves to the Father for the remission of sins and in gratitude for all God's gifts. The priest calls upon the Holy Spirit to bless our material and spiritual offerings. Then, by the words of consecration—"This is my body," "This is my blood"—which recall the words Jesus himself spoke at the Last Supper, the bread and wine become the mystical reality of the Savior. Before our eyes of faith, our humble but meaningful offerings are utterly transformed. While there is no discernible change in the material elements, we believe that *the personal identity of the resurrected Christ* is now present in and through the visible bread and wine. Then, in receiving the bread and wine, we each share in the reality of Christ's presence, as did the disciples at the Last Supper.

In the eucharistic banquet, Jesus gave new meaning to an ancient Hebrew ritual of blessing:

> The procedure in grace before the meal was (as the disciples knew from their childhood onwards) that the head of the house took a loaf of bread, spoke the blessing and gave a piece of the bread to everyone sitting at table, so that by eating of bread each might share in the blessing on the meal. The same thing happened with the cup after the meal. If wine was drunk (which happened only on special occasions, though it was prescribed for the Passover meal), the head of the house spoke the grace over the cup; by passing round the cup all those at table shared in the blessing after the meal. Now Jesus added to the blessing before and after the meal the words of interpretation which explained the bread and the wine as a reference to himself, as the eschatological passover lamb dying for others. The only way in which the disciples could understand this was to believe that with the bread and the wine Jesus was promising them a share in the atoning power of his death. This intention of *personal dedication* may have been the reason why Jesus repeated the words of interpretation in the grace. Each of the disciples was to know that Jesus promised him personally a share in his representative death.[7]

As twenty-first-century disciples, when we eat this bread and drink this cup, we also have a share in the redemptive power of the Lord's death and resurrection. We become active participants in the work of the Savior. We breathe anew the life of Christ's own Spirit. Thus at every Eucharist, the entire drama of our salvation is re-lived from beginning to end.

7. Jeremias, *New Testament Theology*, 291–92.

Moreover, at every Eucharist, we utter the cry of salvation: "Hosanna! Blessed is he who comes in the name of the Lord!" With these words, we anticipate the second coming of Christ at the *parousia* and our own jubilant resurrection from death to life. We look forward to the heavenly banquet, at which Christ will preside as Lord and King over a new creation. Eucharist is Christ's promise that, through the working of the Holy Spirit, our personal identity will be clothed in a gloriously resurrected form. We will receive bodies that can bear being illuminated by the all-consuming life, love, and light of God. On earth we function according to a time/space continuum, unable to defy the laws of gravity and entropy. In the divine realm, there is no time, space, gravity, disorder, or decay. We will be fully animated by the Holy Spirit. We will radiate the light of Christ, not physical light waves, but the *divine* light of wisdom and love. We will not age. The cells of our resurrected body will not die in order for more cells to be born. Yet we will not be static, as that would render us unable to learn or grow or become ever more deeply imbued with the life of God. Rather, the bodily life we experience will be a perfect expression of the wisdom and love, joy and thanksgiving that fill our mind and heart. Will our heart beat? Yes, if Christ's heart does; though not as the heart labors now but rather energized by the pulsing of love. Will we breathe? It seems so. The disciples were breathed on by the resurrected Christ in the upper room and received the Holy Spirit. Indeed, even now, every breath we breathe is a gift of God—the same "breath" that spread over the primal waters and breathed life into Adam and gave life to our bodies at birth. But in the resurrected life we will breathe the breath of the Holy Spirit. We will be wherever inspired thought chooses to take us. In the divine dimension, we will finally become incorporated as full members of Christ's mystical body, celebrating the unity of the children of the resurrection in the greatest possible joy. In short, *we will be transformed* from a mortal union of body, mind, and soul into a whole new and immortal creation:

> "What no eye has seen, nor ear heard, nor the human heart conceived, what God has prepared for those who love him"— these things God has revealed to us through the Spirit; for the Spirit searches everything, even the depths of God. (1 Cor 2:9–10).

Making the Resurrection Real

Quite possibly, the Gospels were written not only to tell the story of Jesus' life, death, and resurrection, but also to inspire early Christians to recognize *their own stories* of meeting Jesus on the road, the mountaintop, in the garden, in the house. For our part, we may lament that we do not have the privilege of following Jesus for three years or more, day in and day out, of seeing him work miracles, forgive sinners, and heal the broken-hearted. We cannot witness him walk on water or multiply loaves and fishes. We cannot peer into his tomb and find it empty of death and full of light. We cannot experience the risen Christ directly. Or can we? Might there be a way to enter into the resurrection appearances so intimately that they could become as real for us as they were for the first disciples? And every bit as empowering?

In addition to the eucharistic liturgy and the practice of the virtues of faith, hope, love, and trust—as well as our daily lives of service to one another—there is indeed a powerful method by which we may come to experience the resurrection of Christ as a living reality: through the daily practice of meditation. This is what Christian contemplatives have been doing for two thousand years. It is never enough to study the Scriptures intellectually; it is essential that we *reflect* on them in order to personalize and internalize them. We may do this through a daily practice of *lectio divina*—divine reading—in which we read a Gospel passage and then reflect on it slowly, quietly, and prayerfully.

We may also go deeper into the stories of Christ's life, death, and resurrection through the medium of *imaginative meditation*. We may place ourselves physically in the gospel scenes. For example, in the resurrection appearances, we may create the time of day, the sight of the empty tomb, the fragrance of spring blossoms in the garden before dawn, the taste of the dust on the dirt road to Emmaus, the touch of the blessed bread, the sound of the Sea of Galilee lapping against the shore, the smell of fish cooking on a charcoal fire. We may ask questions of Mary Magdalene and the other women at the tomb, questions of Peter and the Beloved Disciple, questions of the disciples in the upper room. We may inquire what they were most afraid of, what they hoped for, when exactly they came to believe in the risen Lord and why. We may immerse ourselves in the process of spiritual transformation that the Gospel characters experienced and allow ourselves to feel what they may have felt when the Lord appeared to them in his glorified body.

Our imagination has an extraordinary ability to place ourselves in dramatic scenes, envision the characters, hear the spoken dialogue, and enter into the emotional dynamics of the situation. By creating a vivid scenario, the stories come alive for us; we can experience them in a more intimate way, virtually but also virtuously. As we learn how to do this, we enter more and more fully into the Gospel scenes, no longer mere spectators but active participants, as if we had been there at the time they actually occurred. The resurrection appearances may begin to feel like our own personal stories of coming to faith. Soon, we will want to rest in our favorite resurrection story—allowing it to surround us, flow through us, transform us, all the while being bathed in the radiant light of Christ's outpouring of love. We will believe more deeply not because we have been told to believe, but because we ourselves have been graced by a personal encounter with the resurrected Lord.

The human mind is also capable of stillness and silence. Over time, our imaginative meditations may lead to a desire for the inner quiet of *contemplative prayer*. We may feel inspired to release all images, thoughts, and questions. We may cease using any words at all to pray. Then we wish only to be silent, aware of breathing in union with the breath of the Holy Spirit. We may long to enter into an ever deeper stillness of pure awareness—simply watching the flow of thoughts and feelings, without grasping onto any of them. Then we may more willingly surrender to the divinizing work of the Holy Spirit in our soul, content with doing nothing at all. There, in the depth of silence, we may finally experience the peace that the world cannot give and cannot take away. In that peace, we may be assured that the resurrected Christ *already* lives within us and that we *already* live our resurrected lives within him. Then we may say with Mary Magdalene: "I have seen the Lord" (John 20:18).

> *"I am the resurrection and the life.*
> *Those who believe in me, even though they die, will live,*
> *and everyone who lives and believes in me will never die.*
> *Do you believe this?"* (John 11:25–26)

PART TWO

A Contemplative Practice

By Eva Natanya

1

Preparing to Meditate

JESUS SAID TO HIS disciples, "But whenever you pray, go into your room and shut the door and pray to your Father who is in secret; and your Father who sees in secret will reward you" (Matt 6:6). The spiritual logic is simple. If we have any hope of coming to live a resurrected life, we must do our part in developing an ever more intimate relationship with the Lord, the very one in whose *life* we wish to share. If we can recognize that all our current problems are ultimately a result of our deep-seated spiritual blindness, then we must gradually learn to see ourselves and each other with the mind of Christ. If all the negativity that festers within our subconscious and causes us to harm others, even in the slightest way, is a result of our failing to understand how and *by whom* reality is created in every moment, then we must strive to discover the supreme reason for loving our neighbor as ourselves. And this discovery can only be made in the silent depths of our own hearts.

If we wish to break through to the divine light within, to glimpse the true source of all things, then we must make that inner journey our first priority, every day. Consider for a moment how you manage to make time and mental space for all the things you do in any given day. There are many activities that we perform out of sheer habit or necessity, such as eating, sleeping, bathing, and so on. Other activities may be very deliberate, a result of powerful decisions that we made in the past. For example, think about how you first learned to perform all the tasks at which you are now proficient. Don't take anything for granted. How did you learn to read, to write, to use a computer, to drive, or do any of the things you get paid to do? Was there not some point at which you had to start learning each skill, after which you went about practicing it on a daily or near-daily basis, perhaps for many years, until you became very good at it? On the days when you didn't feel like continuing your training, what motivated you to persevere?

Behavioral psychologists tell us that it takes thousands of repetitions to learn a new skill, and thousands more repetitions to change an old habit. We can all find support for this idea in our life experience. What is perhaps not so obvious to us is that it is the same in the spiritual life. It is not that God is infinitely far away, or that heavenly things are simply impossible for us to understand. It is that our minds are beclouded by bad habits and mental afflictions, the tendency to grasp onto that which cannot really satisfy us, but which then gets in the way of our being able to experience divine inspiration. The fact is that divine reality *is* much harder to perceive than our walls or floors or breakfast table or bed. Thus, rather than leaving our spirituality at the periphery of our "real lives," we must put even greater effort into learning the techniques by which we may draw closer to God—even greater effort than we may have put into learning the kinds of skills that come naturally to human beings in a fallen world. Furthermore, we must be willing to practice such spiritual exercises on a daily basis for the rest of our lives. If we devote enough time to contemplation, if we are patient with ourselves, and if we have proper training and personal guidance, then it is inevitable that we will come to perceive divine realities that most of the world cannot yet see. This is the first step to living genuinely resurrected lives.

Many people think that saints are a chosen few, singled out by God to be channels of divine grace. This may be true, but perhaps many of the saints received revelation simply because they were especially stubborn in their longing, deeply persistent in their seeking. Jesus tells us:

> "Ask, and it will be given to you; search and you will find; knock and the door will be opened for you. For everyone who asks receives, and everyone who searches finds, and for everyone who knocks, the door will be opened. Is there anyone among you who, if your child asks for bread, will give a stone? Or if the child asks for a fish, will give a snake? . . . how much more will your Father in heaven give good things to those who ask him!" (Matt 7:7–11)

Nevertheless, some of us may argue that we have been searching for years, asking with all our hearts, and yet our lives are still filled with pain and disappointment, and the world is still falling apart all around us. We feel no closer to the God we seek. Yet if only we could see things from the divine point of view, perhaps we would know that our efforts have not been in vain, that each step was absolutely necessary in healing our own particular wounds, in purifying our hearts and minds, and in bringing our own path to fruition. For it is crucial to realize that every single thing we are called to do on the spiritual path is for *our* sake, not because the already perfect Lord of heaven and earth has need of it!

The only value in being able to meditate in a steady flow is to gain the capacity to understand something that was always in front of us, but that previously we were unable to recognize. The point of learning how to concentrate perfectly, of spending years of our lives contemplating the sublime teachings of our faith, is simply to prepare ourselves properly, so that the veil of ignorance and delusion may be lifted from our eyes. As St. Symeon the New Theologian wrote concerning what sustained meditation on divine things can effect in the practitioner:

> Therefore he is changed . . . and becomes bolder and more vigorous in the practice of God's commandments. As he fulfills them day by day he is purified anew to the extent that he practices them. He becomes radiant, he is illuminated, there is granted to him to see revelations of great mysteries the depth of which no one has ever seen nor is at all able to see who has not striven to attain the height of such purity. By mysteries I mean things that are seen by all without being understood by them.[1]

Creating the Space

By setting your intention on the simple longing to live as a resurrected being, in the light of Christ, you have already begun to clear a sacred space in your own heart. Yet without a *physical* space of some kind, you may find it very difficult to sustain and develop that intention on the days when it does not feel particularly strong. When we make a loving commitment to another person, our common instinct is to want to build a home together; likewise, when we make a spiritual commitment to seek the Lord, it is vital that we carve out a space within our homes, no matter how small or modest, which is dedicated to nourishing our relationship with him. You may simply set off a corner of a room with a screen or curtain, or else clear a specific area that you will consistently designate

1. Symeon the New Theologian, *The Discourses*, 189.

for the practice of prayer and meditation. It should be a place that is relatively quiet, where you can hope to have at least twenty to thirty minutes of privacy each day. It is important to decorate it nicely, so that it is a space you *want* to go into, a refuge and a place of solace and beauty. Its outer mood should reflect the inner work you plan to do there. Thus it should be simple, clean, free of clutter or excess objects. Just by preparing this holy space, you are already beginning to prepare a mind that will be clean, pure, and clear.

You might wish to place a sacred icon or wooden statue in a prominent and central position within your sacred space, and arrange everything else in an orderly fashion to lead your eye and mind towards that image. This will prepare you for the state of mind you want to reach in meditation, when your eyes are closed, and the image of the divine Face is appearing within the space of your own mind. Place a book of sacred Scripture nearby. It could be the complete Bible, or else a part of it; for example, the book of Psalms, the Gospels, or the Divine Office. It could also be the spiritual writings of a saint to whom you feel a particularly close connection. Then think carefully about which symbol best represents for you the unfathomable qualities of the divine Mind—infinite being, perfect wisdom, unconditional love. It may be a bare cross, the cosmic symbol of both death and resurrection, drawing together all space and time into its single salvific reality. Or else you might choose the form of fire in a candle, a biblically rooted symbol of the Holy Spirit. It could even be a simple bowl or glass of water, reminiscent of the baptismal font, and symbolizing the purity and clarity of Christ's knowledge. Most importantly, it should be a symbol that resonates with you personally, and also evokes divine transcendence in a way that inspires you to look beyond the physical form of the symbol itself.

You might also place some flowers and/or incense on your altar, arranged in a way that feels genuinely beautiful to you. What, then, does such an action demand of faith? Ask yourself: Why is preparing a little altar different from arranging flowers or lighting incense or candles just because *you* like the ambiance they create? What is the difference between a sacred and a secular arrangement? As you reflect upon your answer, the most important thing is simply to take care, to be precise in your movements and loving in your gestures. Let the very act of designing your altar be a kind of dance, a graceful offering of your body's own movement.

Meditation Seating

What kind of posture will you assume, to sit in expectation of divine revelation? The emphasis should be on achieving the position that is most *comfortable* for you, in order that you can be totally still for the duration of your meditation, without being distracted either by pain or by movement in your body. Be willing to spend time trying different possibilities, until you find a suitable posture in which you can sit upright and alert for at least fifteen or twenty-five minutes. With practice, your posture will gradually change, improve, and strengthen, and you will be able to sit for a full hour without moving at all. When you enter into such stillness within your body, then your mind can reach extraordinary places indeed.

You might choose a firm chair, one on which you can sit with your feet planted firmly on the floor, without having to lean against the back of the chair. If this is too difficult, you can use a small cushion to support your lower back. Or you might prefer sitting cross-legged on the floor, on a firm cushion, with sufficient padding under your legs. Do not try to "rough it" on a hard floor. Your legs will quickly fall asleep and your knees and ankles will be sore. You need something soft and supportive under your legs, and you need to be warm enough. The Japanese-style sitting cushion, called a *zafu,* and the rectangular floor mat that accompanies it, called a *zabuton,* are extremely well-designed for this purpose. You might also try a small kneeling bench called a *zaisu,* or else design your own arrangement of pillows, mats, and carpet on which to sit or kneel until you find what works best for you. The most important thing is to have your spine lengthened into its natural upright posture of relaxed vigilance, ideally not leaning back on anything. It may be helpful to arrange your cushion on the chair or floor so that the back of the cushion is slightly higher than the front. This enables your hips to sit just a bit higher than your knees, and tilts the pelvis slightly forward so that it is easier to lengthen the lower back.

A Sense of Presence

Once you have chosen and arranged the seat on which you will meditate, be sure to stand up and step back for a moment, looking at the holy space you have prepared. Rejoice in the gentle beauty of your offerings. Really take time to look at the image you have chosen, and believe that the Lord is already spiritually present in your midst. Always start your session of prayer while standing up, the way a priest does before an altar. Thus you acknowledge that the Lord is already *there*, and it is as though you are waiting for him to take his seat before you. Never just "plunk yourself down" casually, and then expect to have some holy feeling after you get settled. If you were to become aware of the divine presence only *after* sitting down, would you not feel compelled to stand up again, out of sheer respect? Would you dare remain seated if you actually sensed that the Lord had just passed into your room? To acknowledge the divine presence, make a simple obeisance in a way that feels appropriate to you. You might bow slightly from the waist, palms facing each other, pouring infinite honor and reverence into that restrained motion. Or you might bend one knee in a traditional sign of worship. Or you may just lower your head with your hands clasped and say a quiet prayer that expresses your deepest intention, both for your spiritual practice as a whole, and for this particular session of contemplative prayer.

Meditation Posture

Then take your seat with care. Place your left hand in your lap, palm facing upwards, and rest your right one on top of it, allowing the tips of the thumbs to touch lightly. The elbows should be held just away from your body, forming a graceful oval shape from the shoulders to the hands. While there are other conducive positions for the arms, this one is ideal for attaining stable concentration and for enabling energy to flow smoothly throughout the body. Depending on your posture, you might need to place a small pillow or a folded shawl in your lap, to create a smooth resting place for your hands. You should not have to make any noticeable effort to hold your arms in place. Be sure your shoulders are level, neither one higher than the other. As you begin to meditate, and feel as though you are drawing energy up from the earth into your spine, let the neck grow tall and long. This will naturally cause your sternum to lift and your chin to tuck inwards the slightest bit. This is good, but do not exaggerate it. Make sure your head is not tilted too far down, as this can lead to sleepiness. But also check that your head is not tipped backward, as though you were looking at something above you, because this can create unnecessary distraction, not to mention neck pain!

Relax your mouth, even letting it broaden into a gentle smile. The lips should be lightly touching, as leaving the mouth open for an extended period of meditation might cause you to get thirsty. The jaw should be loosely relaxed, and the teeth should not be clenched. There is an ancient tradition that you should lightly touch the tip of your tongue to the roof of your mouth, also to prevent thirst, and the excessive build-up of saliva. For beginners, however, it is not necessary to force this. The mouth should feel relaxed, without any nervous tension in the lips. Most importantly, the flow of the breath should be completely natural and unimpeded, so one should discover for oneself whether it is preferable to breathe through the nose or mouth. Of course, if breathing through the mouth, the lips can open as needed.

Some teachers suggest that the eyes should not actually be closed (as this can lead to sleepiness), but should rather be slightly open, gazing steadily into the space in front of you without focusing on any particular thing. The point is not to be looking at any outer object, since that would become a distraction from one's actual object of meditation. Rather, the purpose is to keep the mind awake and alert, and not confined to the illusion of darkness inside one's head. Yet it can be difficult for beginners to achieve this non-focused gaze in mid-air, and you certainly don't want to go cross-eyed, or build up any tension in the eyes at all. If you can focus better with your eyelids gently closed, that is fine; as long as there is some awareness of light filtering through so that you do not get sleepy. It is most important to keep all the muscles of the eyes loose and relaxed, blinking naturally, without actively focusing on any particular object in the visual field, even though colors and shapes will still appear.

Be Still!

Once you have found your own ideal meditation posture, make a resolution to yourself to *remain in stillness* for the duration of the meditation. There are places our minds can go when our bodies are completely still that it will be impossible to experience if we have disturbed the meditation even once to adjust our position or attend to an itch. It doesn't matter what bodily irritation begins to bother you, what sound is annoying you, whether you are too hot or too cold, restless or uncomfortable: *Don't move!* If you start trying to adjust physically, there will always be something more to disturb you, and you will never gain true stillness.

It is important to be strict with yourself about this, especially if you are meditating alone. When meditating with others, one gains the added incentive not to disturb anyone else's meditation, and this is helpful to teach you just how much you can endure, with no negative consequences. Gradually, you will teach yourself simply to watch each distraction—whether it appears to come from inside or outside the body—simply arise . . . reach its peak . . . and then fade away. If you do not pay much attention to the distraction, it will wear itself out naturally.

It is important to keep to the allotted period of time you have set yourself (even if it is only fifteen or twenty-five minutes). To begin, set yourself very short sessions, so that you are teaching your body this discipline in manageable increments. Gradually you may lengthen the sessions quite naturally, because you *want* to stay longer. However, don't try to sit longer than you can comfortably maintain bright, clear concentration, without building up tension in the body. Also, try to meditate every morning and evening at about the same time. There is power to such ritual habits, and once you find the times of day when your mind can remain clear, without undue sleepiness or disturbance, you will soon look forward to that special, quiet, restorative haven.

Body-Mind Equilibrium

Before we can even discover what our heart longs for; before we can even call on the One who is the source of all we long for; before we can even bring our hearts to pray meaningfully for all those in such deep need, in so many different ways, we must bring our body and mind into equilibrium, into balance. There's a technique, a way of doing this. It will not always have the same effect, because the body and mind are always changing. Still, if we practice consistently, this can become an anchor, a habit, a place of silence and stillness from which the rest of our spiritual life can grow.

When we come to the cushion feeling stressed or upset, even angry, we cannot expect to enter a peaceful and virtuous state of mind right away. Rather, by asking the mind to focus on something as neutral and as immediately close at hand as the *breath*, we give ourselves some space to recover from whatever is disturbing our mind and body. Once refreshed and rebalanced, we can go on to develop the more peace-filled and compassionate states of mind towards which our meditation will ultimately be directed.

Read the following "Awareness of the Breath" meditation several times before attempting to practice it. Perhaps copy some key words on a small card to place in front of you at first, to remind you of each point as you meditate. It's fine to glance down every few minutes to check the next instruction, and then return to your relaxed gaze in which to meditate. Soon you will not need to check the card, and this technique will become a natural and simple means of entering into greater equilibrium of body and mind.[2]

Awareness of the Breath

To begin, become deeply aware of your body; what it feels like to be embodied; what it feels like to inhabit weight, inhabit the experience of solidity, gravity, and to feel how that is distributed upon your seat.

Then be aware of all the fluid aspects of what it is to dwell in that weight. You're not rock solid. So how—without moving, without making any unnecessary movement—can you embody the fluidity that's already there?

As both water and earth are very grounded elements, begin now to be aware of the counterbalance: the upward-moving energies of heat, of fire; or we might say the very *inspiration* that keeps you upright. How is the very posture in which you sit already oriented toward heaven while remaining deeply grounded in the earth?

As you begin to feel a balance between these downward and upward-moving energies, now begin to become aware of the breath, the sheer lightness and motility of the air passing through your whole body.

Without trying to control the breath in any way, simply become aware of how the effects of each inhalation and exhalation reverberate through all the passageways of your body, the veins and arteries, the bloodstream, the cavities of the lungs. How does the experience of breathing enter into your belly, then down to the tips of your toes? Without directing

---

2. Alternatively, if you wish to download audio files of the following meditations, as recorded by Eva Natanya, please visit www.evanatanya.com/resurrectionmeditations.html and enter the passcode: LRLwm2.

the mind anywhere in particular, just become aware of the sensations associated with the breath, wherever they may arise.

Again, without trying to control it in any way, become increasingly attuned to the exhalation, allowing it to reach its full extent, and remaining aware all the way to that end. Then, not forcing in any way the inhalation, allow the breath to return to you . . . as sheer gift.

Let your curiosity follow these subtle movements associated with the breath: along the cavity of the back, through your skull, to the tips of the nostrils. Watch the extent of the sensations associated with the breath all the way down to the tips of the toes, back through your legs, to your fingertips. Still without trying to control it, allow the breath to be its own wisdom to bring your system to equilibrium. Then, in particular, become aware of the rising and falling of your rib cage; but there is no need to think of it as a rib cage. Just try to become attuned to the sensations that your mind associates with chest, in the middle of the body.

At the center of that space begin to feel your spiritual heart. Breathe from there, still watching the rising and falling, the movement of air at the center of the equilibrium of weightedness, fluidity, the energy of heat, and the flow of wind within your body.

Release each breath all the way to the end, holding nothing back. Not pushing. Not forcing. Just giving it away, surrendering all that you are, so that whatever returns is pure gift. Not drawn. Not pulled. Not reclaimed. Simply received. Thus let Spirit heal you, the divine Spirit that knows perfectly how to bring you to balance, if only you allow it. Let the Holy Spirit breathe *you*. . . .

With your mind settled there, try to recall a moment when your connection with Christ Jesus was strongest, clearest; when the presence was so real.

In that moment, what did you see yourself wanting to be?

And how did you feel his presence shaping, modifying, cajoling, or teaching you to become him?

Still remaining aware of your breath, expand your awareness to your whole body again as it is changed by that encounter.

Who is the *you* that Christ sees?

Allow the intensity of that presence, that light within your heart to suffuse your vision of your body; your experience of your body, passing through your images of flesh or bone, irradiating you completely with the crystal clarity of Christ's light: this pure love that is sent to care for everyone.

Let that light fill you now as your breath did before, as though the light is riding on your breath, filling every space and corner of your form with crystal brilliant white light.

Returning your mind to your heart, think of *one person* with whom you'd like to share this experience; one person who you know is in need of such presence, such inspiration, such reassurance.

On a single ray of light imagine that you transmit your own experience of Christ's presence to this person, straight to his or her heart. This light likewise fills this person's body, clearing away all afflictions, worries, confusions, and filling him or her with clarity and divine purpose for existing in this world.

Return your focus to your own light-filled body.

Begin to relax your concentration without losing your awareness.

Then quietly dedicate the power of this meditation: that all people everywhere may find the profound inspiration that comes from intimacy with the divine Teacher, whatever their religion or faith or worldview might be; that all people may know the profound joy of being guided by the heart of perfect compassion, perfect divine love, perfect creativity; and that all our actions may be guided—down to the finest glimmer—by the eyes and ears and knowledge of this divine presence, so that the day may come when all of us may say in all honesty: "I do nothing on my own, I speak nothing on my own, I think nothing on my own, but only in the One who strengthens me."

2

Meditations on Resurrection

GIVE YOURSELF TIME TO practice the "Awareness of the Breath" meditation for several days or weeks, until you sense that your body-mind is able to enter into and maintain equilibrium more easily. *Always begin your meditation practice with at least ten minutes of calming and centering awareness.* This will prepare you to enter into the guided meditations that follow with deeper focus and concentration.

Then, when you feel ready to proceed to the guided meditations, read each sentence or section slowly and reflect on it for a few moments before proceeding to the next one. Perhaps close your eyes so that your imagination can create a vivid picture before your inner eye. Let the image sink deeply into your heart. Rest with the sense of being *in the moment* for as long as you wish before proceeding to the next reflective point. Never feel the need to rush to the next sentence or section. If you do not complete the entire meditation in one sitting, you may return to it later when you are able to complete the whole meditation at one time.

The most important factor is to remain open to whatever the Spirit reveals to you, in whatever way. Stay with that. Heighten your awareness. Breathe in that limitless space. It is holy ground.

Inside the Tomb

It is dark. It is dark in the cave. You are where no living person should be, sitting on a ledge opposite the corpse that is bound in bands of cloth like swaddling clothes. Only the slightest rays of light come through cracks where the giant stone is not quite flush with the opening of the tomb.

It doesn't matter who you are; it doesn't matter that you weren't there historically. You are bearing witness to what was seen by God alone.

We know what it feels like to sit with a sleeping person; even to sit with a very sick person. We know what it is to listen to the quiet breathing; even the labored breathing of someone in pain. But what does it feel like to sit with someone who is dead and utterly hidden beneath his funeral wrappings?

The glances of light, late afternoon light, remind you every once in a while that there is a corpse there, as the light reflects off the white cloth. But there is no movement.

Yet you know there is a presence there.

The corpse is not functioning like a body. There is no metabolism. The cells are not active. The electric signals in the brain have stopped altogether. The blood and water long since flowed out of his side. Urine and feces flowed out, too, when the body gave up its spirit. And yet, the divine Spirit is still close, close to this cleaned-up corpse.

Where is his mind? When the One through whom all things are created is withdrawn from the world, where do all things go for him?

What does he *see* when not in a body?

How does reality appear to the all-creating divine Word when not incarnate?

Rest with him where he dwells beyond breath itself.

Then out of infinite silence there is a shimmer, a vibration of sound and light, more subtle than either one: an expression of the most subtle energy that creates all things. The source of all life.

The wisdom of God dances at a place that is the center of all and has no location because it creates location; it creates all perspective from its own center. And moving, it dances without form and appears in the light of five rainbow colors, beyond all conceptual thought.

It transcends our ability to imagine; and yet for our sake, once again, it takes on the subtlest form of a man, infinitesimally small, yet breaking the boundaries of space.

Divine energy shaping itself as human . . .

Then, in a flash of energy like that of a billion suns exploding, the energy of this divine body irradiates the atoms of the corpse, exploding through the cloths, leaving no trace except an imprint on the shroud.

And entering into the shapes and sizes of our world yet again, a *man made of light* sits on the stone platform opposite you.

Yet light is subtle and light can form the shapes of cells again, the shapes of muscles and bones, the shapes of clothing, no longer made of coarse matter but appearing as coarse matter, irradiated by divine wisdom in a way that is like the incarnation, yet already beyond it.

Gaze upon him in the dark tomb, he who is seen by no one here.

But you see. And he gazes upon you. Without losing the experience of his gaze, watch carefully the reaction in your own heart, the entire demeanor of your being.

Without words or movement, how do you acknowledge him? In this gaze beyond time and space, what does he ask of you? Without words, you know his call: "Follow me."

This blazing form, still so human, rises and steps towards the stone entrance.

And with merely a touch of his hand, the stone falls back.

In the human world, a whole day and another night had passed.

It is dawn.

On the Road to Emmaus

Once again, become deeply sensitized to the experience of being embodied in space. How does that experience come to you?

Try to release the normal conceptions you have of what your body looks like; try to taste the sheer sensations without thinking about them, without imagining them, just being in the shape of tactile sensations that form the image of a body in space.

Gradually find within that space, that living, breathing space, your heart's center, in the middle of your back, just in front of the spine, opposite the sternum, deeper than any physical space can contain.

Make a sincere prayer to the One who resides there, your Lord and Master beyond space and time, to take you into a mystical space where you may meet him in a way that will mark you indelibly forever.

For a brief time, allow all the pain you are aware of today to rise in your heart: your own pain and that of those close to you; that of your city . . . and country . . . and this whole world today.

What does it ask for? Dare to take responsibility for that world as your own, knowing you are both powerless to help and completely empowered to be divine love in that world.

Then recall an experience in your life when you have felt most utterly bereft—of hope, of clarity, of guidance; when you felt there was no one whom you could trust anymore; when that person or people upon whom you thought you could rely were taken from you, in one way or another.

Let that feeling manifest as a desert road, dusty, with nothing around but scrub brush, sand, and rock. A city is behind you; the place you call home is ahead of you. But nowhere feels like home right now.

You are with someone close to you, someone whose companionship offers comfort but does not replace what you have lost. And you are walking . . . walking, trying to make sense of all that has gone before.

Suddenly, another figure comes up beside you, on the other side from where your companion walks. The presence is strong, unexpected, overpowering; strange and familiar at the same time.

And without the usual pleasantries of a passerby on the road this stranger asks you: "What is wrong?" You pour out your heart. All the stories. All the situations. All the background. The story that is eating you up.

When you are out of breath because you've said so much, you come again to the sense of loss. All that you had hoped for is not to be. And you fall silent. Suddenly.

Then the stranger says to you, "Can't you see? That's exactly how it's supposed to be. It's all perfect. Can't you see how each of the prophets of the past had reached such a place himself? Can't you see how the Father has always transformed it?

"And now this Jesus: can't you see how he came to fulfill all the prophecies? How his death took upon himself all of your pain, your hopes, the injustice you've experienced? Can't you see how he gathered that into the heart of his own divine creative force to transmute it all into light? A new creation? Everlasting hope?"

You argue, your heart still clinging to hopelessness, still spinning the story, though it loses its power as you sense there is someone who knows far better what the plan is.

Suddenly the scene shifts. You are near your home. Yet even that doesn't seem familiar anymore. You know you must ask this stranger to stay with you and your companion; this person you feel you've always known. You ask him to rest a while with you. He silently nods his acceptance and comes to set foot in your home.

And so you and your companion go about making a meal, hearts still struggling with the ramifications of what you've heard; so deeply aware of the contrast between your own continued agitation and the profound stillness of your guest who waits quietly at the table where you've offered him a seat.

When the time comes for the blessing, he takes the bread and says the blessing with authority, like one who knows directly the God to whom the prayers are offered. He breaks the bread. Your heart begins to burn. You have seen this authority before . . .

Oh, how you miss him! But the one whom you love is dead.

He could never appear again.

No one like that will come again, and yet . . . here before you, that presence . . . that kindness. As he begins to hand you a piece of the blessed bread, your heart screams: "How could it not be he?"

In the absolute suspension of that moment of recognition, everything is wiped away, all your fears, disappointment, dissatisfaction. Nothing can withstand the truth of this encounter. You cannot take your eyes from him, but somehow, for a moment you are so withdrawn that your eyes must have closed.

When you open them to look at him again, he is gone. The bread is there, the table is there, your companion is there. But there is no trace of him, his clothing, his bag. Nothing. There was no sound. No one got up and left.

Reality itself broke open to receive him.

But you do not feel bereft now. Your heart is utterly at peace. You know what you must do. You and your companion look at each other and smile; you both know. Nothing more needs to be said.

You pick up your travel sack and together walk out into the dusk to proclaim what you have seen.

In the Upper Room

To begin: Let both the breath and the stream of the inner speech of your mind find their natural rhythm in silence, simply watching and releasing the thoughts that flow along with the breath. Let them go, releasing all the way into the exhale, not forcing it, and letting the inhale return, without pulling it. Watch very carefully how the body does this for itself.

Have courage to release all control over the breathing and watch its course throughout your body, wherever it affects you.

Your breath knows how to heal you and bring you to balance, for it is not mere breath but divine Spirit within you; if you can only listen and watch without interfering.

When you are ready you can let just a little light come into your eyes, so that you are fully engaged with the present experience right here and right now. And look into the quality of your mind: relaxed, quiet, clear, not wanting or needing anything else but what is right here.

You can be aware of the movements of thoughts and images; the subjective movements of feelings, reactions; *but they are not you.*

Rest in a deeper perspective, where divine knowing knows all of this, not the same as you and not separate from you.

Become so quiet at the depths of your heart that the Lord can take you anywhere, with no resistance: have no idea that this place is where I am; this time is when I live; this body is who I am. Relinquish it all for a deeper center that makes its own space and time.

And in an instant you are seated with the other disciples, sitting quietly in prayer—though you are aware of the agitation of their hearts around you, the sense of loss and uncertainty, anguish and fleeting hope at the news the women brought. You can watch that anxiety, but not enter into it; it is the anxiety of the whole world at any time, at any place.

You recall being in this room just a few nights before when your Lord and teacher gave you his very identity as food. Now you feel compassion with *his* heart as you become acutely aware of this anxiety that stirs in every person, everywhere. And yet you feel the stillness of his own heart within you, which remains unmoved by that anxiety, even as it dwells in absolute love for all those who do experience it.

Suddenly you hear a gasp from those around you and your eyes shoot open to see the Lord standing in front of you. You could never say later how he was dressed, or even how you knew it was he: a form so replete with divine energy that it explodes all comparison to human perception of a person and a body. And yet there he is, standing there, in space; a person, your Lord.

Peace be with you.

And the peace that was there in your heart is expanded. Yet it is not a passive peace, it is a peace that reaches everywhere; the sheer dynamism of the energy of his presence, the authority that brings all things to perfection and blazes through all fear, all anxiety, all uncertainty.

This light, this energy pours from him, from his heart, from his breath, from every pore of his being. You never knew where it came from, but the Spirit is instantly penetrating each and every one of you.

You realize you closed your eyes for a moment; then you opened them again and he was gone. But everything is different. Everyone else saw and experienced it, too. They begin to talk and exchange, everyone asking questions, trying to express what they saw.

But you remain still and silent, just tasting the vision he gave you: the *glory* from which the whole room, the whole house, all the people there are now arising. You see his creative power dancing through every atom of the table, all your bodies. You see the speech, the vibrations of divine sound. You know without a shadow of a doubt that he is within you, looking upon all this. And you are at peace.

Eventually the sounds of the room subside. You're not even aware of being there in a body anymore. You are resting with the Lord in a space out of time.

Then gradually you feel him place you back in the body you started with, right here, right now, configured to a time and place—his transfigured, glorified, resurrected energy still pulsing within you; his peace still pervading, at the center of all that may move.

Very gently, engage your senses here and now, tasting how it has changed you. And offer the prayer that he may never leave you and remind you always how he entered you, not only in his flesh and blood to eat, but in his glorified body, transmitted through the gift of the Spirit, *his* Spirit.

The Transformation of Thomas

Begin to catch the rhythm of the breath; gently and gradually, joining the mind to these ebbs and flows, letting your whole being unite with the experience of the breath, not blocking thoughts but pouring them into this flow so that they release themselves.

Let the breath sink deep into your belly, the tips of your fingers and toes, not forcing, just allowing, and paying close attention to the end of each exhalation, watching the transition: where does each breath start?

Watch carefully how your body will grant equilibrium to itself, if only you let it.

Let your mind settle in your heart. Become aware of the vast, infinite space there, not enclosed by anything, yet utterly subtle at the core of your being.

Call Christ to be present to you, so that you yourself may be aware of his love, guiding you in every breath.

Ask him to infuse you with *his* love for others, so that you may see the world from within *his* heart.

Then let him pull you through time to be present for his rising, that you also may see and believe.

You are Thomas, one of the Twelve, whose heart has been captured by your Lord and Master. You, also, have given everything to follow him.

And now you are wandering through those streets of Jerusalem alone, your body racked with tears and anger; frustration at the collapse you have just witnessed; the collapse of everything you've believed in. You are burning with a sense of injustice, loss, grief; crying out to heaven, "Why? It wasn't supposed to be like this! Has God lost all power, that the world should overcome him?"

You cannot bear to be with your friends and fellow disciples now. You can't really trust any of them. You feel the doubt tearing through your body; your heart pounding, feeling like it wants to rip you apart. Earlier today, you heard rumors that some women had seen him. You're so fed up with stories. Isn't it clear he died? He's gone.

And so you doubt everything; all that you believed in. Even whether he was the prophet you thought he was. Could you have been so deceived?

As you walk through the alleyways between buildings—those familiar buildings of stone and mortar packed so close to each other—you feel as though they're crushing you. You just keep walking . . . walking . . .

not wanting to be seen but not wanting to be still . . . until you find an empty place at the edge of the city.

You sit down on a rock and collapse, weeping, crying out to your Lord whom you don't even believe in, begging the very one to come who you are sure is gone. But there is only darkness.

Eventually by dawn you sheepishly wander back to the room where the other disciples are staying—you have no other place to go. You share the morning meal with them and they start telling you more stories: that they saw him alive, that he entered the room, that he spoke to them. You are numb. You can barely hear it.

Some gibberish comes out of your mouth about not believing; about wanting to put your hands in his wounds, like a stubborn child. But it doesn't even express your heart, because you can't even feel your heart.

Somehow, you live out the days, finding things to do, finding solace in various tasks to help your brothers and sisters. You realize that that companionship is still there. That brotherhood is still there.

Gradually, the pain in your heart lightens; but there is still a blindness to it—going through the motions of caring and serving, but with no sense of purpose. Only grief. At least you are able to join their gatherings, to listen to their stories with a little less resentment, a little more compassion for their own journeys. So you begin to accept . . . to accept that God is present to them in a different way. Or maybe it's just fantasy.

And so about a week has gone by. Someone is keeping track of the days. And once again you are sharing a meal together. And you remember for a moment what that last meal with the Lord was like. Something happened there. You knew he'd given himself away. You knew he loved you. Could it all have been for nothing?

You close your eyes for a moment, remembering. That longing returns. That crying out in the dark: "Lord, come! If you still exist somewhere, please come!"

Then you hear some commotion, some gasps from your brothers. And your eyes fly open to see him standing there, looking right at you. There's no question that it's he. But it's not just a vision. He's there. Solid in space, standing in the room with you. And you look around at the others. They're all *people*.

You look back at him and see the light pouring from his body, but it doesn't make him any less *solid*. The child in you cannot wait to test what you long to test. And as though reading your mind he says: "Come, put your hands in my hands. Put your hands in my side." Then he holds out his hands to you.

Amidst the image of pierced flesh that has not even healed but has not turned into a scab, that is not like a normal wound: it's like a hole into eternity . . . And amidst the garments (you can't quite see where the garments stop and his skin begins), you see that hole in his side. You feel that if you touched it you would disappear into it. But you dare not touch. You only know.

And in your shame and awe, *you fall flat on the ground.*

You reach forward to touch his feet and without even trying, your fingers slide into the same unearthly wounds in his feet. "My Lord and my God!"

You feel a warmth on your back, an unearthly warmth, but the familiarity of a hand. All that tension, all that blockage in your heart, seems to melt in his hand. He rubs your hair as though you're his child. "It's okay. It's okay. Get up." You remember how you heard him say "Get up!" to so many different people when he healed them. You thought you were strong, you thought you were lucky; *you* didn't have to be healed. You always thought you were there as a hero, to serve his mission. But in that moment, you know how completely you had to be broken for him to heal you. Beyond death itself.

You're vaguely aware of the eyes of your friends and companions on you, but it doesn't really matter. Who can be ashamed in the presence of God himself?

He helps you, still shaking, to your feet, and embraces you. Whatever he is, he lets you hold him, more tangible than anything.

As he releases the embrace, you look into his eyes and he says: "You believe because you've seen me, Thomas. Through you, many will come to believe. They will not see all that you see, but they will believe. And their faith is equal to yours. In fact, greater, because they have *not* seen. But I came because you needed me. You needed to see me like this. So it's alright. Go in peace."

Then he vanishes instantaneously. That reality, that solid, solid man, that strong embrace . . . but he vanishes.

You stagger back to your seat and place your head on the table, so grateful if everyone will leave you alone.

And as you regain your breath, you realize you *are* at peace. There is nothing more to need or long for. You are infused with him. You realize how that embrace was a transmission of his whole being. Because he has transcended matter, the fullness of his presence can enter *your* matter.

And you rest in the pulsing, divine vibration of his love.

Return simply to the breath in your own body now, watching how it has changed, knowing you were there and that you have received that embrace through Thomas, who has preached his Gospel to you through the ages, as the Lord gave him power to do. Let his peace also be upon you; the clarity, inspiration, and purpose that come from meeting the Risen One directly.

And for a moment, send from your own heart the intention to spread this peace, this faith, to all those you know who may need it. Let their names, their situations, arise naturally for you and without thinking in any detail. Just send them this peace.

When you have given it all away, you can gently come back into your body and the room.

At Lake Tiberias

It is dark. The shadows or the silhouette of the mountains reveal the slightest lightening of the eastern sky; the barest blue foreshadowing the dawn. The water is black. There are others in the boat, but everyone is quiet. You are all supposed to be fishing, but no one is very interested in that right now. Your hearts are very quiet, like the sky.

As the boat starts to turn slightly—just a shift in the gentle eddies of the water—you notice a flame at the shore that wasn't there before. You wonder who is setting up a camp at this time of morning. Who would show up now? Gently, almost lazily, you take the oar and start to move the boat closer to the shore. Just that unknown sense of interest: what's going on?

The fire quickly grows. And everywhere there is an unearthly increase of light: dawn can't happen that fast. You suddenly see the figure quite clearly standing there. Better dressed than most fishermen, it seems. He calls out, but it's strange that you can hear exactly what he says; for the distance is still too great. Why can you hear it?

"What have you caught?" It sears your heart. You feel the utter worthlessness of this task of catching fish. You remember the one who showed you a whole other life, inspired you to engage with and care for hundreds of people at a time. When you were with him, you believed that there was another way of living, a goodness so deep, it would transform this world and lead to another. When you were with him, you had felt a love like nothing else. Just that question, "What have you caught?" sears your heart.

You mumble something about there being no fish tonight, but you knew you weren't trying very hard. You didn't say it loudly enough for someone all the way off on the shore to hear. But again, you hear that voice very clearly: "Cast your nets on the other side."

That rough fisherman part of you feels a moment of irony: it's not like the fish stay that close together. If there's nothing on one side, then eight feet away, there's not going to be anything else. But something makes you follow the instruction, without questioning; just something else to do.

Then you hear the clamor of your companions as the giant school of fish appears out of nowhere. You can't even *see* them, but you feel the net starting to get heavier and heavier. Oh, there's the commotion of fishermen. You do what you have to do: set the nets, make sure you don't lose the catch.

And as the boat still drifts to shore, that unearthly brightness increases.

Your companion whispers, "It is the Lord." *Then* you see the figure on the beach. No hesitation. No question. You dive in the water. Shoot towards the shore. Dripping in your outer garments as you stand up in the sand, your voice echoes against the mountainside, as though the very sky were calling out: "It is the Lord!"

You fall to your knees . . .

There is still much commotion as the boat reaches the shore. Pulling down the giant net of fish, the others recognize and pay their obeisance. You help in hauling the net to shore, but your focus remains on the Lord.

You know he is looking at you the whole time, even as he greets the other disciples; as though from every pore of his body is a ray of light searing into you: looking into your eyes, into your heart, into your cells, burning you, purifying you, all that you regret.

You return to your knees for a long time.

You're aware he is talking to the others, cooking fish with them, sharing a meal. But you can't partake. You already knew he was alive, but this encounter is like no other.

Then, at a certain point, he steps aside from the campfire and simply takes your hand and helps you to your feet. And leads you off a little bit.

"Peter, do you love me?"

You begin to feel the whole universe imploding upon your heart, as if he'd told you for the first time what divine love is, as if he's showing you the infinite scope of his mission: hundreds of billions of people and animals, spirits and unseen beings on this planet and many, many other planets. You feel in those words for the first time what his love is.

You want to follow as you always did. Without understanding the cost: "Yes, Lord, you know that I love you." "Feed my lambs."

He has just shown you his lambs for the first time. You cannot imagine how you could care for so many beings.

You long for his comfort. Here you are promising to save the world with him and all you want is some reassurance that you've done well, that you're forgiven, that it's alright. You feel an explosion inside your heart, as though: how could you be worthy of such a task? All you crave is the Lord's love. For yourself.

"Peter, do you love me?" There's a quieting in your heart. Then another explosion: "Yes, Lord, you *know* that I love you!" "Protect my sheep."

Then for a moment you experience the cacophony of conflict, suffering; women crying in labor and in death—Rachel weeping over the loss of her children. You see the span of time: countless wars, lives spent meaninglessly. You see the glimmers of hopes and dashed hopes. You see demons as they are: demons of hatred and jealousy, pride and laziness, desire and doubt entering the hearts of beings, even those who want to do well. You see how those demons entered you when you betrayed him.

You see for the first time what he is asking you to do: to love *even that*. The vision fades. Now all you see are his eyes, penetrating into yours: "Peter, do you love me?"

You can barely breathe. *Lord, you know I would do anything for you.* It rises in your heart to say, *I would die for you.* But you know you've said that before and you failed. So all you can do is answer his question: "You know everything; you know I love you." "Feed my sheep."

Then he places his hand on your shoulder. That supernatural light you had noticed from the beginning, that piercing, burning fire emanating from his body, pours into you like molten lava, filling you from top to bottom, and again, from the bottom to the top, until you feel irradiated from within.

And some part of you knows you are pure, you are forgiven, and you are empowered.

Then standing right there you know you are not Peter. You are you, the one sitting there, the one meditating. You know you couldn't have lived in Galilee at that time, you couldn't have seen him that way. But he is present to you, now. His resurrected body transcends the ages.

You can see the shadows in the rocks where the sand meets the hillside. The dawn is still brightening. You see him vividly there *for you.* He holds out his hands. And you see in his hands all the gifts he's given you in this life, all the teachers, all the guidance, all the experiences that have brought you to this moment of promise: this ability to give him your whole being beyond your being, what you never could have imagined being.

"Follow me."

The whole vision of sea and the boat, your companions, the fire, the fish, the mountains, the sky, all dissolve into his body. His resurrected form blazes a thousand times brighter but also becomes smaller and smaller like a pinpoint of light in front of your heart. And then that light itself enters your heart and lodges there, like a ball of fire within you.

You are aware again of this infinite sea of pain. But you know you can call on his entire being in your heart. You feel as though he is showing you his own sacrifice on the cross. How he took that pain upon himself. Like a billion rays of fire coming toward you, you see the pain of every being—past, present, and future—imploding upon your heart.

But you feel no fear. For you see that he has already transformed it all into the same divine fire. It has no inherently real nature of being suffering. The ignorance that is evil is annihilated.

The energy only fills this heart of love, which again pours outward with brilliant rays of every color of light. And you know that your own heart in some way already touches everyone else's heart, exactly as he has touched yours. Because he is your heart now.

Experience your own body suffused with this light, streaming out in every color, carrying your own radiance with you.

And then let even that vision dissolve, light receding, countless beings receding, until there is just a pinpoint of light at your heart.

Then like a spark evanescing, that, too, disappears.

And you rest in the dawn sky.

Then inhabit your form again. Feel the experience of being in this body. And recall the vibrations of that sublime divine energy, which still suffuses you.

Pray that by the power of divine truth, by the power of the reality of the Risen One, and by the power of your own promise to love and to feed his lambs, that all this may come to pass. And that every living being may experience this peace. Quickly. Quickly. Ever more quickly.

Being the Peace of Christ

Let the breath be . . . and become very sensitive to all the different movements within your body, how they arise to you as sensations, not trying to stop or modify anything, but observing closely, gently, with love and appreciation.

Release more and more deeply into what the breath needs to do for you.

And then once you have gained some stability and equilibrium, from the experience of the breath throughout your whole body, and then in your abdomen, you can raise the level of focus to the tip of your nostrils, still watching the ebb and flow of sensations of the breath, increasing the clarity and the brightness, but without losing the ease, the gentleness.

Be sure to keep the awareness *still* even as the breath comes and goes. Don't follow, just remain the gatekeeper.

Become accustomed to keeping the quality and location of awareness *completely still* even as something as obvious as the passage of breath moves across it.

Then very gently, expand the scope of your awareness again, to take in the whole field of your body.

And very gently let your awareness home in or focus again at the center of your heart . . . pinpointing . . . falling back into ultimate center.

Let the Lord open the space for you to fall into. But as you do, still maintain that stillness of awareness amidst the movements of breath and mind.

And in the depths of that space, knowing you are in the direct presence of your Lord, offer him worship in the way that is perfect for you.

Ask whatever you may wish.

So that it is now not you but Christ. There is nothing for the human you, the old you, to do; nothing to strive for, nothing to modify. Utterly without effort, remain still, not trying to stop anything that arises, but not paying it any attention, resting completely in *his* awareness.

As you are still aware of the rhythm of the breath, you can release completely in the exhalation. And ever so slightly intensify your awareness of Christ's awareness on the inhalation.

As an ordinary person there is nothing we can do to add one whit to Christ's everlasting work; but by surrendering completely to his being, his knowing, his loving, we are at the center of that work without doing anything at all. And ultimately this is the highest service that we can offer to him and to our brothers and sisters.

But as soon as the mind engages as a human in human thoughts, these are not divine thoughts. So, without trying to stop them, we release utterly, without engaging in the human pattern.

And knowing this to be our everlasting kingdom, our timeless dwelling place, there is nothing to fear.

By the power of our resting here, may every living being find this peace, this peace the world cannot give, this peace that he gives to us: in the name of Jesus, the Messiah. Amen.

Empowerment by Fire

First feel the weightedness of your body, reaching down to the core of the earth; the column of energy connecting you to all that is below, rising through the center of your torso, connecting you to all that is above, allowing the energy of your body to settle naturally around this central axis.

Then begin to release the breath, not forcing at all, but allowing it to flow out, the belly to release, the ribs to release, all tension falling out of the shoulders. Let the breath drip down your arms and legs, falling, releasing out of your fingers and toes. And then keeping the mind very still and quiet, clear, watch where the breath starts again, without directing, without thinking you know where the breath starts. Just let it come.

Then follow it out again, all the way. If the breath needs to be short, let it be short. If it wants to be long, let it be long. Just dwell in this cycle over which you have no control, because you've released all control.

Then very gradually begin to watch how the breath itself, the energy of the breath, the sensations of the breath, coordinate with that central axis that you felt at the beginning. How does this experience of the breath naturally rise and fall along the column that grounds you to the earth and connects you to heaven?

As the sensations directly associated with the breath become more and more ingrained, as you become more habitually aware of those sensations, you may be able to distinguish the particular sensations associated with the coming and going of the breath from another, deeper array of movements that may or may not follow the same rhythm. Is there some other energy cycling through you? It is not quite the same as inhalation and exhalation, but still tangible.

Even if you can't quite feel that other flow of energy yet, with the trust that it's there and that with practice you will feel it someday, try to find a current with which that energy would rise from the base of your spine to the level of your heart. And relax into your heart, just in front of the spine, at the level of your sternum, well below the physical organ of the heart.

And resting your mind there, bring to mind your ultimate Teacher, the one who you believe can lead you and show you the way to the fulfillment of every sacred dream you've ever had. Call upon the essence of this Teacher. What are the divine qualities? What is the divine nature that is the source of every goodness for which you hope and which you cannot even imagine yet?

Let that Teacher take you out of time into another time, perfect time, *kairos* time, where a small group of very ordinary people who have had very extraordinary encounters, are gathered together in a room that is very familiar to them. Their hearts are still burning with the wonder and mystery of the appearances they have experienced and others have told them about. They're still sharing their stories.

Some had a vision that they claim makes them believe he is not going to appear again; but of course, others were not there and they still hope he will appear here inside the locked doors once again. Still others weren't even there when he first showed himself in the upper room and are hoping they might get a glimpse. The experiences are so deep and so transformative that everyone would love to have them happen again; for them to go on forever.

So find yourself sitting there with your own longing, your own memories of sacred encounters, transformative experiences, moments of indubitable presence. And sit waiting.

Find the part of yourself that is not worthy; that is afraid of what it would mean to *actually* follow him, *actually* take on the responsibility of an apostle, of an heir, of a child of God. And in your heart, offer up that part of yourself that you think is there, the unworthiness, the littleness, the imperfection.

You can't see him now, but you know he sees you. Feel the gentleness with which he removes from you all that you think stops you from receiving him fully.

You are so absorbed in this conversation, this internal communion with your Lord, that you barely notice the commotion beginning to stir around you. But something makes you aware that the room has changed. There is a moment of many voices talking, whispering: *What's going on?* But quickly that, too, falls silent, as you feel yourself with everyone in the room swept up by an invisible energy, as though you were all being carried in a tornado, brought together as one—swept higher and higher—yet if you open your eyes, nothing has changed, so you close your eyes again to experience it more deeply. This feeling of unity, as though whatever is happening is happening to all at once, as one person.

Then very distinctly, you feel a sharp sensation at the crown of your head, not painful, but impossible to ignore; as though all the subtler energies of your own body are being drawn up to this place at the crown of your head. And simultaneously you are aware that this must be happening to everyone else, as you are caught up in the same wind, the same Spirit.

The sensation intensifies, becoming hotter, as though a candle flame were burning, not upon your hair, but coming out of your own body, yet burning a hole down into you. It's a blissful warmth, a supernatural warmth, boring a hole through your skull, opening a shaft through the center of your body. Surrender to that warmth, that overwhelming love.

The warmth seeps down towards your heart like a river of lava. You don't need to understand it. It seeps the entire length of your body to the soles of your feet . . . and begins to rise again, as if setting your whole body on fire, liquid fire, divine fire.

And you know that every trace of impurity, doubt—everything you hold onto as really you—is being burned away in this sacred crucible of blessing: God himself coming to dwell in you.

Keep relaxing into it, trusting it.

Eventually you find the place again at your heart where there is a brighter light, like a glint of white or gold, and it is the redness of fire. And know that the Holy Spirit has come to dwell in your heart, never to leave you, revealing to you what you were always created to be: the child who is royalty from the day of your birth.

Let that brilliant light shine like sun rays through the fire that still fills you. And know that at the tip of each of those rays, is someone you will care for, someone you will empower, someone to whom you will carry the living experience of the Holy Spirit, effortlessly, without seeking, without striving, but because the Spirit does its work. And surrender completely to that vision, knowing there is nothing else to do.

Gradually let the heat of the fire subside, the light at your heart remain. You open your eyes and see the apostles and disciples, male and female, gathered around you, all with their own unique version of this experience. For now, there is silence, each one absorbing, resting, in the unspeakable glory that has taken place.

Returning to your own heart, recall that there is a different time, a different place in which you know how to function, in which connections are already forged, people with whose hearts you already feel a bond of divine love. So, with the certainty that the Lord has revealed something to you that is no more or less real than your usual world, let the image of the scene dissolve in your heart. Let the Lord take you through time, beyond time. Rest in the eternal time where God's knowledge dwells.

Very gently, let the sensation of embodiment return, the appearances of the room you thought you were in arise again. But know very clearly that you are not the same. Your very being vibrates with divine power, power that can only be used for good, that can only express itself as unconditional love. Trust it.

Then very gently make your own prayer. The Lord has given you himself. His own Spirit courses through your veins, both those physical and those too subtle to be seen. What will you do with it? What promise do you make, which you will never transgress, even when the intensity of this experience has passed? How will you remember, so that you may return?

Make your own intensely private covenant with your Lord. And whisper his name to yourself to seal that covenant.

Devotion and Union

Just watch the dance of the breath through your whole body. Let your belly breathe. Have no expectations for where the breath will show up next. But keep the awareness over the scope of the whole body, letting it bring itself to equilibrium.

The breath may make a sound, but let your mind be silent, witnessing, as though your mind is breathless, watching each moment of this dance that *is* the breath.

In particular, let your rib cage expand, making more and more space around your heart; not controlling, just allowing space by bringing attention to it.

Then just taste, without belaboring it, what your own deepest personal pain is right now. And know how many people, how many living beings, experience something so close, so parallel, to this pain, this fear, this hurt. And know that they are all mirrored within your heart. They vibrate within you, so that what transformation takes place within you must eventually affect them, and vice versa.

So you practice to alleviate the fear, the loneliness, the regrets, the anxiety of all the world. And knowing that Christ has done all these things, has taken on all these pains, has transformed all of them already, call him to the space before you, so that you may look into his eyes.

You can imagine that you are with him in the garden of Gethsemane as tears pour down his face and he sweats drops of blood—or you can let him be with you right here, right now, in a different form. But know that as you look into his eyes that this is the one who has experienced all pain in all time and already knows how it will be glorified.

Pay homage, knowing what it is in him that you honor so completely that you give your whole life to become like that. And then as though all your efforts could take form as a bouquet of flowers or jewels, whatever is lovely to you, see that you present this offering of your life, your day's work—or your week's or month's—and place it all before him, and know that he is pleased.

Then ask him for help with whatever your most urgent concern is. You know something needs to change within yourself, but you can't do it alone. Ask him for help to transform a habit, a pattern, anything that blocks you from reflecting him perfectly.

Now invite him to stay with you and grant you the teachings that can come only from within, the knowledge, moment to moment, where to place your mind, how to think or not to think, how to release, how to focus. Know that these instructions can only arise from him and beg him to be within you as your constant guide.

Then, no matter what scene you have imagined, know that it is a vision; that you are in prayer, in your own time and body, and ask him, along with that vision of his surrounding world, to melt into light and come to bless your heart: pouring through the crown of your head like a baptism, cleansing your whole body, your mind, your speech, and coming to rest within the center of your heart as an orb of pure light, pure Christ presence, the mind of Christ within you.

And let that light of compassion, crystal clear awareness, fill your whole body. You can become aware again of the rhythm of the breath, illuminated by Christ's awareness.

Then, still holding the stillness, the quiet of Christ's awareness within you, the awareness of body and rhythm of breath at a distance, begin to notice the flow of thought and imagery, memory and anticipation, which keeps flowing, through no intention of your own; it just keeps going in the mid-ground.

Watch it now with an almost casual interest. Just letting it be and remaining within the dwelling place of the Lord within you, as though he is watching you, the child, sleep; or you, the child, play. And *you* are now dwelling more with him than just being the child; but you still see the child.

Perhaps the analogy of the shepherd and the sheep is more apt, because you don't have to get involved in the sheep's pains, the sheep's life. You just watch them. Christ's love can embrace us without getting involved in our stories, even though he knows them. So try to find that precise juxtaposition of the unconditional love watching the stories unfold, but without getting inside them; knowing they are *not you*.

Keep returning to the juxtaposition of the stillness and awareness within your heart and the movements within that field of the mind, which you see but do not engage.

Then if there is a particularly strong thought or memory arising, you can take it as your object of investigation. Penetrate it. See through the misunderstandings that make you believe in it in just this way. It can be helpful to have your eyes open and still have that thought or memory arise. And then ask:

Where is it?

Is it inside of you or outside of you?

Is that irrelevant if speaking of the mind?

If it's in the space of the mind, where is that?

Is the space of the mind confined to your body?

If the memory is in the past, where is that?

Likewise, if the anticipation is in the future, does that exist?

And if the memory exists in the present, has it any more reality than a dream?

What is there to hold onto?

Then release it into space, knowing *who* is watching. Rest in him. Just this pure, loving, knowing, embracing presence. Clarifying and releasing in your own rhythm, as though falling back more and more deeply into his presence.

Find again that trust in the depth of your heart that the One who saves all is working there.

See his light shining forth, entering the hearts of everyone everywhere, exactly as he has entered you: telling them, reminding them, teaching them, that he has always already been there.

Know that in the oneness of *his* presence, is the oneness of us all, united like rays of light from star to star, each perfect, each unique. And dwell in the patience that he will transform all for us to see.

Dwelling in the Spirit

The Spirit is speaking. Listen to its subtlest call, as the vibrations of movement through your whole form. There's no need to think of it as a body. It's just an experience. There's no need to think of breath as breath, it's just a movement. But know that it *is* the Spirit.

And listen carefully. Do not disturb its flow.

Do not miss a moment of its movement. Watch it fill you.

If the Spirit is already indwelling within us, the very vibration of our being, and if our experience of matter is arising from the state of our mind, *why are we not in a resurrected body already?* Why do we not experience it all the time?

If matter and spirit can be created anew each moment, and if both matter and mind are decaying each moment, what causes are necessary to experience a transfigured or glorified state of body and mind?

If the depths of our mind, our very capacity to be aware, to be creative, to be in love, is fundamentally not separate from God, where did we go wrong? What makes us think and experience otherwise?

There is something fundamentally wrong with our perceptions, something blocked that we cannot perceive fully. Think of what agony this is: to be infinitely close to God and not realize it. Could it be the source of *all* pain?

Then consider: Is this the condition of everyone we've ever met, everyone we know about, every living creature, infused by Spirit, riding on the breath of Spirit, yet not knowing it; ignorant of the force of the life by which we live?

Is this not grounds for compassion? Unconditional compassion?

No matter how bad it gets, can one blame the blind man for lashing out at what he cannot see?

As you contemplate, do not lose the flow of the Spirit within you. Relax into that flow and let it speak.

Listen carefully to your heart. What is the Spirit that Christ breathes within you asking of you? What does he want for you, from you, in you? Let go of all your ideas. Just listen carefully for what Christ's compassion wants.

Listen to your own mind. It is not easy to hear Christ's voice whenever we want to, is it? Yet we believe he is there. What is stopping us? *Be* the Christ within yourself, standing sentry, bearing witness to all that takes place in you. And from his perspective, with his compassion, let everything else go, without trying to change it. Just watching and releasing.

The Christ who bears witness is absolutely unmoving. Rest in his gaze.

For Christ to remake us, must we not let go of everything we think we are—if all that is only based on a blinded view anyway, a misunderstanding of the very nature of our own body and mind?

And so we die with him and entrust our death to his, vividly, actively, with our whole being.

But when someone dies, he or she is not completely and utterly dead. Something goes on; some energy still infused with the divine life force that never dies. How completely might we be purified when our whole being breaks down to that most subtle layer of life and awareness, falling into the arms of God; when there is nothing left of what we thought we were?

Be swallowed up in the transcendent light that permeates all reality. It cannot be dimmed by the darkest darkness; but none of us ever sees it. The infinite blaze of divine life. All things are seen in this light; all things are purified from the heart of reality that is Christ. The force of life, the force of all matter, and the force of all knowing, loving, creating: inseparable from one another.

You can know this symbolically as a flame at the center of reality, blazing brighter, more clearly with shape and form than the infinite light that covers all space and time: the Light at the center of the light.

When Christ recreates his body, when the Father recreates the form in which his Son lives, it is only for the sake of others. How does Trinity need to be seen in you, *now*?

Become aware again of the form you thought you had, but know that it was never really there as you had thought.

And so it can be *recreated* moment by moment. Let it be infused now with this experience of pure light, filling every pore, every vibration, every sensation.

Let that light blaze forth from you to touch everyone you've ever known or heard of; everyone who needs hope, healing, peace. Be the divine communication to the world; every sound or vibration of this love. Every image that arises of place or people or creatures, let it be suffused with this transmission of divine compassion into form.

Then release the images and simply rest in this presence, always knowing, always perceiving, always loving.

Slowly allow your eyes to open, to bridge into this transfigured world, letting your awareness rest. Letting God see.

Release merely human thoughts, merely human identifications, without modification, without grasping. Letting God be.

Epilogue

The Resurrection Body

Beloved, we are God's children now; what we will be has not yet
been revealed. What we do know is this: when he is revealed, we
will be like him, for we will see him as he is. (1 John 3:2)

HOW WILL WE EVER gain the ability to experience a resurrected body if
we do not even try to imagine it now? If the barrier between our current
ordinary experience and what we shall become is not deliberately placed
there by God, then what more can God do to guide us towards that
place except to show us how to *release* all that is blocking us? This is a
tremendous work not to be ignored. But it will require a steady, untiring
practice; one that is willing to face and gradually let go of all the inner
demons that still prevent us from dwelling, seeing, and living as Christ
dwells, sees, and lives.

If we do not practice, if we do not take the time every day to face
our inner landscape, to allow ourselves to be cleansed consistently by
Christ's presence in us, then inevitably we will continue to spin in our
old habits, fall prey to distraction and busyness, and then find ourselves
worn out each day, with foggy minds unable to think clearly, much less
progress in the path of divine understanding. By not practicing, by not
actualizing the light of the Spirit already present within us, we cannot
help but fall back into thinking of our world as ordinary; of our lives as
but an insignificant attempt at creating meaning within a vast cosmos
of insurmountable, frightening uncertainties; and of our bodies as

something inert and simply material, with no better destiny than to rot in a grave or be burned to ashes.

Yet by practicing consistently, by learning how to dwell without distraction in the peace that already dwells in us—Christ's own peace that surpasses all understanding—we cannot help but receive glimpses of "what we will be." We can begin to believe in the reality of a physical form made of nothing but the effulgence of divine light, and learn, step by step, to embody such a vision of ourselves, even long before the resurrection is enacted fully, for all creation. And by dwelling more and more within these glimpses, more and more they *do* become our own reality, the baseline from which we act and interact in the world.

The details of the spiritual path are many, and a serious practice of contemplation requires the guidance of a wise teacher, one who already knows the exquisite but sometimes disturbing landscape of the interior territory we seek to explore. The meditations offered here are intended simply as a source of inspiration, not as a complete set of instructions for spiritual development. Yet we hope they might offer a template from which you may discover your own very personal experiences of the resurrection narratives. What is most important for now is that each one of us learns to enter the very scenes in which Christ transmits his resurrected reality to his disciples, in the single historical time that is all time.

We suggest that you find your own rhythm, alternating between the imaginative, intensely devotional meditations on Gospel experiences, and resting in the silence and stillness of awareness focused on the sensations of breathing. Do not push to repeat a deeply meaningful experience that may come in meditation; let each day be fresh, without expectation of what may arise. Never miss a day, but allow the balance of your practice to grow organically, without pressure or striving. Trust Christ to guide you in each session of meditation, whether or not you engage in active visualization of a scene of encounter. The process is long-term; we are changed by the consistency of dedication, the pure intention of our hearts, and the infusion of divine grace to which we open ourselves when we surrender completely to Christ's love within. Once we gain stability in our meditative concentration, the sky is the limit for the authentic understanding that will grow. So do not lose heart; practice without ceasing until the actual resurrection dawns. For this is the imperative of our lives, to prepare for what Christ has always been preparing for us. And for which he begs us to be ready.

Listen! I am standing at the door, knocking;
if you hear my voice and open the door,
I will come in to you and eat with you,
and you with me. (Rev 3:20)

Bibliography

Adler, Cyrus, and Emil G. Hirsch. "Shemoneh 'Esreh." In *The Jewish Encyclopedia*. New York: Funk and Wagnalls, 1901–1906. http://www.jewishencyclopedia.com/articles/1398-amidah.

Aeschylus. *The Eumenides*. Vol. II. Edited by Jeffrey Henderson. Cambridge, MA: Hárvard University Press, 2008.

Allison, Dale C. *Resurrecting Jesus: The Earliest Christian Tradition and Its Interpreters*. London: T & T Clark, 2005.

Alsup, John E. *The Post-Resurrection Appearance Stories of the Gospel Tradition*. Stuttgart: Calwer Verlag, 1975.

Aquinas, Thomas, Saint. *Summa Contra Gentiles, Book Four: Salvation*. Translated by Charles J. O'Neil. Notre Dame, IN: University of Notre Dame Press, 2016.

———. *Summa Theologica: Supplement to the Third Part*. Translated by the Fathers of the English Dominican Province. Edited by Anthony Uyl. Woodstock, Ontario: Devoted, 2018.

———. *Opusculum 57, In festo Corporis Christi* in *Liturgy of the Hours, Feast of Corpus Christi*. Totowa, NJ: Catholic Book, 1990.

Aristotle. *De Generatione et Corruptione*. Vol. II. Notre Dame: Notre Dame University Press, 1981.

Arkani-Hamed, Nima. "Messenger Lecture 1." Cornell University Cornellcast: October 18, 2010. http://www.cornell.edu/video/nima-arkani-hamed-quantum-mechanics-and-space-time.

Asaad, G., and H. Shapiro. "Hallucinations: theoretical and clinical overview." *American Journal of Psychiatry* 143.9 (1986) 1088–1097.

Athanasius. *De incarnatione*. http://www.newadvent.org/fathers/2802.htm.

Augustine of Hippo, Saint. *The City of God*. Translated by Marcus Dods, DD. Peabody, MA: Hendrickson, 2017.

———. *The Confessions of St. Augustine*. Translated and edited by Albert Cook Outler. Mineola, NY: Dover, 2002.

———. *The Enchiridion on Faith Hope, and Love*. Translated by Bruce Harbert. Edited by John E. Rotelle, OSA. Hyde Park, NY: New City, 1999.

———. *On the Trinity*. Edited by Gareth B. Matthews. Translated by Stephen McKenna. Cambridge: Cambridge University Press, 2002.

———. *Saint Augustine Tractates on the Gospel of John 112–24; Tractates on the First Epistle of John.* The Fathers of the Church Vol. 92. Translated by John W. Rettig. Washington, DC: Catholic University of America Press, 1995.

———. *Sermons on Selected Lessons of the New Testament.* Translated by Richard Gell Macmullen and Edward Bouverie Pusey. Altenmünster: Jazzybee Verlag, 2017.

Brown, Raymond E., SS. *The Gospels and Epistles of John: A Concise Commentary.* Collegeville, MN: Liturgical, 1988.

———. *An Introduction to the Gospel of John.* Edited by Francis J. Moloney. New York: Doubleday, 2003.

———. *An Introduction to the New Testament.* New York: Doubleday, 1977.

———. *A Once and Coming Spirit at Pentecost.* Collegeville, MN: Liturgical, 1993.

———. *A Risen Christ in Eastertime.* Collegeville, MN: Liturgical, 1991.

———. *The Virginal Conception and Bodily Resurrection of Jesus.* New York: Paulist, 1973.

Brown, Raymond E., and John P. Meier. *Antioch and Rome: New Testament Cradles of Catholic Christianity.* Mahwah, NJ: Paulist, 1982.

Bultmann, Rudolf. *History of the Synoptic Tradition.* Translated by John Marsh. Peabody, MA: Hendrickson, 1963.

———. *New Testament and Mythology.* Translated and edited by Schubert M. Ogden. Minneapolis: Fortress, 1984.

Bynum, Caroline Walker. *The Resurrection of the Body in Western Christianity, 200–1336.* New York: Columbia University Press, 1995.

Cantalamessa, Raniero. *Easter: Meditations on the Resurrection.* Translated by Demetrio S. Yocum. Collegeville, MN: Liturgical, 2006.

Carmichael, Joel. *The Death of Jesus.* New York: Macmillan, 1962.

Carnley, Peter. *Resurrection in Retrospect: A Critical Examination of the Theology of N. T. Wright.* Eugene, OR: Cascade, 2019.

Catchpole, David. *Resurrection People: Studies in the Resurrection Narratives of the Gospels.* Sarum Theological Lectures. London: Darton, Longman & Todd, 2000.

Chardin, Pierre Teilhard de, SJ. *The Divine Milieu.* New York: Harper, 1960.

Cole, K. C. "In Patterns, Not Particles, Physicists Trust." *The Los Angeles Times*, March 4, 1999.

Conzelmann, Hans. *1 Corinthians: A Commentary on the First Epistle to the Corinthians.* Translated by James W. Leitch. Edited by George W. MacRae, SJ. Philadelphia: Fortress, 1975.

Craig, William Lane. *Assessing the New Testament Evidence for the Historicity of the Resurrection of Jesus.* Lewiston, NY: Edwin Mellen, 1989.

———. *The Son Rises: The Historical Evidence for the Resurrection of Jesus.* Chicago: Moody, 1983.

Dahl, Murdoch E. *The Resurrection of the Body.* London: SCM, 1962.

Davies, Jon. *Death, Burial and Rebirth in the Religions of Antiquity.* Abingdon, UK: Routledge, 1999.

Davis, Stephen T. *Risen Indeed: Making Sense of the Resurrection.* London: SPCK, 1993.

Dillon, Richard J. *From Eye-Witnesses to Ministers of the Word: Tradition and Composition in Luke 24.* Rome: Biblical Institute, 1978.

Dodd, C. H. *The Parables of the Kingdom.* New York: Charles Scribner's Sons, 1961.

Donahue, John R., ed. *Life in Abundance: Studies of John's Gospel in Tribute to Raymond E. Brown.* Collegeville, MN: Liturgical, 2005.

Epiphanius. *The Creeds of Epiphanius*. www.ccel.org/ccel/schaff/creeds2.iii.i.xii.html.

Eusebius. *Church History*. Book 4, chapter 4. www.newadvent.org/fathers/250104.htm.

Feynman, Richard. *The Feynman Lectures on Physics*, Vol. I–4. Caltech Video: 1961–63. https://www.feynmanlectures.caltech.edu/.

Fiorenza, Elizabeth S. *In Memory of Her: A Feminist Theological Reconstruction of Christian Origins*. New York: Crossroad, 1983.

Fredriksen, Paula. *Jesus of Nazareth, King of the Jews: A Jewish Life and the Emergence of Christianity*. New York: Vintage, 2000.

Geach, P. T. *God and the Soul*. London: Routledge & Kegan Paul, 1969.

Gersten, Dennis, MD. *Are you Getting Enlightened or Losing your Mind? A Spiritual Program for Mental Fitness*. New York: Crown, 1997.

Getty, Mary Ann. *First Corinthians, Second Corinthians*. Collegeville, MN: Liturgical, 1991.

Gleiser, Marcelo. *The Island of Knowledge: The Limits of Science and the Search for Meaning*. New York: Basic, 2014.

Habermas, G. R. *The Risen Jesus and Future Hope*. Lanham, MD: Rowman and Littlefield, 2003.

Harmless, William, SJ, ed. *Augustine in His Own Words*. Washington, DC: Catholic University Press, 2010.

Hays, Richard B. *First Corinthians: Interpretation*. Louisville: Westminster, 1997.

Homer. *The Iliad*. Vol. II. Edited by C. P. Goold. Cambridge, MA: Harvard University Press, 1999.

Irenaeus of Lyons, Saint. *Adversus Haereses*. In *The Ante-Nicene Fathers* Vol. 1, edited by Alexander Roberts and James Donaldson. Grand Rapids: Eerdmans 1996–2001.

———. *Against the Heresies* Book 3. Ancient Christian Writers Vol. 64. Translated and annotated by Dominic J. Unger, OFM. New York: Newman, 2012.

Jeremias, Joachim. "Die älteste Schicht der Osterüberlieferung." In *Resurrexit*, edited by Édouard Dhanis, 194. Rome: Libreria Editrice Vaticana, 1974.

———. *The Eucharistic Words of Jesus*. London: SCM, 1966.

———. *Jerusalem in the Time of Jesus*. Philadelphia: Fortress, 1967.

———. *New Testament Theology: The Proclamation of Jesus*. New York: Scribner's, 1971.

———. *The Parables of Jesus*. London: SCM, 1972.

Johnson, Luke Timothy. *The Real Jesus: The Misguided Quest for the Historical Jesus and the Truth of the Traditional Gospels*. New York: HarperCollins, 1997.

Jones, Alexander, ed. *The Jerusalem Bible: New Testament*. London: Darton, Longman & Todd, 1966.

Josephus, Flavius. *Jewish Antiquities* books 1–3. Translated by H. St. J. Thackeray and Ralph Marcus. Cambridge: Harvard University Press, 1978.

———. *Jewish Antiquities* books 4–6. Translated by H. St. J. Thackeray and Ralph Marcus. Cambridge: Harvard University Press, 1930.

———. *Jewish Antiquities* books 12–13. Translated by Ralph Marcus. Cambridge: Harvard University Press, 1943.

Kaufman, Gordon D. *Systematic Theology: A Historical Perspective*. New York: Charles Scribner's Sons, 1968.

Keck, Leander E. *Proclamation Commentaries: Paul and His Letters*. Philadelphia: Fortress, 1979.

Kelly, J. N. D. *Early Christian Doctrines*. San Francisco: HarperSanFrancisco, 1978.

Laird, Martin, OSA. *Into the Silent Land: A Guide to the Christian Practice of Meditation.* Oxford: Oxford University Press, 2006.

———. *An Ocean of Light: Contemplation, Transformation, and Liberation.* Oxford: Oxford University Press, 2018.

———. *A Sunlit Absence: Silence, Awareness, and Contemplation.* Oxford: Oxford University Press, 2011.

Lapide, Pinchas. *The Resurrection of Jesus: A Jewish Perspective.* Translated by W. C. Linss. Minneapolis: Augsburg, 1983.

Laverdiere, Eugene, SSS. *Luke: New Testament Message 5.* Wilmington: Michael Glazier, 1980.

Léon-Dufour, Xavier, SJ. *Resurrection and the Message of Easter.* New York: Holt, Rinehart and Winston, 1971.

Licona, Michael R. *The Resurrection of Jesus: A New Historiographical Approach.* Downers Grove, IL: IVP Academic, 2010.

Linde, Andrei. "The Universe, Life, and Consciousness." In *Science and the Spiritual Quest: New Essays by Leading Scientists,* edited by W. Mark Richardson et al, 188–202. London: Routledge, 2002.

Liturgy, of the Eucharist. www.catholic-resources.org/ChurchDocs/Mass.htm#Eucharist.

Longstaff, T. R. W. "The Women at the Tomb." *New Testament Studies* 27.2 (January 1981) 277–282. Published online by Cambridge University Press, February 2009. https://www.cambridge.org/core/journals/new-testament-studies/article/women-at-the-tomb-matthew-281-reexamined/E69EFAB5CF63BB2B2408D7CCFA95FE98.

Lüdemann, Gerd.*The Resurrection of Christ: A Historical Inquiry.* Amherst, NY: Prometheus, 2004.

MacMullen, Ramsey. *Christianizing the Roman Empire (A.D. 100–400).* New Haven, CT: Yale University Press, 1984.

McIntyre, J. "The Uses of History in Theology." *Studies in World Christianity* 7.1 (2001) 8.

Moloney, Francis J., SDB. *Belief in the Word: Reading John 1–4.* Minneapolis: Fortress, 1993.

———. *A Body Broken for a Broken People: Eucharist in the New Testament.* Peabody, MA: Hendrickson, 1997.

———. *Love in the Gospel of John: An Exegetical, Theological, and Literary Study.* Grand Rapids: Baker Academic, 2013.

———. *Sacra Pagina: The Gospel of John.* Collegeville, MN: Michael Glazier/Liturgical, 1998.

———. *Signs and Shadows: Reading John 5–12.* Minneapolis: Fortress, 1996.

NET Bible®. Biblical Studies, 2018. http://bible.org.

O'Collins, Gerald, SJ. *Believing in the Resurrection: the Meaning and Promise of the Risen Jesus.* Mahwah, NJ: Paulist, 2012.

———. *Easter Faith: Believing in the Risen Jesus.* Mahwah, NJ: Paulist, 2003.

———. *The Easter Jesus.* London: Darton, Longman & Todd, 1973.

———. *Jesus Risen.* Mahwah, NJ: Paulist, 1987.

Olsen, Carl E. *Did Jesus Really Rise from the Dead? Questions and Answers about the Life, Death, and Resurrection of Jesus.* San Francisco: Ignatius, 2016.

Origen. *Commentary on Matthew.* In *The Ante-Nicene Fathers* Vol. X, edited by Allan Menzies, DD. Grand Rapids: Eerdmans, 1995.

———. "Commentary on Psalms." In *Origen (The Early Church Fathers)*, translated by Joseph W. Trigg, 69–72. Abingdon, UK: Routledge, 1998.

———. *Contra Celsum*. Translated by Henry Chadwick. Cambridge: Cambridge University Press, 1953.

———. *De Principiis*. Edited by G. W. Butterworth. New York: Harper & Row, 1966.

Perkins, Pheme. *Resurrection: New Testament Witness and Contemporary Reflection*. New York: Doubleday, 1984.

Pesch, Rudolf. *Das Markusevangelium*. 2 vols. Herder's Theologischer Kommentar zum Neuen Testament. Freiburg: Herder & Herder, 1977.

Philo of Alexandria. *The Works of Philo Judaeus: The Contemporary of Josephus*. Vol. II. Translated by C. D. Yonge. London: George Bell & Sons, 1894.

Pitre, Brant. *The Case for Jesus: The Biblical and Historical Evidence for Christ*. New York: Image, 2016.

Plato. *The Dialogues of Plato*. Vol. 2. Translated by Benjamin Jowett. London: Sphere, 1970.

———. *Phaedo*. Translated by David Gallop. Oxford: Clarendon, 1975.

Polkinghorne, John. *Quantum Physics and Theology: An Unexpected Kinship*. New Haven: Yale University Press, 2008.

Price, Simon F. R. *Religions of the Ancient Greeks*. Cambridge: Cambridge University Press, 1999.

Rolf, Veronica Mary. *An Explorer's Guide to Julian of Norwich*. Downer's Grove, IL: IVP Academic, 2018.

———. *Julian's Gospel: Illuminating the Life & Revelations of Julian of Norwich*. Maryknoll, NY: Orbis, 2013.

———. *Suddenly There is God: The Story of Our Lives in Sacred Scripture*. Eugene, OR: Cascade, 2019.

Saki (H. H. Munro). *The Chronicles of Clovis*. London: The Bodley Head, 1912. Reprint, North Charleston, SC: CreateSpace, 2010.

Schlatter, D. H. *Der Evangelist Matthäus*. Stuttgart: Calwer Vereinsbuchhandlung, 1929.

Schmisek, Brian. *Resurrection of the Flesh, or Resurrection of the Dead: Implications for Theology*. Collegeville, MN: Liturgical, 2013.

Schnackenburg, Rudolf. *The Gospel of Matthew*. Translated by Robert R. Barr. Grand Rapids: Eerdmans, 2002.

Schneiders, Sandra M., IHM. *Jesus Risen in our Midst: Essays on the Resurrection of Jesus in the Fourth Gospel*. Collegeville, MN: Michael Glazier/Liturgical, 2013.

———. "The Resurrection (of the Body) in the Fourth Gospel: A Key to Johannine Spirituality." In *Life in Abundance: Studies of John's Gospel in Tribute to Raymond E Brown*, edited by John R. Donahue, 168–98. Collegeville, MN: Liturgical, 2005.

———. *The Revelatory Text: Interpreting the New Testament as Sacred Scripture*. Collegeville, MN: Michael Glazer/Liturgical, 1999.

———. *Written that You May Believe: Encountering Jesus in the Fourth Gospel*. New York: Crossroad, 2003.

Sirilla, Michael G. "Divinization for the New Evangelization." In *Divinization: Becoming Icons of Christ Through the Liturgy*, edited by Andrew Hofer OP, 95–115. Chicago/Mundelein, IL: Hillenbrand, 2015.

Symeon the New Theologian. *The Discourses*. Mahwah, NJ: Paulist, 1980.

Teeple, Ryan C., et al. "Visual Hallucinations: Differential Diagnosis and Treatment." *Primary Care Companion to the Journal of Clinical Psychiatry* 11.1 (2009) 26–32.

Tertullian, Quintus Septimius Florens. *Treatise on the Resurrection*. Edited by Ernest Evans. London: SPCK, 1960.

von Rad, Gerhard. *Old Testament Theology*. Vols. I & II. Translated by D. M. G. Stalker. Peabody, MA: Prince, 2005.

Waterman, M. M. W. *The Empty Tomb Tradition of Mark: Text, History, and Theological Struggles*. Los Angeles: Agathos, 2006.

Wedderburn. A. J. M. *Beyond Resurrection*. London: SCM, 1999.

Williams, Rowan. *Resurrection: Interpreting the Easter Gospel*. London: Darton, Longman & Todd, 1982.

Wright, N. T. *History and Eschatology: Jesus and the Promise of Natural Theology*. Waco, TX: Baylor University Press, 2019.

———. *Paul: A Biography*. New York: HarperOne, 2018.

———. *The Resurrection of the Son of God*. Minneapolis: Fortress, 2003.

INDEX

Made in United States
North Haven, CT
06 May 2022

18957161R00157